The Archaeology of Utopian and Intentional Communities

The American Experience in Archaeological Perspective

UNIVERSITY PRESS OF FLORIDA

Florida A&M University, Tallahassee
Florida Atlantic University, Boca Raton
Florida Gulf Coast University, Ft. Myers
Florida International University, Miami
Florida State University, Tallahassee
New College of Florida, Sarasota
University of Central Florida, Orlando
University of Florida, Gainesville
University of North Florida, Jacksonville
University of South Florida, Tampa
University of West Florida, Pensacola

THE ARCHAEOLOGY OF UTOPIAN AND INTENTIONAL COMMUNITIES

STACY C. KOZAKAVICH

Foreword by Michael S. Nassaney

———★———

University Press of Florida
Gainesville · Tallahassee · Tampa · Boca Raton
Pensacola · Orlando · Miami · Jacksonville · Ft. Myers · Sarasota

First cloth printing, 2017
First paperback printing, 2023

28 27 26 25 24 23   6 5 4 3 2 1

Library of Congress Cataloging-in-Publication Data
Names: Kozakavich, Stacy C., author. | Nassaney, Michael S., author of
    foreword.
Title: The archaeology of utopian and intentional communities / Stacy C.
    Kozakavich ; foreword by Michael S. Nassaney.
Other titles: American experience in archaeological perspective.
Description: Gainesville : University Press of Florida, 2017. | Series: The
    American experience in archaeological perspective | Includes
    bibliographical references and index.
Identifiers: LCCN 2017030471 | ISBN 9780813056593 (cloth) | ISBN 9780813068978 (pbk.)
Subjects: LCSH: Collective settlements—United States—History. |
    Utopias—United States—History. | Archaeology—Research—United States. |
    United States—History.
Classification: LCC HX653 .K69 2018 | DDC 307.770973—dc23
LC record available at https://lccn.loc.gov/2017030471

The University Press of Florida is the scholarly publishing agency for the State University System
of Florida, comprising Florida A&M University, Florida Atlantic University, Florida Gulf Coast
University, Florida International University, Florida State University, New College of Florida,
University of Central Florida, University of Florida, University of North Florida, University of South
Florida, and University of West Florida.

University Press of Florida
2046 NE Waldo Road
Suite 2100
Gainesville, FL 32609
http://upress.ufl.edu

CONTENTS

FIGURES

FOREWORD

America was founded on dissent and has continued to attract social, religious, and political dissidents seeking fertile ground to sow new ideas
about how to live in community. But even as America served as a beacon
for the world's tired, poor, and homeless imaginaries, once transplanted to
the shores of this haven, the drudgery of daily life coupled with the inequities of new class relations re-created some of the conditions that propelled
many to flee from their original homelands. Yet others—driven by a vision
to abandon the shackles of greed, ignorance, avarice, and ennui—formed
intentional communities and implanted themselves in places physically
apart from mainstream society in an effort to realize their beliefs about
proper social relations. Typically, they aimed to embrace new ways of being
that would liberate them from the oppression and dehumanization that
accompanied capitalism, patriarchy, and individualism as they aimed to
transform the dominant culture.

Various groups at different historical moments worked to found a more
perfect union while holding divergent values. Many were committed to
hard work and spiritual purity, and grounded their beliefs in active choices
regarding settlement location, building design, and consumer goods needed
to sustain their own versions of life, liberty, and the pursuit of happiness.
A common practice of the dominant society is to point a discerning finger
toward these social experiments, savor their supposed failure, and cast as-
persions on those who would dare to attempt to live according to alternate
values as a smoke shield to obscure the flaws of mainstream society.

I first became familiar with intentional communities in the early 1970s
in conjunction with the counterculture movement. The idea of moving

from a congested mill town in southeastern New England to the verdant hills of New Hampshire, Vermont, or upstate New York had a certain romantic appeal, though my middle-class values kept me closely tethered to family, school, and a part-time job in my father's five-and-dime store. In my later teen years, I would on occasion escape my sheltered existence for a long weekend to a temporary utopia among swarms of rock music aficionados where I could temporarily "turn on, tune in." I always returned to my reality, secretly envying those who had cut their bourgeois ties to build a new society. A more serious foray into communal living came when I discovered archaeology and lived on multiple occasions for several months with field crews who shared an ideology, or at least a work ethic, to retrieve the detritus of daily life from a wooded river valley in southwestern New Hampshire and later a plowed field on the Illinois prairie. Of course, I always considered this to be an extended apprenticeship and not a permanent condition in which my coworkers and I would cohabit indefinitely. Moreover, I can say in hindsight that much of this was merely adolescent angst and rebellion.

We would be foolhardy to confuse these trivial (but personally formative) experiences with the very serious and long tradition of utopian and intentional communities that social scientists—archaeologists among them—have studied in earnest since at least the 1980s. In *The Archaeology of Utopian and Intentional Communities*, Stacy Kozakavich joins this scholarly tradition, as she juxtaposes the goals of intentional communities and their material expressions. Archaeology is a particularly informative tool in this study because the avowedly ideological nature of intentional communities had a far-reaching influence on the ways in which they manipulated the material world. Communalists often grounded their beliefs in practice by constructing roads and landscapes; building houses and organizing space; and producing, selecting, and consuming goods that were consistent with their values and beliefs. And through its recursive power, architecture—as one form of material culture—expressed communal beliefs, while it simultaneously acted to "codify and shape members' behaviors" in (sometimes) predictable ways.

Unlike some segments of society that intentionally hide their actions (for example, freedom seekers on the Underground Railroad), many intentional communities published their own newspapers and compiled regular reports, to produce a rich documentary record that can be tapped for data on self-perception (and sometimes self-deception). But Kozakavich reminds us of the necessity to balance deliberate self-reporting (often favorable, for obvious reasons) and the skeptical writings of journalists from the outside with the concrete but fragmentary evidence from material culture to more closely apprehend daily lived experiences of community members.

Kozakavich begins with a clear definition of what she means by intentional communities, which allows her to leave the occupants of prisons, dormitories, crew housing, and other temporary and involuntary associations for others to study. For her, intentional communities are composed of members united by a common vision of an ideal society and/or by a shared commitment among voluntary residents to provide an alternative to unacceptable conditions in the mainstream. In addition, their settlements are designed with permanence in mind and physically or geographically separated from those they aim to transcend. If social critique is inherent in intentional communities, we might expect colonies to form in the greatest numbers and varieties during historical periods characterized by economic crisis or divisive social conflict. Yet closer inspection reveals that there have always been intentional communities. Predictably, their forms, motivations, inspiration, and dominant values are varied. Early religious communities that archaeologists have studied include Ephrata, Shakers, Harmonists, Inspirationists, Zoar Separatists, Moravians, and Bishop Hill colonists, to name just a few. These early efforts set a precedent for subsequent intentional communities in the American cultural landscape. The nineteenth century saw various alternative developments, often in the face of the impersonal and alienated relations that obtained under industrial capitalism.

Many of the secular variants sought transformation from a "disappointing present to a glorious future," aiming to reshape society in the image of an ideal. Their very existence stands as a critique of their culture of origin. Despite efforts to operate outside the surrounding society, they retain legal and economic ties that allow their continued operation. For Kozakavich, this speaks to the connectedness of intentional communities both across time and space. Members corresponded and learned from each other. They also retain the ideological tinges of wider society, such as gender divisions and racial biases. Material disparities between ideals and practices become apparent through archaeological investigation. The challenge is to go beyond these discrepancies to understand how members experienced life in past intentional communities, and how those experiences changed over time in response to broader changes at the community level and beyond.

Intentionality is apparent in the materiality of countless community members' actions, from building foundations to bottle caps, animal bones to smoking pipes. Contextual relationships among varied objects can provide evidence of where and when community guidelines were practiced, and how individuals and families mobilized the material world—not always in compliance. Material evidence of practices that vary from those specifically required by community protocols can reveal the tension between the real and prescribed behaviors for individual members. Ceramics found in areas where Shaker women laundered clothing suggest that work took precedence over communal dining. The presence of a key at Kaweah may have been used to lock away private property, just as an 1884 nickel points to the persistence of a cash economy, despite the communal practices espoused by the membership.

Research designs can be oriented to examine various salient questions such as how a colony's vision and environmental factors work together to structure a community's material world, in terms of physical layout, architectural plans, and public and private spaces. We can ascertain competence in building abilities and the presence of adequate resources to execute building plans as envisioned. For example, the paucity of material remains and evidence of deliberate dismantling of buildings and the recycling of nails at Kaweah reveal a level of impoverishment, despite claims to the contrary. Locally produced goods and those brought from outside sources can be distinguished, along with their distribution among colonists. Food consumption from individually sized, single-portioned cans at California's Llano del Rio Cooperative Colony (ca. 1914–1917) indicates an avoidance of communal meals and the ability to dine alone. Careful contextual analysis is necessary before we assume that objects were adopted with all the connotations of capitalism. Just as trade goods were reimagined by their Native American users, so too did communalists impose new meanings on the objects they used in daily life.

The challenge in interpreting the archaeology of utopian and intentional communities is in some ways no different than any interpretation of the past. How do we construct a narrative that is true to the communalists and presents their pasts as they were, rather than how we think they should be? How do we portray intentional communities in ways that do justice to their founders, adherents, and descendants? Perhaps this is particularly difficult because intentional communities have always been used as a foil for the dominant society. Efforts have been made repeatedly to discredit intentional communities and point to their failures. Yet, as Kozakavich notes, their historical contribution lies in the continuous recall of utopian possibilities. Archaeology is well positioned to keep those hopes and dreams alive as we uncover the detritus of everyday life and connect the past to the present by highlighting the influence that intentional communities had on forming the America we live in today. Social Security and other New Deal initiatives are safety nets inspired by intentional communities that close the gap between rich and poor, or at least keep greater numbers of citizens from falling below the poverty line. By contributing to a historical narrative that pays due diligence to our forebears, we participate in an emancipatory and activist archaeology that empowers those whose voices were silenced. We also gain a deeper appreciation for a more inclusive American experience and a better understanding of myriad contemporary forces that simultaneously aim to reveal and obscure our contested history and its archaeological expression.

Michael S. Nassaney
Series Editor

ACKNOWLEDGMENTS

Communities of the past have sparked my interest for more than twenty years, perhaps rooted in all the delicious slices of Doukhobor bread I ate at the Saskatoon Exhibition as a child, or in a visit during my teen years to a Hutterite Colony in Saskatchewan where we learned that the enigmatic women in polka-dot headscarves we'd occasionally see in city stores were part of something much larger. For encouraging my first archaeological look at the Doukhobors I owe a debt of gratitude to Margaret Kennedy and the faculty of the University of Saskatchewan Department of Anthropology and Archaeology. The staff at Western Heritage Services provided the crew, laboratory space, and specialized expertise for the 1996 study of Kirilovka, Saskatchewan. Thad Van Bueren bravely corralled a handful of us who worked at community sites to share our ideas in a themed session at the 2001 Society for Historical Archaeology conference in Long Beach, California, and then persevered for five years while we molded our papers into a themed volume for *Historical Archaeology*. Heather Van Wormer introduced me to the Communal Studies Association, an organization whose conferences redefine what *community* can mean in the professional and academic world.

The Kaweah Colony Archaeology Project, discussed in chapter 6, relied on help from many individuals and institutions. Thanks to Laurie Wilkie for advising and advocating for me in the Department of Anthropology at the University of California, Berkeley. The Bancroft Library and Tulare County Historical Society provided funding and access to unparalleled archival sources. Thomas Burge, Ward Eldredge, and William Tweed of Sequoia National Park, and Duane Christian and Kimberly Cuevas of the Bureau of Land Management in Bakersfield shared local expertise and resources in helping to establish the project. Many residents of Three Rivers, including Sophie Britten, Jim Barton, Wilma Cauling, Marge Ewen, and Elena Broslovsky, shared knowledge and coffee. Sarah Barton Elliott and John Elliott keep the spirit of *The Kaweah Commonwealth* alive. Jay O'Connell offered his expertise and encouragement as a fellow scholar of Kaweah. Fieldwork depended on the generous access provided by Frank T. Elliott III and the Elliott Land and Cattle Company, and the hard work of volunteer crew members who braved mud, heat, and poison oak to collect data: Cheryl Smith-Lintner, Kim Christensen, Stacey Lynn Camp, Joann Grant, Rachel Giraudo, Tara Evans, Amanda Hallstrom, Katie Sprouse, John McWilliams, Chris Sheklian, Don Huff, Callen Huff, Phil Huff, Jonathan and Mona Maynard, Chris Avery, Miriam Lueck-Avery, Jan English-Lueck, Karl Lueck, Eilene Lueck, Kathleen Kubal, Chris Lloyd, Trish Wittenstein, Rita Pena, Josie Perez, and Dave Grant.

This volume was slow in the making, and I have deep appreciation for Thad Van Bueren's recommendation, Sarah Tarlow's early conversations with me about writing on this topic, and Michael Nassaney's invitation to contribute to his series and his patience in waiting for the final product. Many fellow archaeologists and historians offered information about intentional community studies. James Kopp of Lewis & Clark College, Vincent Birdsong of the Florida Bureau of Historic Preservation, Linda Pansing of the Ohio History Connection, Edward Safiran at Bishop Hill State Historic Site, Mark Johnson at the Illinois Historic Preservation Agency, Floyd Mansberger of Fever River Research, and Scott Heberling of Heberling Associates, Inc. all shared research findings and access to reports. Michael Strezewski, Kim McBride, and Don Janzen gave their time for helpful conversations about their own research perspectives.

Several institutions granted permission for reproduction of images from their archival collections. Maps and photographs from the Beinecke Rare Book and Manuscript Library, Yale University; the Thomas Fisher Rare Book Library, University of Toronto; the Massachusetts Historical Society; the National Air Photo Library of Canada; Library and Archives Canada; and the Saskatoon Public Library Local History Room illustrate and enhance this work immeasurably. The Library of Congress Geography and Map Division, Historic American Building Survey, and Work Projects

Administration Poster Collection, as well as the Internet Archive, provided invaluable digital research sources. Special thanks to Andy Sewell of Hardlines Design Company and Bruce Aument of the Ohio Department of Transportation for sharing images from their investigations at Union Village, Ohio; and to Breck Parkman for allowing use of images from Olompali State Historic Park.

Much gratitude to Eleanor Katari, whose editorial eye and word-charming skills helped smooth the draftiest drafts into something more coherent. Reviewers Lu Ann De Cunzo and Kim McBride offered invaluable suggestions for shaping the final version.

I am indebted most to my family, who have supported me throughout the writing process. My mother, Elaine Kozakavich, answered my calls on her Saskatoon local history expertise with enthusiasm. My father, Ron Kozakavich, distracted me just enough with good fish stories. My husband, Peter Merholz, has accompanied me on many travels to community sites around the country and has graciously endured my delves into places and people of the past. Jules and Dorothy remind me every day that no matter how hard it can be to work for a better shared world, it's still worth trying.

INTRODUCTION

Encountering Community

Intentional communities have a long history in North America. We can follow a winding and colorfully stranded thread from today's ecovillages, cohousing complexes, and collective farms through the countercultural communes of the 1960s and 1970s, to the socialist experiments on either side of the turn of the twentieth century and the vibrant rural religious communalists of the Second Great Awakening. How far back does this thread go, and where and when did it start?

Some would argue that group settlement based on shared ideals began in the early days of European settlement on the continent, with the arrival of Pilgrims at Plymouth Rock and the Puritans of the Massachusetts Bay Colony. Each could be construed as having much in common with later, more explicitly idealistic settlements, as these colonists shared strong religious beliefs at odds with the Church of England and fled here in search of the physical and metaphysical space to live according to their shared convictions. Yet the 41 passengers who originally signed the Mayflower Compact consisted of both Saints and Strangers—pilgrims who were searching for religious freedom as well as tradesmen and adventurers whose primary focus was a good return on their investment. The Civil Body Politic outlined in the Mayflower Compact established the Pilgrims' government at Plymouth Plantation but in doing so explicitly recognized the ultimate sovereignty of King James. The religious communalists of Plymouth and Massachusetts Bay have counterparts in the profit-focused entrepreneurs of Jamestown. The Virginia Company of London's ca. 1607 Jamestown settlement, as well as the Puritan and Pilgrim colonists' voyages and villages, operated their efforts as common stock operations in early years. In doing so they maintained written inclusion of English stockholders, and labored for the personal enrichment of a body of overseas investors whose contribution to the work of community building was based on the financial expectation of high returns (Hinds 1908:13–14). Evoking Puritan leader John Winthrop's biblically inspired 1630 exaltation that the Massachusetts Bay Colony be "as a city upon a hill" glosses over the financially motivated aspects of these migrant groups' origins and actions.

These dualities—cooperation and competition, communalism and capitalism, the collective and the individual—are intertwined in the roots of our historical understanding. In our current configuration of society, capitalism and individualism are seen as foundational ideologies. Their counterparts are considered weak, ancillary, subversive, or even "un-American." Yet to think of this outcome as inevitable is to engage in a failure of historical imagination on a grand scale. The collective impulse has long been strong in North American history, and to discount its influence is to give short shrift to the many communities and associations that have worked hard to embody and live out their various versions of that ideal.

Donald Pitzer, a modern historian of communal settlements, recognizes that the Pilgrim separatists' and Puritans' short-lived communal economies, developed primarily to ensure their survival on North American shores, were nonetheless important in setting the stage for the following nearly four centuries of American communal societies (Pitzer 1997:6). These initial iconic colonies were just a few among many foundational examples of alternative economies and idealistic social designs that populated the seventeenth and eighteenth centuries. The ascetic residents of Bohemia Manor, a Protestant Labadist community in what is now Maryland, found refuge in the earliest days of American settlement, from 1683 to 1727. Members were monastic in their practices but severed ties to structured church institutions. English social reformer James Oglethorpe was inspired by the plight of his country's worthy poor and jailed debtors in developing his vision for the Georgia Colony and its founding city of Savannah, established in 1733. Many nations among North America's indigenous peoples demonstrated forms of collective social organization and resource sharing that were unfamiliar to European eyes, and yet were, in their contexts, the dominant societal pattern rather than alternative subcultures. North America was never settled as a single, unified community with shared goals. The contrasting threads of individuality and collectivism have created a space where individuals have the freedom to choose to pursue collective goals. Since the early days of European contact, this continent has offered fertile ground, both literal and figurative, where experimental communities could attempt to take root and grow.

The sixteenth-century voyages of discovery and early years of seventeenth-century colonization expanded the boundaries of the known world, and also provided new realms for the literary imagination. Idealistic authors brought the reading public's awareness to the idea of new lands and distant indigenous populations, who were sometimes romanticized as being free from the maladies of European society. Storytellers traveled uncharted fictional distances for readers in a concrete world whose mapped expanses still contained enough unknowns for the imaginary to be discovered someday as real. With the maps being redrawn every day, finding heaven on earth may have seemed like only a matter of time. Sir Thomas More's 1516 *Utopia* retells the fictional travels of its protagonist to an uncharted island whose inhabitants have built their society in ways that eliminated his perceived flaws of contemporary England: inequality, avarice, and war. James Harrington's 1656 *Commonwealth of Oceana* demonstrated qualities of an ideal society that would later be fundamental to the thinking of Thomas Jefferson when drafting America's Declaration of Independence (Kopp 2009:25). Writers later in the nineteenth century, when more of the globe had been charted by travelers over sea and rail, still found their perfect societies in faraway places just outside the realm of known geography. Etienne Cabet's 1840 *Voyage en Icarie*, William Dean Howells's 1894 *A Traveler from Altruria*, and Charlotte Perkins Gilman's 1915 *Herland*, for example, all recount the experiences of travelers to, or visitors from, isolated countries. Edward Bellamy championed a different and more fanciful kind of travel than across oceans or mountains. His 1888 *Looking Backward 2000–1887* took its protagonist, Julian West, across time into the future of Boston, Massachusetts, to demonstrate how close we could get to an ideal society in only five generations. Bellamy's imagined future depended as much on liberating technological developments and advances in knowledge as it did on the will of the people to achieve a just society. Many of these fictional treatises were intended to inspire readers to incite change from within their own societies, with thinkers drawing inspiration and energy from eighteenth-century national-scale revolutionary social movements in North America and France. Some readers, however, may have taken as the moral the idea that a perfect society was achievable only in isolation. For others, the impetus to travel away from unbearable flaws may have been greater than the will to fight against established powers.

The combination of a vividly drawn example of a perfect society and opportunity of space for settlement may have felt like a clarion call to try to achieve the dream. Alternative communities are often held up by the mainstream merely as a foil to the values of American capitalism. This does a disservice to their own internal perception of themselves as radical change agents, working to remake this world or embody the next. Their stories, and the stories of all of North America's intentional communities, are continuously and strongly interwoven into the fabric of our modern nations.

Our study of these idealistic groups, or intentional communities, sits at an intersection of two main bodies of historical thought: that of utopian and radical philosophies, and that of cooperative social structures and movements. Understanding these communities' efforts contributes to our own deeper understanding of American history by holding up a lens for us to the varied perceptions and perspectives on fractious issues of the past.

This volume explores how archaeological approaches have contributed to our understanding of intentional communities throughout American history. By accessing material records and interrogating documentary sources, scholars such as archaeologists, architectural historians, geographers, and others can bring balance to our perspectives on unconventional communities. Both written and oral histories can be fractured or biased, tending toward either hagiography or vilification, and are informed by the imperfect human memories of survivors and successors. By balancing instances of deliberate self-reporting, such as the glowing reviews found in a colony's own self-published newspaper, and the skeptical analyses of journalists from the outside with the concrete but fragmentary evidence from material culture, we can come one step closer to understanding community members' daily lived experiences. With what we learn, we can attempt to tell anew the stories of these once radical groups and the role they played in nation building.

Archaeologists, in particular, are accustomed to belaboring the details. We physically go to the places of past community, incorporate the views of multiple historical voices and modern specialists, and look holistically and synthetically at the evidence. We look not only at the words written by community members and their observers but also at the remains of the material world they built within the structures of their belief. Our inclusive approach to sources provides evidence from the broadest scale of settlement patterns that span multiple states to the tiniest lost button from a quiet hillside. At these shifting levels of focus, different stories and questions emerge about the subjects of our study. Among our responsibilities to this evidence, and to the people whose lives left the traces in our midst, is to organize and approach it with a mind to questions that matter. Throughout the following chapters, we see how today's archaeologists formulate these questions and frame windows to deepened understanding.

It continues to be problematic that many archaeologists focusing on intentional communities are either cultural resource management professionals with limited timelines and budgets or students with finite academic careers. In these roles we can thoroughly research and document specific community sites and local cultural contexts but may lack the opportunity or scholarly interest to look beyond the most common primary and secondary sources in building interpretive contexts. Our piecemeal work then goes only to our clients, regulatory agencies, or academic departments, too often below the radar of researchers building ideas about other intentional communities. It is the rare cultural resource management report, like that from Andrew Sewell and Bruce Aument's Union Village Shaker project for the Ohio Department of Transportation, that becomes easily publicly available. All too often little publicity or notice carries knowledge of intentional community studies outside of their immediate geographic area or scholarly niche. One objective of this publication is to collect and briefly present as many examples as possible of archaeologists' work on intentional community sites and spaces in the United States. Of course, some publications have been inaccessible and some reference leads ran dry. There are undoubtedly more studies out there to find and incorporate into our shared body of knowledge, but the hope is that this volume's references can offer a start to those wishing to establish a foundation upon which to build future work.

The first chapter in this volume, "Building the Ideal," introduces readers to the concepts of utopian societies, communal groups, and intentional communities as applied in American scholarship, and presents commonalities shared by groups that we can define as intentional communities. Examples from early religious congregations, social and spiritual reform groups, and socialist experiments illustrate the varied sources of inspiration and broad geographic spread of American intentional communities from the eighteenth to the twentieth centuries. Chapter 2, "Understanding Communities," discusses scholars' approaches, past and present, to the study of American intentional communities and outlines the strengths of taking a scaled archaeological perspective in our view of community artifacts, buildings, and spaces. An archaeological and historical discussion of the Doukhobor Village of Kirilovka in Saskatchewan, Canada, provides an example of how viewing community pasts at three different scales—those of the artifact, built environment, and cultural landscape—allows us to see how community ideals were simultaneously made real and challenged within historical groups. As Nan Rothschild and Diana diZerega Wall express in their 2014 macro- and microscale approach to the archaeology of American cities, people interact in different ways with broadly constructed artifacts like whole cityscapes and smaller artifacts and places that comprise the stories of individual human lives. The connections between these scales are inseverable, and we (as both archaeologists and participants in the world) simultaneously interact at multiple scales, shifting our attention and action among them. At the broadest scale of landscape, explored in chapter 3, "Maps of Idealism," archaeologists develop deeper understandings about community space management by integrating documentary evidence such as maps and prescriptive literature with traces of structured past environments such as roads, paths, and building foundation remnants. The lens zooms closer for chapter 4, "At Home, Work, and Worship," which addresses how built environments fostered togetherness and reinforced separateness among Shaker, Amana Inspirationist, Oneida Perfectionist, Brook Farm, and Ephrata Cloister families. Chapter 5, "Material Visions," focuses on how the artifacts made, bought, and used by intentional community members participated in building, demonstrating, and dismantling the connections between members and their beliefs. California's late nineteenth-century Kaweah Co-operative Commonwealth offers a reintegrated view of scaled archaeological approaches to intentional communities in chapter 6, "Seeking Kaweah." The concluding chapter, "Remaking Communities," suggests how archaeologists of intentional community can fully and respectfully illuminate the pasts of the groups whose lives and legacies we study. It seeks to begin a conversation about how archaeologists might contribute our interpretations of past communities' material evidence to social action in the present.

Throughout this volume there are three main points I hope to communicate. First, the archaeological study of intentional communities is not a new phenomenon. For more than four decades, Shaker, Moravian, and other religious community sites have drawn the attention of researchers seeking ways to expand our knowledge of these early residents through the remnants of their material culture. Starting in the early 1980s, as broader paradigms in historical archaeology shifted, more thoughtful theoretical and interpretive approaches brought to the forefront new ideas regarding our understanding of intentional communities. Today our cumulative body of work reflects some of the breadth of community forms and possible methodological approaches from which to move forward. Second, the ways that intentional communities' goals and ideals interact with and are represented in their members' material worlds are not consistent across all scales of analysis. Archaeologists can generally agree that the consciously expressed beliefs shared by members of an intentional community shape the group's physical world, and the physical environment constrains and influences the expression of a group's belief. How this occurs, and what information we can glean about the interactions between those ideals and the lived environment, can vary significantly depending on the spatial scope of our investigative perspective. I offer the model of narrowing telescopic lenses, starting with the broadest focus on communities' interactions with the landscape, then narrowing in to look at the architecture of residential buildings and spaces, and ultimately down to the level of interaction with the smallest artifacts of daily life, from buttons to tobacco pipes to household tableware. Finally, to focus too much on communities' firm historical starting and ending dates is to discount the lingering impact of their founders' ideas. Many communities can be shown to be continuous and integrated, existing in the ideas and actions of their members after moving on, and in connections with other communities across the nation. Their ideas provoke our response, sometimes in the direction of change. Are we, or should we be, activist voices in presenting these groups' histories? If we aren't conscious and intentional in our relationship to the people and the materials they left behind, we risk misinterpreting and misrepresenting a group's ideas and the statements they attempted to make about the mainstream world within which they lived. It is imperative that, as scholars, we approach our work with both rigor and reflexivity, and attempt to track our own biases as we work at the level of the landscape, the built environment, and the artifact to interpret the historical legacy of intentional communities in North America.

1

———★———

BUILDING THE IDEAL

What should we call groups of people who choose to separate themselves from their broader surrounding society and live together according to shared social, economic, or religious principles? Any definition will necessarily exclude some and obscure obvious differences between others, but groups by establishing basic criteria the linkages between communities can be made stronger, and the distinctions between communities inside and outside the category become clearer. Archaeologists have used the terms *utopian communities*, *intentional communities*, and *communal societies* to refer to groups fitting this basic description, but these terms are not interchangeable. Although often overlapping in applicability, each of these three terms has its own specificities.

Utopian?

In his seminal work *California's Utopian Colonies*, historian Robert V. Hine succinctly defines a utopian colony as

> a group of people who are attempting to establish a new social pattern based upon a vision of the ideal society and who have withdrawn themselves from the community at large to embody that vision in experimental form. (1983:5)

Hine's description is robust and precise, and it is the one I rely on most heavily in this volume. But outside those narrow parameters, when we use the word "utopian" to describe a movement or idea, what do we usually mean? More often than not, the term is applied to ideas that we consider untenable under present circumstances. They're more optimistic than realistic, usually lying somewhere on the scale between good-hearted folksiness and dangerous revolution.

The first published use of the term "Utopia" was in 1516, as the title of Thomas More's Latin-language fictional account of the eponymous island, and in the past five centuries the term has been applied and misapplied widely. "Utopia" has become perhaps the most widely understood reference for a perfect place that does not exist, as built into the word's Greek etymology are the concepts of place (-topia) and either nonexistence (ou, arguably More's original intent) or goodness (eu-). An archaeological consideration of utopian sites and spaces hinges on the assumption that people working toward a specific idea were aiming for eu- rather than ou-topia; that rather than creating a perfect nowhere, they were seeking to establish a real and tangible location for their perfect society. Whether their goals for societal change were simply to establish their own ideal community or to completely reform mainstream society through their philosophy and practice, they needed to start with a concrete physical place.

Subsequent utopian literature and experimentation echoed More's aspirations to achieve a world free of political tyranny, poverty, and social ills. The specifics would vary, of course, as any particular Utopia's characteristics always arise in response to aspects of the larger society with which it's contrasted. Movements as broad as the period of voyage and discovery that led to European settlement in and migration across the Americas, Franklin D. Roosevelt's New Deal communities and projects, and faith in digital technological advances to change modern society have been described as utopian in their impulse and nature.

Nonetheless, the term "utopian" doesn't work as a broad philosophical description of communities' structures or goals, even if applied in its most generic sense, removed as far as possible from More's original imaginings. Many of the groups discussed in this volume weren't acting within or according to the Western utopian tradition of thought and literature, and were in fact motivated by radically different methodologies and goals. Religious groups with roots in schism from institutionalized churches developed according to different principles than social movements informed by secular theorists, and the goal of sectarian freedom from religious persecution engenders a different path to the future than a vision of global freedom from wage slavery. Communities throughout American history sometimes grew from a combination of both religious and secular influences, as many groups combined aspects of spirituality or sectarian beliefs with a desire for social and economic reform.

Rather than attempting to bend the concept of utopia to fit the myriad possible forms of community, as some scholars choose (Rhodes 1967, as echoed in Kopp 2009), let's hold to the concept of *utopian* as an idea that applies better to some communities than others. It can be seen as an activating impulse that informs and inspires community building, rather than a stricture that defines the community's final shape. Geoffrey Hewitt, Australian archaeologist and researcher of the Herrnhut commune, emphasizes this aspect of *intent* when citing James Metcalf and Elizabeth Huf's book about the same community. They write: "Utopian refers to the *intention* to achieve an ideal society, not to the outcome of the attempt" (Metcalf and Huf 2002:2, cited in Hewitt 2007:108 [emphasis Hewitt's]).

Communal?

The now biannual journal *Communal Societies*, produced by the Communal Studies Association, has provided a platform for discussion of communal societies past and present since 1981. Jonathan G. Andelson, a scholar of Amana Colony history and an early communal studies contributor, has written that a communal society is a

> full-featured or institutionally complete ongoing social form in which the bonds connecting the members to one another and to the group as a whole are, whatever else they may be based on, based on feelings of fellowship. (2002:131)

Like Hine's definition of a utopian colony, Andelson's definition of a communal society deeply informs the work in this volume. Most important for consideration here is his concept that communal societies are institutionally complete—that they include the necessary structures and services to fully operate outside of mainstream society. These structures and services can include health care facilities and practitioners, schools and educators, as well as specialists in the range of trades and skills necessary to support the community's chosen economic and social goals. Also, though "feelings of fellowship" are difficult to confirm in our historical studies, it may be allowed that a sense of fellowship is more likely to be fostered by voluntary communities where members share basic common principles, and where adult members must consciously choose to join the group.

However, the word *communal* necessarily implies a level of resource sharing and economic interdependence. Not all of the groups discussed here intended to be truly communal, or stayed communal throughout their time together. Some societies expressly denied that they were communal in nature, organizing instead as cooperatives or joint stock corporations while sharing resources in daily practice. Communal and cooperative groups routinely negotiate and reevaluate the structures of sharing and collectivity that define their internal economic principles and separation from the mainstream. Structures for economic and social sharing have been expressed as an almost infinite range of possibilities, from groups in which individuals and families contribute funds, goods, or labor to the community while maintaining largely autonomous living arrangements, to those that attempt a complete dissolution of the nuclear family into a collective that holds all economic and material resources in common. This spectrum of ways that sharing can be expressed in communities makes the term "communal" too specific to be universally applicable here. As with "utopian," we will observe communalism as a quality and goal of some communities discussed here but not a necessary qualification.

Intentional?

The term I use to refer to the groups included in this volume is *intentional communities*. This concept, as understood here and shared by scholars and community members alike, connotes a planned residential grouping whose members share basic social and/or religious and/or economic values, and intend to create a living alternative to the mainstream of which they were previously a part. Donald E. Pitzer, historian and cofounder of the Communal Studies Association, finds use of the term *intentional community* as far back as 1958, when members of existing communal groups chose this term to describe their own diverse network of communities (2012:xxiii). In working archaeologically, our view of such communities requires that they be tied to a specific physical place, and thus a necessary element is that members need to live together in close proximity, away from the general public.

Anthropologist Susan Love Brown, also a frequent contributor to *Communal Societies*, defines an intentional community as

> one that is purposely and voluntarily founded to achieve a specific goal for a specific group of people bent on solving a specific set of cultural and social problems. . . . Fashioned according to the needs and beliefs of their founders and subsequent members, these communities help to resolve issues that do not affect the general public as critically. (2002a:5)

Brown exposes both the strengths and weaknesses of the term in her broadly inclusive definition. The concepts of purposefulness and voluntarism are key here, as is the idea that communities form in response to a particular perceived problem or issue. However, the term can admittedly seem too vague. Aren't all settlements intentional to some degree? Embracing this vagueness can lead to definitions like that proffered by Gregory Claeys and Lyman Tower Sargent, editors of a useful reader on utopian thought. For their purposes, intentional communities are "groups of five or more adults and their children, if any, who come from more than one nuclear family and who have chosen to live together to enhance their shared values or for some other mutually agreed upon purpose" (1999:4). According to this definition, anything from a college dormitory to a monastery to a tech startup's incubation house could be an intentional community. It can be useful to identify how different groups use coresidence to achieve particular goals, but within this volume we need to create more specificity about what intentional communities are, and what they are not. Drawing from Hine's, Andelson's, and Brown's definitions, we can clarify that intentional communities are:

> composed of members united by a common vision of an ideal society, and/or by a shared commitment to provide an alternative to unacceptable conditions in the mainstream;
> voluntary for resident members;

built with the goal of permanence;

institutionally complete in design or intention; and

physically or geographically separated from mainstream society.

There are no limitations on specifics of economic form, family structure, philosophical beliefs, or religion, as will be demonstrated by the spectrum of examples in the following pages.

A Cycle or a Thread?

In his discussion of debris left behind by members of Northern California's Chosen Family commune, archaeologist Matthew Brunwasser describes the years between 1967 and 1969 as "a period of political turbulence, intergenerational conflict, and cultural experimentation that shaped modern America" (2009:30). He's right of course, and though the intensity of communal growth between 1965 and the early 1970s outstripped that at any other time in American history (Brown 2002a:8), Brunwasser's statement can be applied equally well to nearly any period that spurred the growth of intentional communities in the United States.

Whether they attempt to completely reject mainstream thought or simply focus energy toward a reinterpretation of mainstream-compatible ideas, intentional communities critique dominant society. They bring together members who collectively embrace a shared vision of a perfect (or at least improved) social order but also who reject certain prevailing cultural or economic norms such as competitive individualism (Fogarty 1990:4). If critique of the mainstream is inherent in intentional communities, it makes sense that colonies tend to form in the greatest numbers and varieties during historical periods characterized by economic crisis or divisive social conflict (Brown 2002b:154; Shor 1997:xv). Beginning an alternative community at a time of social tension and upheaval is an act of criticism and defiance of what the group's founders see as an untenable situation. The scale of radicalism varies by group and philosophy, as some communities seek only to protect their right to live according to their own beliefs unhindered by the state or social norms. Others plan to set an example by which to transform society entirely. Archaeologists of the Llano del Rio Cooperative Colony Thad Van Bueren and Jill Hupp write that the common theme shared by varied alternative communities is their opposition to dominant social values, expressed in their "efforts to create new social orders or revive traditional ones that fall outside of accepted norms" (2000:25).

Numerous scholars have worked to develop time frames or cycles of community development through North American history, and certainly some periods saw more communities form than others. Of the brewing religious fervor that bubbled over between the 1820s and 1840s, historian Ronald G. Walters writes, "It is difficult at first to see much coherence in anything so varied as antebellum communalism. The communities themselves ranged from highly structured to utterly unstructured, from theological to free thinking, from celibate to 'free love'" (1997:41). This variability continued during the socialist impulse of the 1880s and 1890s, and the back-to-the-land movement of the 1960s and 1970s. Despite these broad time frames of increased community development, though, there has scarcely been a time during which no communities started or continued. Shaker villages, the Amana Colonies, Harmonists, and others bridged the Civil War years and extended through the changing social and technological landscape of the late nineteenth century. A handful of socialist and spiritual colonies founded in the decades around 1900 were sustained through the first decades of the new century. I agree with Charles LeWarne, scholar of Washington State's historical intentional communities, when he writes, "I am inclined to minimize the cyclical view and to see the communitarian movement as a thread—albeit having varying shades—that is constantly present and running through the American experience" (1995:xii). Perhaps the most uniting feature of American communities, then, is their very ubiquity in our shared history, fluorescing more brightly during some periods but consistently enlightening alternate possibilities.

Many Paths to the Ideal

What follows is an introduction to a few groups motivated by religious, spiritual, and secular ardor, focused on those whose places and materials have been studied from an archaeological, or in some cases cultural geographical, perspective. The earliest communities to seek refuge and find the potential to build new social forms in the United States were religious sectarians whose flight from persecution led from western Europe and

England to the northeastern states. Later movements born from American experiences created new spiritual and social forms that questioned the growing nation's direction. Socialist philosophy and speculative fictions informed other groups, inspired to seek economic fairness and equality. As settlements moved toward California's shores, so did the impulse to remake society. In the last century and a half the western states provided the space for associations that combined spiritual principles and economic ideals in new and inspired amalgamations. These examples are but a few among the hundreds of experimental communities that graced the American landscape through the past three centuries, though even in their small number they represent a broad variety of the philosophies and community shapes that existed in our past. The map and gazetteer presented in the appendix show the locations and provide some basic details of each of the communities discussed here and in the following chapters.

Spiritual Revivalism

Shared religious conviction in the face of persecution by nonbelievers provided the impetus for North America's earliest intentional communities. During the era of colonial settlement, religious colonists seeking refuge on American soil fled a climate of intolerance and their experience of persecution in seventeenth- and eighteenth-century Europe. Especially in Germany, religious sectarians who would not serve compulsory military duty, swear allegiance to secular governments, or send their children to schools run by the state-sanctioned churches were harassed by military, church, and law enforcement officials. They were ostracized and decried by their nonbelieving neighbors. Some were imprisoned, like Harmony Society founder George Rapp, or were beaten or fined for their unwillingness to cooperate. Several small groups of Dutch Mennonites, French millenarians, and German Pietists formed short-lived associations such as the Woman in the Wilderness community, Johannes Kelpius's collection of mystical cave-dwelling hermits, in the northeastern United States before the turn of the eighteenth century. More permanent group settlements, such as the ascetic and celibate Ephrata Cloister of Lancaster County, Pennsylvania, began in the early 1700s (fig. 1.1). Ephrata's most devout brothers and sisters wore monastic robes, eschewed basic comforts in their foods and furnishings,

Figure 1.1. An Ephrata Cloister interpreter wearing the white robes of the Ephrata Community's celibate members shows the author to the 1743 Sisters' House. Photo by Peter Merholz, 2003. Used with permission.

and rose nightly for prayer services intended to apprehend Christ's Second Coming.

At the turn of the nineteenth century, as the Ephrata Community was entering its final decline, most of the intentional communities forming in the United States still had in common a deeply religious nature. Of these, the best known in popular memory is probably the Shakers, or the United Society of Believers in Christ's Second Appearing (as they became officially known after 1823). In 1773 "Mother" Ann Lee, then 43 years old and living in Manchester, England, gathered converts to help realize her spiritual vision of a Christian sect led by a dual male-female godhead. Fueled by inspiration from the "Shaking Quakers" sect, the United Society was nicknamed "Shakers" for the energetic dancing that was part of their group worship. Lee brought a handful of her followers with her to New York State in 1774 to recruit new members and establish their celibate, egalitarian heaven on earth. Villages gained momentum and membership as the Protestant revivalism of the Second Great Awakening burned through the hearts of American religious seekers. By the late eighteenth and early nineteenth centuries, there were at least 20 Shaker communities between Maine and Kentucky, acting as havens for the devout and the desperate alike. Evangelical where the Age of Reason was rational, the Second Great Awakening brought emotional participation and the democratization of religious practice to followers disillusioned with the rigid authority structures of traditional churches. Like Johannes Kelpius and Conrad Beissel, Mother Ann Lee and her followers rejected the formalities, hierarchies, and worldly affiliations of institutionalized churches in favor of building more personal relationships with the spiritual through lived, not just professed, faith.

Though generally represented in broad public understanding as monolithic, deeply conservative, and stunningly simple in dress, decor, and demeanor, the Shakers were among the longest-lasting and broadest geographically spread of American intentional communities. Their villages lasted long enough to experience significant changes in the degree and nature of authoritarian control over brothers' and sisters' daily lives. As many Shaker communities' membership numbers were buoyed by the broad periods of religious revival across the nation, the concomitant increase in uninitiated recruits necessitated the revision and reassertion of behavioral and religious norms. The guidelines for acceptable practice and conduct, in the form of the Millennial Laws, were issued and amended multiple times between the late 1820s and the end of the nineteenth century. In addition to the wide time span of their settlements, Shakers also extended their reach across a vast territory, with villages in the states of Maine, New York, Massachusetts, New Hampshire, Connecticut, Ohio, Indiana, Kentucky, and Florida. Differences in thought, interpretation, and practice between

Figure 1.2. Shaker Church Family Dwelling House, Canterbury, New Hampshire, built 1793. Photo by author, 2003.

distant nodes of the community were inevitable, as residents drawn from the local populations brought their own foodways, customs, and building techniques to their new lives as Shaker brothers and sisters (fig. 1.2).

Although in current popular memory the Shakers are remembered for their simply designed and elegantly crafted furniture and housewares, their shared commitment and resources enabled them to attain high levels of commercial output of food and seed, and the production and sale of patent medicines. Food historian Ruth Ann Murray writes, "The Shakers were driven by the need to survive, inspired by their faith to work to their full potential, and aided by a lifestyle that made specialization and large-scale economies possible" (2012:40). Individual Shakers were largely identified as farmers and craftspeople, because at the time in which their communities were thriving, most of the population of the United States consisted of farmers and craftspeople. Through the decades, Shakers were early adopters of technological changes as well as initiating their own innovations that, though now seen as representing a wholesome practicality, at the time were cutting-edge innovations that contributed to the group's economic survival. The well-known flat brooms, apple peelers, and paper seed packets developed by Shaker hands are relatively easy to display as artifacts of their ingenuity, but Shaker builders and mechanics also contributed their own ideas in delivering steam and water power and facilitating large-scale laundry washing. Murray believes that

> had the Shakers first emerged in 1974 America, they may have attracted software developers, financial investors, and engineers to their ranks. They may have retreated into communes and produced computer operating systems, high speed microchips, or provided trustworthy financial services. (2012:230)

The same might be said of a great many other nineteenth-century intentional communities whose memory we indelibly associate with "simpler times" and old-fashioned technologies. What looks quaint to modern eyes may have been radical at the time.

Like their distant predecessors at Ephrata, the nineteenth-century's German-speaking Pietist communities also thrived as communally based Christian separatist settlements who sought refuge and acceptance in the United States from persecution in Europe. These include the Harmony Society in Pennsylvania and Indiana, the Separatists of Zoar in Ohio, and the Community of True Inspiration at Amana, Iowa (Herson et al. 2013; Pitzer 1997). With roots in Pietist thinkers and radicals in the Württemberg region of Germany, these groups differed in the application of their beliefs but shared philosophical origins, language, and ethnic heritage.

George Rapp, a Pietist visionary born in Germany in 1757, visited the United States in 1803 with the intent to secure an ideal location for his prospective community. He was joined the following year in Butler County, Pennsylvania, by 450–500 German immigrant followers. The group rejected the established Lutheran Church of the late eighteenth century and sought to achieve spiritual perfection through earthly communal living. They hoped to create a "model Christian republic" like that espoused in the 1619 book *Christianopolis* by Andreae, and influenced by German philosopher Johann Herder's idea of the Humanität (Pitzer 1979; Strezewski 2013:7). Harmonist tenets included the idea of spiritual perfection, which consisted of conversion from sin and personal communication with God; and millennialism, preparation for Christ's Second Coming. Charter members of the village of Harmony, Pennsylvania, renounced private property in exchange for the security and salvation of religious community. In 1814, Rapp and the Harmonists moved en masse from their first settlement in Pennsylvania to seek increased isolation from outside sources of temptation and scorn, settling the town of New Harmony on Indiana's Wabash River. Moving again a decade later, Harmonists designed and built the town of Economy, Pennsylvania, on the principle of order in their piety, laying out the town in four quadrants and including homes for 119 families (fig. 1.3). It also included what became the most memorable lasting feature of the town existing today, George Rapp's extensive and symbolic garden, planned and planted adjacent to the leader's house.

Another radical alternative to the institutionalized Lutheran church in Germany, the Inspirationist sect, or Community of True Inspiration, was founded in that country around 1714. Members established their first communal settlements and industries more than a century later in leased German monasteries and a former Moravian settlement. By the early 1840s, government persecution and hostile neighbors, angry about the Inspirationists' refusal to participate in military service, convinced many of the sectarians to emigrate to the United States with leader Christian Metz. Their first North American settlement was founded at Ebenezer, New York, in 1843. In 1855, Metz and his followers moved again, from Ebenezer to Amana, Iowa, in search of greater isolation from worldly contact and influences (see #18 in the Appendix). Over the following decade, more families moved from Ebenezer, ultimately settling in seven villages in and around Amana, with a combined population of 1,228 (Andelson 1986:45) (fig. 1.4).

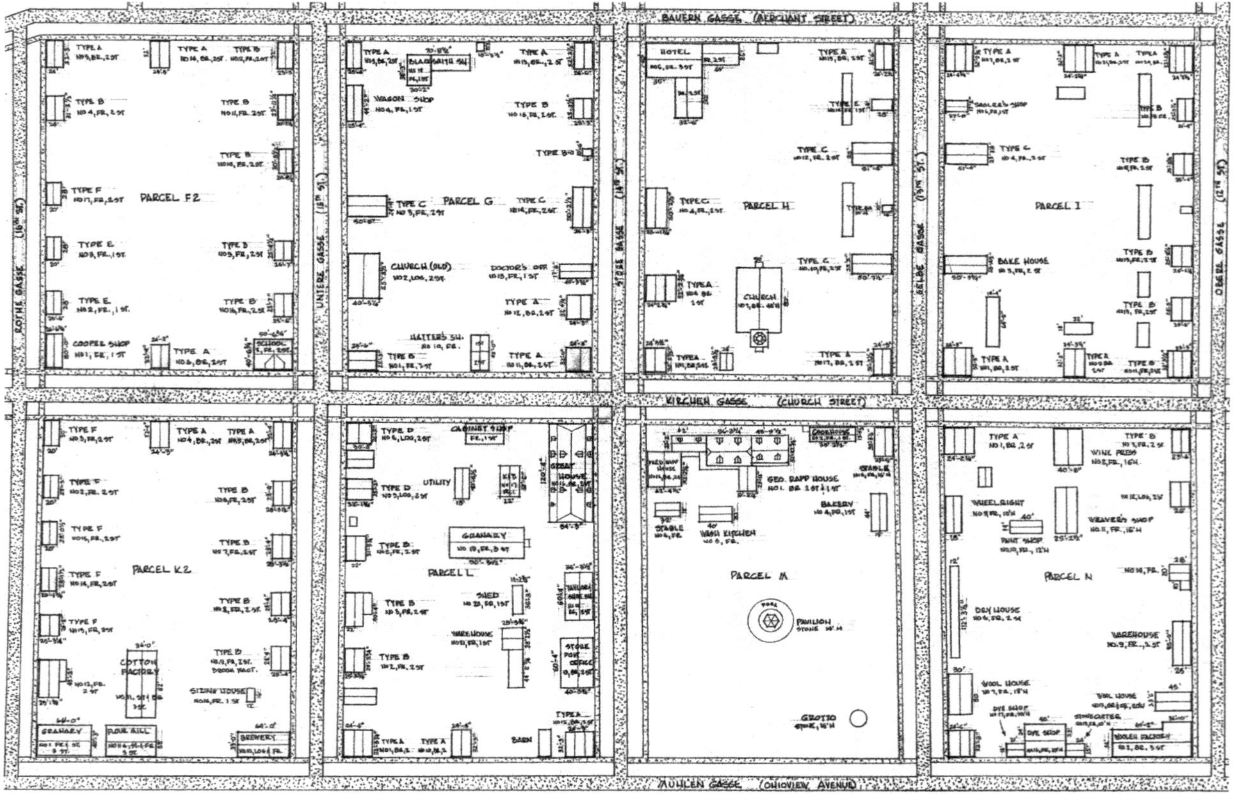

Figure 1.3. Excerpt from the plan of a section of the Harmonist village of Economy, Pennsylvania, showing evenly sized and spaced blocks and buildings. Drawn in 1967 by Paul D. Fackler and William Hartlep, Carnegie Institute of Technology for the National Park Service Historic American Building Survey. Library of Congress HABS PA,4-AMB,1- (sheet 2 of 5).

Figure 1.4. Plates in a Middle Amana print shop type tray, from publications made by Amana's printers after dissolution of the communal structure in 1932. The print shop houses a working hand-set press and Linotype machine. Photo by author, 2014, reversed to show plates as they would print.

The southern German Christian separatists who settled Zoar, Ohio, in 1817 and officially became the Separatist Society of Zoar in 1832 also fled persecution in their country of birth for rejecting the established church and refusing to send their children to church-run schools or to participate in military service (see #12 in the Appendix). The basic principles of their faith included rejection of religious ceremony and structured leadership. Under the guidance of their appointed leader, Joseph Bäumeler (spelled Bimeler in most American publications), members established the society's communal structure in 1819 in response to economic necessity. As a communal enterprise, the approximately 225 members were able to cultivate more land and operate craft workshops to support themselves in their pursuit of their faith more effectively than they would have as individual families. Multiple families shared large residences, but each family cooked for itself and tended to its own laundry, and after 1845 children older than three years were raised within their birth families rather than communal houses. Visitor Charles Nordhoff observed when researching his 1875 report on *The Communistic Societies of The United States* that the overall cleanliness and orderliness of the village of Zoar lacked the attention to detail of more fully communal groups such as the Shakers (1966:111). However, he could not deny their economic strength, and estimated their total property to be worth over a million dollars (Nordhoff 1966:103).

German-speaking Moravians who settled in Georgia, Pennsylvania, and North Carolina in the mid-eighteenth century followed a religious movement called the *Unitas Fratrum*, related to that of the Pietist brethren of Ephrata, Zoar, Amana, and New Harmony but with roots reaching back earlier than Lutheranism, to fifteenth-century Prague. These villagers embraced communalism to ensure the economic survival and physical safety of members while extending the reach of their faith (Hinds 1908:14–15). While Moravian immigrants were seeking to escape from persecution in their settlement in Saxony, missionization also served as a main impetus for their movement throughout Europe, to the United States, and across the world. In the desire to teach their faith to indigenous groups and to unite other Christians, Moravian missionaries between the mid-eighteenth and late nineteenth centuries built stations in Greenland, Labrador, southern Africa, the Caribbean, and Australia, in addition to their American settlements.

Within each Moravian town, members were organized and segregated according to gender, marriage status, and age-group categories called "choirs." In the early years of settlement in Bethabara and Salem, North Carolina, choir members lived, worked, and worshipped among those most similar to themselves in the community. As decades passed, more nuclear families lived in their own homes rather than shared accommodations, and more craftspeople pursued work for their own income rather than strictly for the Church coffers (Gutek and Gutek 1998:26). Nonetheless, the choir system is perpetuated today in the Moravians' cemetery, or God's Acre, at Salem, where burials are arranged chronologically and each newly departed individual is interred among his or her own choir.

Bishop Hill, Illinois, is a final example to be discussed here of a Pietist-inspired religious community related to the German groups presented above. These Swedish separatists coalesced around 1830 in Hälsingland, central Sweden, led by charismatic preacher Eric Jansson, with his own particular version of perfectionist Pietism and pursuit of communal living. Faced with persecution for their beliefs and for heretical acts such as Lutheran book burning, about 800 members of the group traveled to Illinois between 1846 and 1848 (Nordhoff 1966:344) (see #16 in the Appendix). At its height of activity between 1850 and 1855, their community had more than two dozen buildings, including a church, brickworks, sawmill, flour mill, hotel, and a large dining hall and residential building affectionately referred to as Big Brick, with 72 apartments on the upper floor for member families, as well as an attached bakery and brewery. Families lived in both individual homes and shared apartment buildings, ate together in the dining hall, and shared all assets—agricultural fields and stock—in common (Nordhoff 1966:346). Their community's structure lasted less than two decades.

These earliest religious communities—Ephrata, Shakers, Harmonists, Inspirationists, Zoar Separatists, Moravians, and Bishop Hill colonists—set a precedent for intentional communities in the American cultural landscape. While deeply religious, they were more than monastic enclaves; they offered fully functioning alternative residential and economic systems for believers. Each sought the difficult balance between interaction with mainstream communities through trade and compliance with local laws, and maintaining a separate togetherness.

Passionate Reform

Overlapping in time with the primarily religious communities of Shakers, Moravians, Harmonists, and others in the first half of the nineteenth century were dozens of communities based upon principles of social reform, both secular and spiritual, whose founders and philosophies were rooted more firmly in North American cultural movements than in European religious dissidence.

In 1841, minister and social reformer George Ripley and a group of like-minded thinkers calling themselves the Brook Farm Institute for Agriculture and Education purchased about 200 acres of farmland near Roxbury, Massachusetts, for their Transcendentalist experimental community (see #15 in the Appendix). Theirs was not a unified vision, nor was it representative of the Transcendentalist movement as a whole, which was, loosely speaking, "inspired by similar critiques of industrial capitalism grounded in evangelical Unitarian values" (Preucel and Pendery 2006:16, citing Francis 1997). Some members joined to escape the poverty spreading in the wake of the economic crisis of 1837, while others had more literary or artistic interests, and many young people came only to attend the well-known boarding school operated by the group (Savory 2013:7). In 1844, Brook Farm's few dozen residents adopted Fourierist principles, which stressed greater communalism and egalitarianism, in an attempt to maintain their social experiment economically by encouraging disciplined work and increasing productivity (Preucel and Pendery 2006:13). An economically and emotionally devastating fire in 1846 effectively ended Brook Farm's community.

Oneida Community founder John Humphrey Noyes, born in 1811, became a licensed preacher by the age of 23. Early in his young career, he began preaching the idea of perfectionism—that he, and all Christians, were inherently perfect and free from sin. To this then-marginal view he added the idea that the Second Coming of Christ had already occurred, and that therefore humans should live as if in heaven on earth. Within this heaven there was no traditional marriage or individual property, and thus individuals must live communally as one family. A small community living along these lines began to coalesce in Putney, Vermont, in the 1840s, but the community's outraged neighbors eventually threatened Noyes and several other members with arrest for adultery, necessitating an expeditious change of location. In 1848, Noyes established the Oneida Community 200 miles to the west in New York State (see #17 in the Appendix). For 30 years the community maintained their whole-group family structure, until mounting mainstream opposition and critique led Noyes to flee to Canada, and the remaining residents chose to dissolve the community into a joint-stock company.

Joseph Smith Jr. was born in 1805 in Vermont. Like George Ripley and John Humphrey Noyes, he grew up in the tumultuous revival frenzy of early nineteenth-century upstate New York. In the fervor of his spiritual enthusiasm, the young Smith recorded a series of visions he experienced beginning in 1820 and continuing for several years, slowly revealing to him what would become the *Book of Mormon*. With a small but growing body of followers, Smith organized the Church of Jesus Christ of Latter-day Saints (LDS) in 1830, relocating from New York State to escape persecution and to be with supporters in Kirtland, Ohio. Further years of hostility from non-Mormon populations in Ohio and Missouri pushed Smith and his converts to what would become Nauvoo, Illinois, in 1839. In 1844, disillusioned former Mormons and their non-Mormon allies created a fledgling newspaper, the *Nauvoo Expositor*, whose first and only published edition revealed Smith's polygamous practices and intimated that he was attempting to act as an infallible, divinely inspired monarch. Smith ordered the destruction of the press, which his followers carried out and for which he was arrested. Tensions escalated wildly, and Joseph Smith and his brother, Hyrum, were dragged from the jail where they were being held and murdered by an angry mob. In the wake of what followers perceived as a double martyrdom, devoted apostle Brigham Young took control of the young church and led followers to abandon Nauvoo by 1846 and trek to the Salt Lake Valley. Young oversaw the expansion of Mormonism into hundreds of new communities built across the Great Basin states. An ideal plan envisioned by Joseph Smith for the City of Zion served as a rough guide for constructing many of the new western Mormon towns.

In 1894, physician and "post-Christian" religious socialist theologian Dr. Cyrus Teed led his followers, who knew him as Koresh, from New York and Chicago to southwestern Florida. Here they would establish an egalitarian communal settlement that members of the Koreshan Unity called their New Jerusalem. Teed had been recruiting his disciples since the 1870s, attracting followers with beliefs that included the idea that Earth was a hollow sphere, with the lands, seas, and humans residing on the inside of the sphere and the half-light, half-dark sun at its center (fig. 1.5).

Ripley, Noyes, Smith, and Teed each drew on spiritual and social undercurrents of nineteenth-century America to craft the new belief systems that would structure their followers' lives. Unlike the European religious communities discussed above who shared religious and cultural roots in Germany and Sweden, and who moved en masse to settlements in the United States, the Oneida family, Brook Farm, the Mormons, and the

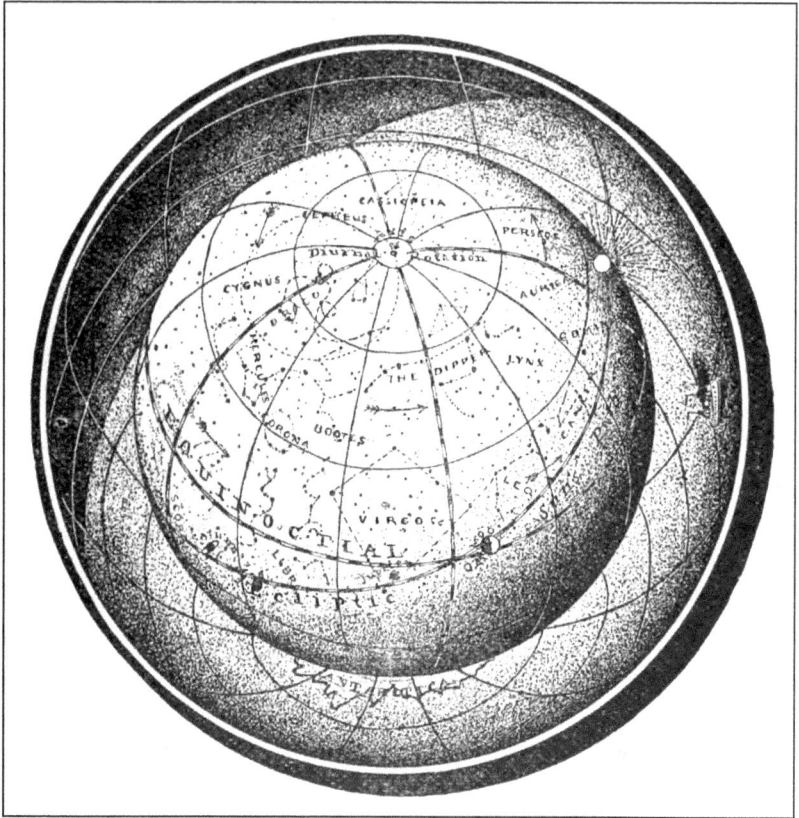

Figure 1.5. This graphic, titled "In the Hollow of His Hand: The Heavens in the Earth," from Cyrus Teed's 1905 *Cellular Cosmogony, or, The Earth a Hollow Globe*, shows how Koreshan Unity members visualized astronomical features within the bounded universe of the concave earth. From the collection of the University of California, digitized by Google and available as an electronic document at the Internet Archive (archive.org).

Koreshan Unity settlers coalesced as uniquely American phenomena. As different from one another as they were from the earlier religious communities, groups such as these four exemplify the variability and integration of spiritual and secular ideals that characterized subsequent American intentional communities.

Socialist Fictions Made Real

Thomas More's sixteenth-century travel account of *Utopia* is only one early example in a loosely bounded tradition of fictional accounts of ideal places. Intellectual historians Gregory Claeys and Lyman Tower Sargent pull the roots of the utopian vision in the Western tradition back as far as the Greek poet Hesiod's eighth-century B.C. visions of the golden age of the first mortals, *Works and Days* (1999:7), earlier even than Plato's oft-cited fourth-century B.C. *Republic*. Though long in history and abundant in imagination, speculative utopias gained the most traction as community inspiration much later, when mid-nineteenth-century writers such as Charles Fourier and Étienne Cabet inspired French readers exhausted by waves of civil war. In general, these utopian fictions envision communities that, if not fully secular, don't include organized religion as part of their fundamental structuring principles. Utopian fictions, like Étienne Cabet's 1840 *Voyage en Icarie* and later in the century Edward Bellamy's 1888 *Looking Backward* and William Dean Howells's 1894 *A Traveler from Altruria*, are proscriptive in nature, describing the details of daily life and social structure in such color and clarity that readers are sometimes inspired to try to make the vision they've read about real.

Among the earliest groups inspired by socialist literature to establish communities in the United States, the Icarian movement was borne out of social upheaval in France during the first decades of the nineteenth century. Writer Étienne Cabet gained a devoted following with his articles in the newspaper *Le Populaire*, and his 1840 utopian novel, *Voyage en Icarie*. Cabet's fictional land was a modern industrial paradise where unpleasant work was performed by machines, leaving only safe and enjoyable tasks for human laborers. Cities would be clean and beautiful, the petty vagaries of fashion eliminated, and the arts and sciences accessible and beneficial to all. Central to his ideal was the eradication of inequality, private property, and money.

Cabet himself discouraged real-world experimental communities. He believed that Fourierists, Saint-Simonists, and even contemporary and intellectual compatriot Robert Owen's colonists at New Lanark, Scotland, and New Harmony, Indiana, were wasting their effort on communal experiments when they should rather have focused on disseminating their doctrine more broadly, in order to initiate a decades-long process of change throughout whole nations (Sutton 1985). Nonetheless, supporters urged Cabet to materialize his vision by building real communities. Swept up in the enthusiasm of his new followers, in the late 1840s Cabet moved with a group of prospective communal settlers to Nauvoo, Illinois, which had been abandoned by most of its Mormon founders over the previous five years. The Icarian settlement at Nauvoo resulted in schism between Cabet's followers and those who resented his authoritarianism, and was followed by short-lived experiments in St. Louis, Missouri, and Chelthenham, Illinois. Cabet died among his minority of Icarian followers in St. Louis in 1856, and the majority of colonists from Nauvoo relocated to land that they had acquired near Corning, Iowa. By 1880, factionalism within this group created two separate communities, of which the more radical Jeune Icarie group relocated to Sonoma County, California, with the hope of establishing a new Icaria. They acquired an 885-acre ranch south of the town of Cloverdale and built their "Icaria Speranza" along the west side of the Russian River, along a small drainage that still bears the name Icaria Creek. Icarians' choice of California for their new colony had as much to do with the political climate as the temperate Mediterranean weather, as the San Francisco Bay area at this time had an active socialist community (Anderson 1995:25; Hine 1983:65; Sutton 1995:34). The Cloverdale experiment lasted until around 1886, and the Corning, Iowa, settlers maintained their community until about 1898. As they moved across the United States, Icarians remained committed to the French language, and as Missouri communications scholar Steve Wiegenstein argues, their devotion to French identity and customs kept Icarians at a distance from their English-speaking neighbors (2006:291).

Though not separated by language from their American neighbors, the English gentlemen farmers of Rugby, Tennessee, kept their distance by maintaining the upper-class affectations of their upbringing. Between 1880 and 1887, these "second sons," mobilized by English novelist Thomas Hughes, attempted to become a kind of new landed gentry away from a homeland that offered them no such opportunity.

Spreading Westward

Between the American Civil War and the First World War, communities spread farther into western North America than in previous decades. During this time, the West Coast, Great Basin states, and northern Mexico germinated communal experiments with a spectrum of identities and ideals encompassing Mormons, Molokans, vegetarians, Theosophists, Little Landers, and socialists, all inspired by different philosophies to remove themselves from mainstream society to form colonies with different goals (Hine 1983; Miller 1990). Eminent historian of California's communities Robert V. Hine writes that among late nineteenth-century West Coast intentional communities, "the thought patterns resulting in communitarian experiments became far more numerous" even than in the eastern states in the first half of the century (1983:4). With the exception of Aurora, a community in the Willamette Valley of Oregon established in 1856 by millennialist minister William Keil, intentional communities on the West Coast flourished later in time than those in the eastern United States.

Many of these growing experiments were deeply inspired by European socialist philosophy and developments in the labor movement in response to declining social and economic conditions for working-class residents of industrializing cities. Works inspired by Marxist theory, such as Laurence Gronlund's 1884 *Cooperative Commonwealth*, addressed growing industrialization and economic disparity in European and North American cities. The stories and ideas espoused in utopian fiction and socialist literature of this era appealed primarily to wage-earning middle-class families whose financial aspirations could not keep up with the pace set by the growing wealth of America's industrialist and mercantile barony. Farmers and small business owners, increasingly limited by banks and railroad companies, were attracted to many utopian authors' antimonopoly ideas (Passet 2005:308).

Founders of one of the better known of California's socialist experiments, the Kaweah Co-operative Commonwealth, hoped to directly involve author Laurence Gronlund in their community, as his 1884 *Co-operative Commonwealth* informed much of Kaweah's philosophical structure (see #22 in the Appendix). A writer for the colony-published newspaper, the *Kaweah Commonwealth*, crowed in March 1890 that a gratifying fact exists in this, that Laurance [sic] Gronlund the author of "Co-operative Commonwealth" has applied for membership in the Kaweah colony, thus recognizing the virtue of its organization as founded upon the principles enunciated in his own work. (15 March 1890)

Executive members of Kaweah prepared to provide funds for his travel to California, and to free elected offices for the author to assume upon his arrival, but Gronlund and his wife never came to the colony. The Kaweah Colony's efforts will be discussed in more detail in chapter 6.

Not far from Icaria Speranza, the westernmost outpost of the French socialist Icarians, the Northern California Christian socialist community of Altruria was inspired by William Dean Howells's 1894 utopian novel *Traveler from Altruria*. A rural answer to Edward Bellamy's future utopia in Boston, Altruria's strength was based on the altruism of its members (Claeys and Sargent 1999:301–302). For two years the small membership of less than two dozen attempted to maintain a cooperative settlement under the direction of Unitarian minister Edward Byron Payne. Though lasting only briefly, Altruria's attempt inspired socialist lawyer, politician, and activist Job Harriman to later found the Llano del Rio cooperative experiment in Los Angeles County (see #28 in the Appendix).

Harriman started the Llano del Rio Cooperative Colony in 1914 when, after losing his presidential election bid as Eugene Debs's Social Democratic Party running mate in 1900 and failing in other political efforts, he decided to demonstrate socialism in a practical form (fig. 1.6). Organizers acquired land in northeastern Los Angeles County, in the southwestern Antelope Valley, at the western edge of the Mojave Desert. Though the colony actively pursued agricultural and industrial goals, and printed voluminous promotional literature, loss of water rights in the arid California location and internal struggles between members spurred the colony's move to New Llano, Louisiana, in 1917. By the time the California colony folded, it owned over 2,000 acres of land and controlled a lumber camp, a cattle camp, and two limestone quarries (Van Bueren and Hupp 2000:14).

A more aesthetic example of Southern California's community history, the American Theosophical Society headquarters at Point Loma, near San Diego, was an architecturally eclectic artistic and spiritual community

Are You An Undesirable?

HAVE you been an agitator in your vicinity? Have you struggled and worked to make things better for humanity? Have you developed a spirit of altruism, and thus become a rebel against the oppression of the capitalist autocracy? Have you been honestly and earnestly spreading the doctrine of discontent with the system of the despoilers? Have you talked and agitated for the coming co-operative system? If so, you have friends and comrades and loved ones, but you are undesirable so far as the capitalists and parasites are concerned. If you have achieved this much we want you to go a step farther. We want you to come to the Llano del Rio Community where we are making a great demonstration of the co-operation for which you have worked.

You see the future alike of farmers and city mechanic. You see the centralization of wealth and the crushing down of the middle classes. You see expropriation and disemployment. You see your comrades go down and under in the fierceness of the struggle. Surely you are tired of the struggle in the competitive system, where remains the inexorable the law of tooth and claw.

Why not cast your lot with your comrades who for eighteen months have borne the brunt of the hardships in pioneering at the Llano del Rio Co-operative Community in Los Angeles County, California.

If you are tired of being exploited and robbed and want to get the field social product of your efforts, turn to pages 15, 16, 17, 18, 19 and 31 of this magazine and read the story of the wonderful progress that has been made by the Co-operative Community founded by Job Harriman. If you are interested write for our booklet, "The Gateway to Freedom."

Sandbox and Irrigation Gates

"Modern society conducts its affairs under circumstances which create and maintain an ever increasing burden on all humanity. Man sustained in youth by the illusion that ability or good fortune will ultimately reward him with happiness through material success, learns sooner or later, that no peace can be his until the unmoral conditions of commercialism and industrial competition are removed."—From the Community Constitution.

LLANO DEL RIO COMPANY

Membership Department

924 Higgins Building   Los Angeles, California

Figure 1.6. An advertisement for the Llano del Rio Company encourages socialist agitators and frustrated laborers to join their cause. From the September 1915 issue of the Llano del Rio Company's newsletter, the *Western Comrade*, page 32. Digitized by the California State Library, available as an electronic document at the Internet Archive (archive.org).

occupied by as many as 500 members between 1897 and 1942 (see #24 in the Appendix). Like Llano del Rio, it is an example of those communities whose active spans extended through times less associated with the social and economic upheaval from which intentional communities often develop

The Chosen Family commune is a final California example, and was one among hundreds from the florescence of rural communes where (mostly) young people of the 1960s and 1970s went to get back to the land, "turn on, tune in, drop out" (Leary 1966), and escape the urban blight growing through these decades. In a faint echo of the Brook Farm colonists' burned Phalanstery, the Chosen Family's communal structure could not recover from the devastating effects of a 1969 fire in their home.

Echoing the variability of earlier American-born communities at Oneida, Brook Farm, and Estero, California's intentional communities represent a wide range of ideals from Kaweah's and Llano del Rio's socialism to the Theosophists' artistic spiritualism, to the Chosen Family's reaction to postwar American conservatism. These are only a handful of examples from dozens of West Coast communities, most of which have not yet been studied by archaeologists.

Connected Communities

Intentional communities in the United States were never completely isolated, despite the mythology of otherworldliness and separation that surrounds them in our historical imagination. Whether local or national in their goals, intentional communities share that their existence stands as a critique of the culture from which their members came but within which they must still operate, both legally and economically. Each group exists in dialogue with the larger surrounding society, and continues to build and maintain legal and economic relationships that allow its continued operation. Many groups must participate with national, state, and local legislative bodies by paying property taxes, recording real-estate transactions, and registering vital statistics. And most, if not all, groups continued to purchase some goods and services while offering or selling others outside their ranks.

Just as significant as these economic and legal connections are the shared beliefs and implicit assumptions that members carry with them into their intentional communities, which may or may not be called into question by community philosophy. Southern California's 1914–1917 Llano del Rio colony is remembered as an example of early feminist theory and practice for its association with Alice Constance Austin, an architect whose home and city plans envisioned women's liberation from doing their own cooking and laundry. The intended labor distribution at Llano included job rotation, opportunities for the aged to work in apprenticing, and women's ability to work in any trade. This last goal, however, wasn't even supported by the group's own industrial school, which divided its learning opportunities by gender—limiting girls to education in more traditionally female, domestically oriented occupations "like cooking and sewing" (Van Bueren and Hupp 2000:20). In practice at Llano, the gendered divisions of labor experienced by members before colony life were reproduced in the new community. Journalist A. R. Clifton reported in 1918 that, at the industrial school, "the boys did a large amount of the construction work in providing buildings for this center, and the girls cooked and made many of the clothes for the boys as well as for themselves" (1918:86).

Ethnic and racial biases, both implicit and explicit, were also carried into community life in more than one instance. While nothing about the philosophical basis for the Llano del Rio colony was racially discriminatory, founder Job Harriman explained that applications from "Negroes, Hindus, Mongolians, and Malays" were turned down "not due to race prejudice but because it is not deemed expedient to mix the races in these communities" (Llano del Rio Company of Nevada 1916:2). Also in California, leaders of the 1888–1892 Kaweah Co-operative Commonwealth touted the value of laborers' equality while simultaneously engaging with the anti-Chinese movement that was intertwined with organized labor in the state. Their boast that their wagon road stood as "the greatest monument ever erected to cooperation by a white civilization" (Kaweah Commonwealth, 12 July 1890) reminds us that there is no objective concept of utopia. Visions of a perfect society are necessarily in dialogue with those aspects considered imperfect in any particular time and place, while incorporating elements of belief that would have no place in a society of our own intentional design.

While maintaining connection to the world from which they are setting themselves apart, intentional communities also build connections to other like-minded communities through shared spaces, ideas, and membership.

New Harmony, Indiana, provides but one example of two different kinds of connections—sequential location overlap and member interrelationship. The original town site of New Harmony was built by Pietist members of the Harmony Society in 1814 and was occupied for a decade before its residents returned to Pennsylvania. The next occupants were members of Robert Owen's secular experimental community who, though their organized attempt at social reform lasted only a few years, inspired others to pursue a path to community. English heiress and reform enthusiast Frances Wright drew experience, support, and fellow members from Owen's New Harmony for her own later community at Nashoba, Tennessee, which she founded in 1826 to provide a home and work for African American families freed from enslavement (Egerton 1977:22–23).

Historian Peter Hoehnle's work demonstrates that the Amana Society of Iowa and its New York predecessor, the Ebenezer Society, were connected by an extensive network of intercommunity economic and intellectual contacts. For Ebenezer and Amana, a commitment to communitarianism was in some cases a more important determinant of contact than any similarities in faith or vision, as Amana's German Inspirationists exchanged communication, goods, and members with the Zoar community, Shakers, and secular Icarians (Hoehnle 2000:74). The Shakers' primacy and longevity as an example of a Christian communal society was such that aspiring society founders like Chicago-based Cyrus Teed and Annie G. Ordway, who later steered the Koreshan Unity Settlement in Florida, approached the Shakers for guidance and acceptance. Teed and Ordway's 1892 visit to the Shaker village of New Lebanon, New York, after which Teed was admitted to the Shakers' novitiate order and Ordway became an elder, is described in the October 1892 issue of the Shakers' publication *The Manifesto* (220, 230). Teed had also sought the support of the Harmonist Society at Economy, Pennsylvania (Gutek and Gutek 1998:208).

Serial and concurrent intentional community memberships such as Frances Wright's, Annie Ordway's, and Cyrus Teed's were common. Several former Harmonist Society members traveled with self-styled Christian leader William Keil to Aurora, Oregon, in the early 1850s. Job Harriman (O'Connor 2000:107), who would later found the Llano del Rio Cooperative Colony in Southern California, was associated with the Altruria Colony, a Christian socialist intentional community in Sonoma County (ca. 1894–1896). At the same time, former Kaweah Co-Operative Commonwealth Colony (ca. 1888–1892) members and supporters J. G. Clark, W.C.B. Randoph, J. Q. Henck, George R. Moore, and C. S. Preble participated as members of Altruria (O'Connor 2000).

This interconnection of colonies demonstrates the presence of a larger network of intentional communities, within which the success or failure of a single experiment did not necessarily indicate a failure in the cause as a whole. As Otohiko Okugawa writes in a 1983 paper that diagrams the multiple connections between several nineteenth-century communities,

> the types of interrelatedness and the patterns of migration clearly show that even when a group did not "survive" it often went on to live again in another commune—usually a related one. The larger communitarian world can thus be viewed as a living one that maintained its vitality well beyond the late nineteenth century and well beyond the usual terms of death and survival. (1983:82)

For groups whose community was built based on specific social, religious, or economic ideals, the intention can long outlast and outgrow a community built around it.

Temporary Utopias

As the concept of what constitutes an intentional community has been subject to some ongoing discussion, it seems prudent here to provide examples of some potentially confusing cases of categorization. I would argue that the following three specific types of organization, while they share some outward structures and commonalities, cannot be considered intentional communities: residential institutions, company towns, and intentionally temporary or demographically bounded communal experiments.

In her contribution to *The Archaeology of Institutional Life*, Sherene Baugher includes communal societies in her broad definition of "institutions" to be included in the book's scope, encompassing "those institutions that control people's behavior and daily life" (2009:5). Her specific examples from archaeology include Lu Ann De Cunzo and colleagues' 1996 landscape archaeology study at Father Rapp's garden in Economy, Pennsylvania; David Starbuck's 2004 book *Neither Plain nor Simple: New*

Perspectives on the Canterbury Shaker; and Matthew Tomaso's 2006 work at the "quasi-utopian" company town of Feltville, New Jersey (Baugher 2009:7). The volume's focus is upon those institutions that sought to reinforce mainstream societal values and either reintegrate or reform individuals to become good citizens according to broad social standards. Almshouses, workhouses, asylums, prisons, and schools were institutions within which inmates exercised limited control, primarily by choosing which guidelines to follow and which to openly contradict or quietly disregard (see Casella 2007). In describing the Ephrata Cloister, the eighteenth-century German Pietist community he spent over a decade researching in Lancaster County, Pennsylvania, archaeologist Stephen G. Warfel writes in the same volume that the community was "not an intentional community per se" (2009:138), rather that the group more closely suited anthropologist Harry Holbert Turney-High's 1968 definition of an institution as "a ritualized system of groups in equilibrium organized around goals considered too important to trust to informality" (1968:346). Identification is a matter of opinion, however, as the Ephrata Cloister is also featured as the first example in Gerald and Patricia Gutek's detailed 1998 guide to museums and historical reconstructions of intentional community, *Visiting Utopian Communities*. Some scholars clearly consider certain intentional communities to be institutional in nature. However, this does not mean that residential institutions are necessarily intentional communities.

Institutional residential establishments can seem similar to intentional communities in many aspects. An orphanage or asylum's architecture and infrastructure may bear similarities to that of a Shaker dwelling house or other communal space where lodging, dining, sanitation, and other needs are managed at a large scale to serve a concentrated population. As archaeologists of institutional life have demonstrated, the architecture and landscape of prisons, asylums, schools, and hospitals can be used to structure residents' behavior by reflecting and instilling certain basic societal principles of order and acceptability (Beisaw and Gibb 2009; Casella 2007). However, while residents in penal, educational, and health institutions are intended to be temporary inmates, members of intentional communities as defined here are expected to make a permanent commitment to resident membership. In a 2002 discussion of sociogenesis and schismogenesis in intentional communities, Jonathan Andelson writes that most "intentional communities reject the notion that their existence is inevitably temporary and instead embrace a separate existence as the goal state" (2002:134). Without collective commitment to permanency, prospective members would be unlikely to make the necessary personal and material sacrifices for membership.

Perhaps more important, while intentional community members seek either to create an alternative society or to reform society at large in the image they have designed, institutional inmates are intended to be personally reformed according to the image considered acceptable by the mainstream society, which they are expected to aspire to rejoin. Intentional communities seek to reshape society in the image of an ideal; institutions seek to reshape individuals to the expectations of society. Prison convicts are incarcerated for a discrete period of time, after which they are released back into mainstream society—either repentant and reformed or bound to revisit prison. Boarding school students are in training to become productive members of mainstream society. Psychiatric patients are hospitalized to help them reestablish "normalcy," and those who can't must remain inmates, at arm's length from the rest of society, under the care of guardians who act as enforcers of accepted mainstream behaviors. Even monastic institutions allied with large churches, which seem uncommonly separate from the world outside, can be understood as integral to networks of spiritual teaching and practice that support more than they question or critique secular society.

Company towns, though structured intentionally for economic and social outcomes, also do not fit the present definition of intentional communities. Martin Gibbs, in his discussion of the mid-nineteenth-century mining town of Gwalla in western Australia, argues convincingly that company towns such as Gwalla and the mill town of Feltville, New Jersey, were designed to provide a comfortable and predictable environment in which resident employees could be expected to optimize their work productivity (2010:611). Jane Eva Baxter expands this idea in her 2012 look at Pullman, Illinois, a company town established in 1880 to closely manage the lives of the Pullman Palace Car Company's factory workers in the interest of increased productivity. The design of Pullman was nothing if not intentional—with scaled housing quality and placement mapped directly to occupational status, and comprehensive services ensuring that residents could access everything, and only those things, conducive to what company managers considered a wholesome and temperate lifestyle. The community aspect is what was truly lacking. Residents paid high rents to the Pullman company, which planned to recoup the costs of building the town, and the only common factor shared by all who lived there was their common employer. Residents weren't permitted to sit on porches or congregate in public spaces, and the only parks were located under the watchful gaze of the highest status employees' homes (Baxter 2012:659). Archaeological evidence from Pullman's public spaces and backyards shows barely any pre-1900 debris, let alone evidence that workers used spaces in unsanctioned ways during the company's ownership of the town. An extreme example of corporate planning, Pullman was less a workers' community than a laboratory for class-based antagonization that contributed significantly to the 1894 Pullman Strike.

In a few interesting cases, temporary cooperative or communal settlements approximate intentional communities in their commitment to offering alternative social models. Age-specific cohousing and temporary cultural festivals might encourage alternative economies and cohabitation, but they do so without requirements for institutional completeness or permanent participation. Society as a whole doesn't need to be reproduced in the age, gender, and occupational composition of these groups, because all-encompassing societal change isn't their goal. A dusty week in Burning Man's "experiment in temporary community dedicated to radical self-expression and radical self-reliance" (Burning Man Project 2016) may change the personal perspective of many participants and create a global social network of like-minded art enthusiasts, but it has yet to offer a permanent and institutionally complete alternative to mainstream society. As such, it provides a wonderfully vivid example of the difference between temporary utopian vision and lived intentional community.

Other Lands

This volume limits its scope to intentional communities in North America, particularly in the United States, with only brief forays into Canada and Mexico. This limitation is one of practicality, and is not by any means intended to assert that intentional communities formed only on this continent. A great many communities throughout America's past had their origins in Europe, either in philosophical inspiration or actual physical settlements. Religious and social persecution did not force all utopian groups to relocate overseas; many grew and remained within the borders of Great Britain and continental Europe. A few examples include England's anarchist cooperative Clousden Hill in Northumberland (ca. 1890s–1900) and the Whiteway Colony in the Cotswolds, founded in 1898 and still operating, and France's anarchist Free Society of Vaux (ca. 1903–1906) and Aiglemont (ca. 1903–1907). Some of the groups that originated in European countries before starting North American communities, such as Moravian missionaries, Mennonites, the Bruderhof, and Molokans, also settled broadly on multiple continents as land and potential members were found. Hewitt and others remind us that "there were literally dozens of cooperative homestead associations and village settlements within the Colony of Victoria (now part of Australia) alone, during the closing decade of the nineteenth century" (Hewitt 2007:108). Within the same hemisphere, Lucy Sargisson and Lyman Tower Sargent's 2004 volume *Living in Utopia* is dedicated to New Zealand's intentional communities of the past and present. Nations of the early colonial world offered exceptional havens for intentional communities with inspirations off- and on-shore, as they provided the space, both geographical and social, within which communities could assert their ideals. While intentional communities have been a strong thread woven through the development of modern America, they're certainly not a uniquely American phenomenon.

Our Dystopian Preoccupation: Success and Failure

Intertwined with any popular discussion of attempts at intentional community are the questions of how and why each community through American history has, seemingly inevitably, failed. The reasons for colony dissolution are as many and varied as different colonies themselves, and often involve complex combinations of internal disputes, external political and economic relationships, and geographic or climatological contingencies. A few scholars have attempted to generalize about which qualities seem to make some colonies more successful than others. Historian Ronald Walters proposes that the shared language, extended family relationships, and rural

European background strengthened bonds among German pietist community members (1997:48). Internal homogeneity, then, combined with distinct differences or deviations from the external society, contributed significantly to communities' success. Psychologist Leigh Minturn's 1995 study of modern (later twentieth-century) communes, though, provides a different view. Her results indicated that predictors of commune success include formal leadership, shared religious orientation, joint property ownership, isolation from outside media, and distinctive restrictive customs. Cultural homogeneity, communal work efforts, and inconsistency of ideologically based decision-making were present in unsuccessful communes.

Donald Pitzer's approach of "developmental communalism" (1997) contextualizes the idea of intentional communities' success or failure within each specific group's ability and willingness to transform in response to changing conditions. This way of looking at communities tends to view groups and their members as active participants in community formation and re-formation, rather than as passive victims of inevitable failure. Pitzer further argues that those groups who stubbornly held to communal practices within changing environments may have undermined the larger ideal that group living was originally intended to serve. In this view, some groups must fail as communities to ultimately perpetuate and communicate their vision. If maintaining the communal structure was secondary in importance to developing whatever ideal brought members together in the first place, and if a community's ideas live on through members' influence after the community itself disbands, we must temper our enthusiasm to call it a failure. Dolores Hayden eloquently remarks that she is "willing to define as a success any group whose practices remain provocative even after the group itself has disbanded" (1976:6). Her wording is significant. Groups need not fully integrate their beliefs into mainstream thought and practice to have been a success; it is enough if their actions in pursuit of their ideals have provoked ongoing conversations about the worth and achievability of those ideals within the larger society.

To be realistic, not all groups will succeed in either community or ideational form. The great majority of those ever attempted have been all but forgotten, but those discussed here, whose places and debris have been reimagined through archaeological perspectives, have a chance to provoke our thoughts once again. The following chapter provides an introduction to some of the ways archaeologists, anthropologists, historians, and other scholars have approached intentional communities since the nineteenth century, from descriptive travelogues informed by firsthand observation to modern analyses of centuries-old technologies.

2

———★———

UNDERSTANDING COMMUNITIES

For as long as there have been intentional communities in the United States, these groups have attracted attention from scholars and the public eager to learn about the radicals in their midst. Anthropologists, geneticists, historians, geographers, psychologists, sociologists, and others are drawn to the study of how communities form, function, and eventually fade. The writings devoted to describing individual communities are too numerous to discuss here, though excellent bibliographies listing many of these accounts have been compiled by Timothy Miller (1990), Donald Pitzer (1997), and Richard C. S. Trahair (1999). The discussion here focuses on writers who have taken on the broader task of writing about multiple communities, whether in an encyclopedic or analytical way.

Contemporary Observers

Starting in the middle of the nineteenth century, journalists and other interested parties visited settlements across the nation, putting their observations into print with the various goals of educating the public, informing governmental policy, and instructing current and future community members. The earliest well-documented attempt to chronicle American intentional communities was by A. J. Macdonald, a Scottish-born printer and proponent of Owenite (following the ideas of Robert Owen) and Fourierist (following the ideas of Charles Fourier) communities who solicited questionnaires from community residents and personally visited dozens of groups between 1842 and 1854. During his years of study, he amassed notes about nearly 80 different communities and associations. Macdonald died of cholera before he could complete and publish his work, but John Humphrey Noyes, founder and leader of the Oneida Perfectionist community in New York, sought out his collected papers to provide a starting point for his own 1870 book, *History of American Socialisms*.

From the beginning, most writers have been clear that their purpose for studying intentional communities was not simply an intellectual exercise. There was often a didactic or prescriptive aspect to their chronicles, rather than a purely analytical one. Macdonald's "letter of inquiry," which he distributed to current and former community members, expressed his hope that the planned publication would guide other hopeful groups "like a light-house, pointing to the rocks on which so many have been wrecked, or to the haven in which the few have found rest" (quoted in Noyes 1870:4). Noyes's own appropriation of Macdonald's materials diverges from this broadly inclusive and optimistic stance by discounting in his own discussion all groups not aligned either with Owenite or Fourierist principles of association. As the driving force of the Oneida Perfectionist community, which operated in New York starting in 1847, Noyes positions his work as an evaluation of these two strains of thought by which to contrast his own presumably more thorough and potentially successful model. Modern labor historians have also been critical of Fourierist experiments, though not as examples of imperfectly realized community plans as Noyes does but as distractions from the important working-class solidarity building being undertaken at the time by union organizers (Boyer 1997:x; Guarneri 1991:4). Appealing more to middle-class intellectuals than actual workers, Fourierist promises failed to offer the concrete connections and protections that unions could offer nineteenth-century industrial laborers.

Following only a handful of years behind Noyes's 1870 *History*, journalist Charles Nordhoff's 1875 *The Communistic Societies of the United States* is more in line with Macdonald's generally sympathetic nonparticipant observational scholarship. Nordhoff personally visited more than a dozen communities, and in his volume presents and weighs their comparative strengths as potential avenues for offering viable, meaningful alternatives to wage labor for members of the American working class. His detailed commentaries continue to be useful to scholars of the Amana Inspirationists, Oneida Perfectionists, Separatists of Zoar, Shakers, and others.

Oneida community member William Hinds also raised his scholarly voice on the topic of then contemporary and historical communities with his 1878 *American Communities*, published by Oneida's own Office of the American Socialist. He followed this volume with updated revisions in both 1902 and 1908, which were published by a Chicago press following the Oneida colony's collapse. Hinds's 1908 revision is probably the most comprehensive view of intentional communities published up to that time, including descriptions of more than 45 different groups. His brief closing section, entitled "Inductions," reads as an undiscouraged, though cautionary, endorsement of communal living. He writes:

> That an ideal Community is an enlarged home, or aggregation of happy, intelligent, virtuous households, with enlarged dwellings, domains and workshops, multiplied labor-saving appliances and increased facilities for improvement and happiness, wherein all strive for the common good; and such a home will be as much superior to the single household in all that makes life worth the living as it excels the latter in means and numbers; but if, perchance, the demon of strife enters and continues to assert itself in the enlarged home, then its miseries will be multiplied in the like proportion. (Hinds 1908:592)

Ernest Wooster's 1924 *Communities of the Past and Present* is a collection of Wooster's own interviews and descriptions, coupled with large blocks of text taken directly from previous authors' work, such as Hinds's *American Communities*. Published by the Llano del Rio Cooperative Colony, at New Llano, Louisiana, the book is prefaced by an introduction written by Llano founder Job Harriman. Wooster presents just over 40 communities as examples for comparison to his own community of New Llano, which (unsurprisingly, perhaps) is presented as being the closest to ideal. This work may be the most excoriating indictment of others' failures produced from within the community of communities.

Skeptical and Sentimental Recollections

A few overviews of nineteenth-century communities were produced in the mid-twentieth century, trailing by a few decades the active communal experiments they discussed while preceding the florescence of communes to come in the 1960s and 1970s. While not solely dedicated to intentional communities, Alice Felt Tyler's 1944 *Freedom's Ferment: Phases of American Social History to 1860* devotes a section of seven chapters to what she calls "Cults and Utopias," including a discussion of the well-documented groups founded before 1860. Her use of the term "cults" betrays her scholarly attitude toward intentional communities, of which she writes that the "idea of progress carried to the extreme of belief in the possibility of perfection was a heady wine, causing in many men an emotional intoxication that led to a confused view of the world about them. From this very confusion came numerous new religious cults and social experiments in communal living" (Tyler 1944:46).

Widely acknowledged as the first comprehensive historical overview devoted exclusively to communal experiments to have been written by a modern scholar, Arthur Bestor's 1950 *Backwoods Utopias* is still cited as a foundational work by eminent scholars in the field (Pitzer 2012). Mark Holloway's 1966 *Utopian Communities in America, 1680–1889* originally bore the main title *Heavens on Earth*, and removal of this title—for whatever reason it was really done—represents well what's written inside. Holloway seems to only grudgingly acknowledge the enthusiasm it required to establish an intentional community. His roughly thematic and chronological discussion of a broad range of communities portrays the communal movement in the United States as essentially dormant, with the Israeli kibbutzim and French Communities of Work as the most vital contemporary examples of communal effort (Holloway 1966:231). Looking to the future of such experiments, Holloway writes with restrained optimism that, in the absence of unforeseen wars or other upheaval, future community development will draw on the syndicalist and socialist forms demonstrated by these precedents (1966:232).

Robert Hine first published his extensive and thoughtful *California's Utopian Colonies* in 1953, and in his second edition of 1983 was able to preface his previous work with a reflection on the communal experiments in the state between the mid-1960s and mid-1970s. Drawing deep distinctions but also a few parallels between the nineteenth- and early twentieth-century California communities and those countercultural outposts that arose 70 years later, Hine highlights the variability in inspiration and structure among historical communities at differing points in time.

Comparative Analyses

Rosabeth Moss Kanter's 1972 *Commitment and Community: Communes and Utopias in Sociological Perspective* spearheaded a more broadly evaluative approach to historical communal groups by positing mechanisms that contributed to community longevity. Though the usefulness of her approach has long been questioned by other scholars with interests other than questions of success, failure, and longevity, Kanter's work contributed substantially to the growing tradition of methodologically rigorous scholarship on a topic frequently seen as outside of or extraneous to significant mainstream history. In more recent decades, scholars of intentional communities have sought out patterns and models for explaining the processes of community formation and dissolution, produced encyclopedic collections describing the hundreds of American intentional communities founded in the past two centuries, and continued to produce detailed descriptions and comparisons in focused case studies of individual communities.

Carl Guarneri's *The Utopian Alternative: Fourierism in Nineteenth-Century America* is a thorough view of Fourierist endeavors in the United States between 1820 and 1880, and places into historical context this significant utopian socialist movement that is often now thought of as merely an "entertaining sideshow" to the development of modern American society (1991:xi). In this consideration, the intentional communities—phalanxes, when established according to Fourier's principles—were only part of the nationwide expression of the associative impulse. Guarneri argues that utopian socialists were "makers of history rather than its fugitives," with Fourierism as a significant theme in the development of American society (1991:6). In his 1990 *All Things New: American Communes and Utopian Movements, 1860–1914*, Robert Fogarty also seeks to assert intentional communities' relevance to the continuous process of American history-building. In this overview of the social place and impact of the roughly 140 colonies founded between 1860 and 1914, Fogarty picks up the historical thread after the heyday of the most well-known intentional communities of the pre–Civil War era. He goes on to demonstrate that the waves of community-founding fervor observed by some historians as discrete historical periods are subject to too many exceptions. Instead, in Fogarty's view, colony organization was constant, diverse, and socially responsive and relevant throughout the last half of the nineteenth century and into the twentieth (1990:2). This perspective echoes that of Tel Aviv University scholar Yacov Oved, who begins the first chapter of his 1988 *Two Hundred Years of American Communes* with the statement, "Since 1735 there has been a continuous and unbroken existence of communes in the United States" (1988:3). Historian Paul S. Boyer asserts this idea, too, in his 1997 introduction to Donald Pitzer's *America's Communal Utopias*, stating that "while communalism enjoyed its greatest efflorescence in the 1820–50 era (with a second wave in the post-1960 years), it has never been absent from the American experience" (Boyer 1997:xi). Clearly, there were periods throughout history in which more intentional communities formed than others, but Fogarty, Oved, Boyer, and others are right to remind us that, while community formation may have varied in type and intensity in response to prevailing social and economic conditions, it has never been absent from our social landscape.

Geographer Brian J. L. Berry's 1992 *America's Utopian Experiments: Communal Havens from Long-Wave Crises* lists and discusses a number of communities in varying depths, and posits the theory hinted in his title that the periods most fertile for the growth of intentional communities correspond to times of economic deflation. Berry's argument is soundly refuted by historian Edward K. Spann, author of the 1989 *Brotherly Tomorrows: Movements for a Cooperative Society in America, 1820–1920*. In his review for the *Annals of Iowa*, the State Historical Society of Iowa's quarterly journal, Spann implies that Berry's economically deterministic thesis approaches the category of "snake oil" in its usefulness to predict and explain the rise of communities (1994:371). Their disagreement could stem from the authors' differing intellectual perspectives on intentional communities. Berry's economic approach is more dispassionate toward communal groups, seeking broad economic patterns that transcend, and at the same time discount, the specificities of intentional communities' motivations and goals. Spann's perspective as a historian of nineteenth-century social movements, however, is sympathetic and even optimistic toward the potential of future intentional communities.

Published in 1997, Donald Pitzer's edited volume *America's Communal Utopias* brings together the topical expertise of 17 scholars of specific communities, ranging from colonial communalists to twentieth-century

Koreshan Unity members, allowing a deep level of context to be explored. Moving forward with his concept of developmental communalism, advanced over the preceding decade, Pitzer espouses a view of communities that highlights their dynamism through, and sometimes beyond, shifting levels of commitment to structured communal sharing. A developmental approach helps us to view communities' impacts and successes in terms of what they themselves hoped to achieve, rather than by measures of communal lifespan. Pitzer also provides what he calls "the most complete list of American communal utopias ever printed" as an appendix to the edited volume, including over 40 pages of communities founded before 1965 (1997:12). This in itself is something that many scholars have attempted but only imperfectly achieved. In their long-term commitment to thoroughness, Pitzer and his contributing colleagues have made a lasting gift to scholars of intentional communities.

Paul Boyer's foreword to Pitzer's 1997 volume is a call for a comprehensive historical view of communal societies, which Boyer sees as lacking in the scholarly literature so far. While many worthy individual community histories have been written, "isolated communities or movements are rarely seen as comprising a distinctive historical phenomenon whose ideological underpinnings, organizational strategies, and complex interconnections can be studied systematically and traced over time" (Boyer 1997:x). Frances Robert Shor's *Utopianism and Radicalism in a Reforming America: 1888–1918*, released the same year as Pitzer's volume, enters into this perceived void with thematic chapters exploring women's participation in developing utopian visions and African American utopias, as well as anarchist and socialist motivations for experimental community (1997). Shor, however, limits his time period to a 30-year stretch, a reasonable accommodation that allows him to go into greater depth than a broader study could likely achieve.

Timothy Miller's 1998 *The Quest for Utopia in Twentieth Century America*, Volume 1, *1900–1960* is similarly limited in its focus, stretching from communities founded in the years between the nineteenth-century religious revivals and socialist solutions to industrial capitalism, to the countercultural communes of the 1960s and 1970s. Miller is able to carefully demonstrate that intentional communities were a continuous social reality throughout this period of the nation's history. Land-holding agricultural associations, Christian communes, and artists' colonies of the first decades of the twentieth century were often less obviously radical in their critique of mainstream society than earlier or later intentional communities, while still exploring and demonstrating aspects of communalism. Without attempting to instigate an entirely new social order, these early twentieth-century experiments sought alternative ways for individuals and families to live together in the modernizing world (Miller 1998:vxii–xviii). They were, nonetheless, intentional communities in form, eschewing pure individualism in favor of coresidence with shared goals and purposes. Miller's second volume, presumably outlining intentional communities from the 1960s to the present, has yet to be published.

The following decade, Robert P. Sutton produced his two-volume *Communal Utopias and the American Experience*, with the first volume on Religious Communities, 1732–2000 (2003) and the second on Secular Communities, 1824–2000 (2004). Sutton, whose own focus of scholarship has been on the nineteenth-century Icarian communities inspired by Etienne Cabet's writing, is perhaps the first scholar to fully extend the historical view of communal experiments from the eighteenth into the latter half of the twentieth century in this extensive, though largely descriptive, biographical-style text. The extensive time period Sutton covers is explored at the cost of the analytic extent of Shor's and Miller's volumes.

This brief overview of scholars' work on the topic of intentional communities clearly demonstrates some of the challenges in writing toward depth and comprehensiveness, objectivity and compassion, when considering multiple historical groups. No individual should expect to comprehensively and meaningfully capture the full significance of intentional communities throughout American history. Rather, in the spirit of our subjects, each writer acts as a member of a community of interest, their individual work contributing to the strength of the overall body of understanding.

Archaeology as a Tool for Learning about Intentional Communities

Scholars of intentional communities experience the same limitations of documentation and memory that constrain the knowledge and interpretations of all historical researchers. As historians, we are always dealing with a filtered and fragmented past. Access to literacy and the means of recording have never been equally distributed across societies, limiting the range of voices heard by listeners in the present. Memoirs and oral history interviews can be selective and self-censored, or reflect a subject's later interpretation of events. The specifically ideological nature of intentional communities amplifies this potential for written records to reflect highly subjective realities. When everything depends on the rightness of an idea, it becomes more important to perpetuate and promote that idea than to document the daily struggles that show how difficult embodying that idea may be. On paper, at least, the dream is always still possible to achieve.

Contemporary documentary sources from within intentional communities may be saturated with the emotional and spiritual fervor, or even overt propaganda, of their members. From the outside, cultural misunderstandings and sheer xenophobia may color contemporary sources. Many communities that were extant through the mid-nineteenth century were avid printers and publishers, producing periodicals and special volumes devoted to disseminating knowledge about their particular religious or social cause. Circulations varied, but it was not unusual for community newspapers to be distributed to financial supporters and like-minded associations across thousands of miles. Local and national mainstream newspapers sometimes featured occasionally accurate, but just as often scandalously inaccurate and ill-informed, portrayals of communities of interest to their readership.

The biographies and attitudes of colony founders like the Harmony Society's George Rapp, Llano del Rio's Job Harriman, and the Kaweah Co-operative Commonwealth's Burnette G. Haskell are relatively well documented in their own preserved writings and scholars' later considerations. Even in place-based secondary approaches, the leaders' personal stories of inspiration, organization, and implementation often dominate the focus. In Gerald and Patricia Gutek's 1998 historical travel guide, *Visiting Utopian Communities*, for example, in their delineation of the historical backgrounds of each community, the biography of each leader exceeds discussion of other members' lives and experiences by many pages. Learning about the day-to-day realities of community members is comparatively difficult, leading to an imbalance in secondary literature that disfavors the mundane details that structured the social life and everyday experiences in community homes and workplaces. LouAnn Wurst's study of Gerrit Smith's Temperance Hotel in Peterboro, New York, employs "a relational approach that directs our attention away from Gerrit Smith as a famous businessman and philanthropist and towards the struggles within the community in which he lived," and offers an example we can follow in studying intentional communities (2002:170). No matter how egalitarian a community's policy and practice are, leadership with charismatic appeal and deep conviction to the cause is fundamental to group formation. The challenge, as Wurst sets out for us, is to illuminate the experiences of community members without losing sight of the leaders' importance.

Using the methods and approaches of historical archaeology, scholars can provide additional ways to better balance the strengths of different voices from communities' pasts. By pulling together multiple lines of evidence, including written accounts, photographs, maps, landscapes, architectural remains, and material culture, our goal can be to understand how members experienced life in past intentional communities, and how those experiences changed over time in response to broader changes at the community level and beyond.

Finding the Ideal

The history of North American intentional communities is more than two centuries long. Even though the history of scholarly archaeological investigation of these communities is somewhat shorter, we now have more than five decades of archaeological studies on which to build a groundwork for our future explorations. Writing in the early years of historical archaeology's development as a discipline, Vincent P. Foley lauded the potential of this growing branch of archaeology as it gained "respectability" and separation from avocational practitioners. In the early 1960s, Foley supervised excavations at the ca. 1754 Moravian water works in Bethlehem, Pennsylvania, and at the time of writing was optimistic about the project's potential to contribute knowledge not available in the Moravians' extensive written records.

The site of the Swedish Christian immigrant colony of Bishop Hill, Illinois, holds the likely distinction of being the intentional community site studied earliest by archaeologists. From 1947 to 1952, Richard Hagen undertook investigations into the Colony Church site at Bishop Hill, in large part to inform building restoration. This and subsequent work from this site exemplify the motivations for and approaches to archaeological research typical of projects at many community sites conducted through the late twentieth century: driven in part by the motivation to create and re-create tourist-friendly historical sites, they focused on mapping and description with the intent of building restoration, rather than on artifact-level interpretation or analysis attempting to explore the structure of colonists' daily lives. In the first half of the 1970s, fieldwork over several seasons undertaken by faculty and students from nearby Knox College worked toward gathering information for building reconstruction and restoration at the Bishop Hill site. These included locating and excavating the early 1850s Bjorklund Hotel's privy (Wilson and Wilson 1973), its stable (Van Ness 1973), basement stairwell, walkway, and fence (Wagner 1975). John Wagner expanded beyond the hotel in the 1974 field season to find locations of several outbuildings associated with the church lot, excavate a brick-lined colony-era well on the lot, and determine if a staircase had been built to the church basement. Despite Hagen's claims in the late 1940s and early 1950s that he had found such a feature, Wagner writes that there is no evidence of a basement staircase along the wall of the church that was tested. In 1975 Wagner's crew investigated the locations of a public freight scale and bandstand in the town's public square, and trenched through a filled ravine in an ultimately unproductive search for evidence of the hillside dugouts colonists built for shelter though their first, devastating winter. These field projects were designed as ground-level architectural history studies to locate, expose, map, and describe building remains.

A 1994–1995 excavation project at the Boys' Dormitory site at Bishop Hill was also run as a field school, this time for Black Hawk College in Moline, Illinois. This project mirrored the 1970s-era investigations in its focus on building restoration. At the behest of the historic site's planners, the project was conducted in preparation for the removal of a postcolony addition to the dormitory. Unlike earlier projects, which had focused on broad-scale excavations and mapping of architectural features, this excavation uncovered more information at a finer level of resolution. A considerable quantity of artifacts related to the young colony men's occupation of the dormitory were recovered from what was estimated to be less than a 5 percent sample of the building's site (Safiran 1996:14). Principal investigator Edward Safiran stops short of detailed analysis of the artifact assemblage, which includes ceramic tableware and food preparation vessel fragments, personal items such as buttons, smoking pipe fragments, and medicine bottle fragments, as well as architectural debris. The significant finding in this report seems to be recognition of the potential for future archaeological studies.

Floyd Mansberger's 2002 archaeological data recovery plan was also designed in the service of building restoration, as it was prepared to facilitate engineering evaluation of the Bjorklund Hotel foundation in advance of repair. In addition to his interest in the locations of buried structural remains, Mansberger notes that proposed data recovery may encounter artifacts that could be used "not only to date the events associated with these surfaces, but also to assess the character of the events and/or activities associated with these surfaces. Artifacts from these various middens may shed light on the functional evolution of the yards around the structure through the years" (2002:4). This more recent work at Bishop Hill approaches an attempt to interpret the daily lives of the village's residents in ways that past efforts, primarily intended to inform building reconstruction, could not.

While Bishop Hill might have been approached earliest, Shaker villages are by far the most extensively studied of intentional community archaeological sites, more so than any other group. Kim McBride's investigations at Pleasant Hill, Kentucky, have been among the more thoughtful and productive contributions to the study of Shaker sites (see #9 in the Appendix). She has worked extensively with the nonprofit organization the Shaker Village of Pleasant Hill to explore many aspects of the area, including the site of the 1810 meetinghouse, the 1812 Centre Family Dwelling, an outdoor worship area known as Holy Sinai's Plain, the West Lot laundry, and several other building foundations and activity locations. Not far away, in Ohio, Bruce Aument, Andrew Sewell, and their colleagues' 2009 report on 2005 fieldwork at the North Family Lot portion of Union Village is an example of how archaeological thinking—and the federal regulation of Section 106, a portion of the 1966 National Historic Preservation Act (NHPA) that requires federal agencies to consider the effects of their undertakings on historic properties—provided the impetus and the opportunity to revisit Shaker sites and access a deeper level of information and analysis than had previously been available (see #8 in the Appendix). A team of archaeological specialists conducted cultural resource management studies for a highway construction project across a portion of the former village location. The project agency, the Ohio Department of Transportation, made the novel decision to disseminate the resulting four-volume report electronically. This is unusual, as cultural resource management technical reports are more often confidential documents available only to clients, involved public agencies, and committed researchers as permitted by the State Historic Preservation Officer. In preparing and publishing their report, the authors set out to lay a groundwork for future investigations, as well as to actively try to demystify the Shakers (Aument and Sewell 2009:12). It is true that for many of us, the images that come to mind when thinking of the Shakers are of beautifully simple wood furniture, peg rails, flat brooms, and bonnets. It is too easy to imagine that the lives of their creators were filled with the same peaceful grace and simplicity of design. Aument and Sewell's first and broadest success is to show us—literally—the foundations of the walls that held up the peg rails that housed the shops where the brooms and the bonnets were made. By bringing our attention down to the level of the concrete detail, the authors help imbue our vision of the Shakers of Union Village with all the daily routines, messiness, and change that necessarily exist when imperfect people live in the same place for 90 years (Aument and Sewell 2009:2, 43).

Despite three decades of attention at Pleasant Hill alone, Kim McBride was quoted in a 2012 *American Archaeology* article about her own two decades of work at the village as saying, "The Shakers are pretty well known and pretty well studied from an historical standpoint. . . . From an archaeological standpoint, not so much" (Burton 2012:37). Unfortunately, she has a point. But this situation may be attributable less to a lack of data and more to an inexplicable reluctance on the part of archaeologists to fully take advantage of and access previous work in their field. Researcher Joseph Grygas opens the abstract to his 2011 State University of New York at Albany master's thesis on Watervliet Shaker Village with the statement, "To date, Shaker archaeology is currently in a relatively primitive stage" (2011:ii). Following David Starbuck's example, Joseph Grygas studied refuse from a sheet midden outside of the Second Church Family Dwelling House at Watervliet, New York (see #5 in the Appendix). He reviewed previously unanalyzed collections and conducted a small survey and testing program around the location of the Second Church Family Dwelling House. Working at the western extent of the Shaker domain, far from Watervliet, undergraduate thesis researcher Daniel Tallent developed a predictive model of sorts for interpreting Shaker remains at South Union, Kentucky (see #10 in the Appendix). He expects that Shaker sites will lack the "metallic clamps and fixtures" typical of commercially produced furniture, as Shakers produced their own furniture using all wood joinery; he posits as well a dearth of those items of personal adornment—such objects as jewelry and ornate clothing buttons—overtly prohibited in Shaker communities (Tallent 2009:44). Yet Kim McBride's and David Starbuck's extensive previous work has already clearly addressed expectations and evidence at Shaker sites, exploring the ambiguities of meaning that small objects can hold in Shaker contexts. Scholars focusing on Shaker sites and materials must be expected to find, read, and build on one another's work, and senior scholars need to do more to promote one another's foundational studies. Barring this basic attention to the necessary work of building a rigorous and reflexive community of scholarly debate, the field may continue to seem "primitive" to those entering its ranks. Hopefully, by bringing together citations from archaeologists working at intentional community sites across the United States, volumes like this one may provide an entry point for those seeking to review existing literature and approaches.

Meaningful Action

What can the archaeological study of an intentional community provide to expand our understanding of the past? For all the weaknesses in Mark Leone's assumptions about the roles of primitive technology in intentional communities, his concept of sacred technology—defined as "material culture and built environments which had sacred practice interwoven into their making" (1977b:88)—is a useful one. Material culture connects us to the ways in which people interacted with the physical world around them, often in ways that, to most of us, seem habitual and routine. We make dinner. We wash the dishes. We put on our clothes. But in each intentional community there are tasks and practices that take on new meaning within the group's lived philosophy. Special significance is attributed to an action or item whose meaning is relatively recently and quite specifically defined in relation to belief. Dietary practices connected to a community's ideals might include vegetarianism, communal cooking and eating, or commitment to complete self-sufficiency through agricultural production. The composition of the household and shape of the home were frequently important to restructuring society according to a community's plan. Routes of travel through and around communal spaces, the use of individual or shared work spaces, even daily clothing and habits could all potentially be defined or constrained by the community's ideals. Kentucky archaeologist Kim McBride writes that

> archaeological remains at Shaker sites may be unusually amenable to interpretation precisely because the Shakers made conscious and deliberate efforts to demonstrate their beliefs about religion, relationships between people, and relationships to God in their day-to-day actions and in the physical things they created. (1995:404)

Daily acts were made special in their performance according to community standards, and the resulting products held the significance of their makers' context of belief. Drawing from Julia Hendon's (2000) concept of mutual knowledge, Heather Van Wormer takes this idea of the sacredness of daily acts through to these same acts becoming once again routine—taken for granted—in their new form. According to Van Wormer, the "architects of intentional communities are hoping to achieve the mundane . . . In order for their worldview to be truly accepted, and thereby ensure its survival, that worldview must permeate every aspect of life, and become unmarked, and in this way routinized" (2004:176). Products and activities weren't simply delineated by a community's guidelines—the activities themselves discursively and recursively reinforced these guidelines to the members undertaking them. Community cohesiveness was a dynamic process. Sharing a meal at the communal table cemented the bonds of association and reminded diners that they weren't alone in their quest for a better world. Tying on your bonnet with a pink ribbon reminded you, and everyone around you, who your Moravian choir sisters were and what was expected of you as an unmarried adult woman. As members worked to construct the built environment, they collectively made their world according to their shared principles. Though writing from the perspective of architectural history,

Dolores Hayden's reminders that shared labor concretely constituted the Shaker world are equally relevant to archaeologists:

> Every Shaker design expressed its makers' internal dual sensitivity to real and imaginary, earthly and heavenly space. Each member, part of the living building, was engaging in a physical labor fully identified with life's ultimate purpose, translating visual concepts into physical reality, helping to transform earthly millennial communities into the New Jerusalem. (1976:100)

While the Shakers' motto "Hands to work, hearts to God" puts their labor into the realm of the sacred, in secular socialist communities engagement in labor was no less significant. Communities such as the Kaweah Cooperative Commonwealth defined themselves by their recognition of the practice of labor. The time members devoted to building and maintaining colony infrastructure was rewarded as the basic unit of exchange value in Kaweah's internal economy, so daily work became tied inextricably with members' interdependence and commitment to the cause. Colonists' labor was part of a collective performance intended to display and reinforce group unity, both to members inside and to potential donors and recruits outside the community. The products of colony labor—newspapers from the print shop, cabbages from the garden, and miles of gravel road—could be held up as representations of the benefits of collective labor. Withholding work took on significance, too, as a meaningful statement against colony management and values.

Questioning Community

Material correlates of community members' actions, from building foundations to bottle caps, can provide evidence of where and when community guidelines were practiced, and how the material world was mobilized to create a new society. Alternatively, material evidence of practices that vary from those specifically required by community protocols can reveal the tension between lived reality and prescribed ideal for individual members. Often the most memorable interpretations that archaeological studies contribute to the broader understanding of intentional communities is the frequent disparity between explicit ideals and policies and actual practices (Starbuck 2001, 2004; Tarlow 2006; Van Bueren and Tarlow 2006). Finding the differences between what was written and what was wrought isn't peculiar to community studies; it has long been considered a strength of the archaeological perspective. As students, we all learned how William Rathje's Garbage Project famously exposed the disparity between modern American consumers' reports of their food and beverage consumption and the consumption quantities indicated by their trash output (Rathje et al. 1992; Rathje and Murphy 1992). We felt like we had been let in on a secret—that only archaeologists could uncover what really went on behind the closed doors of the ages. But is whether or not community members obeyed the rules we think they were expected to obey the most interesting question we can ask?

Even in the communities whose members are most tightly bound by religious faith, social conviction, shared language, and cultural history, archaeology may reveal that individuals and families had different ways of materially engaging with their belief and identity as part of the group. The most potentially interesting questions along this track address how the community negotiates the tensions that these differences can cause. Are there reiterations of shared ideals to emphasize collective standards, as with the Shaker Millennial Laws, or do group expectations flex to accommodate members' on-the-ground experiences and priorities? Change happens where ideology and action meet, and in the material remains we can see what's left behind by ideologically informed action and reaction.

Dynamic Idealism

Community building wasn't a static goal but an ongoing process that required members to develop basic infrastructure and services, negotiate what was communal and what was private, design and implement educational programs for new and existing members, and maintain a sense of physical, intellectual, and emotional progress toward their ultimate goal, whether that goal was an ideal society, heaven on earth, or a well-earned idyllic afterlife. Changes in group ideals over time and across space provide worthy challenges for archaeological study. When documentary sources and field conditions are good, archaeology's diachronic perspective can work to enhance our understanding of how changes in group ideals were materialized in the physical world. When our sources are limited, it behooves us to remember that developing community ideals, writing about those ideals, communicating the ideals to members, and enacting the ideals in daily life were stages in a process that progressed at variable rates across space and time.

In some cases, changes within communities occurred in ways that may be largely invisible in the documentary record. Heather Van Wormer provides an example of such a case at Mary's City of David, where the physical structure of the community and its relationships with the outside world changed drastically after controversial founder Benjamin Purnell's death in 1927, and its 1930s split and transition from being the House of David to Mary's City of David. Internally produced documentary records show little change in structure and content. She cautions that failing to consider material culture in examining this era of the group's history would cause misunderstanding of the community's redefinition and neglect "its central significance in defining community identity and promoting *communitas*" (2004:162).

To guide archaeologists in choosing which questions to ask of the material culture of intentional communities, Sarah Tarlow, Thad Van Bueren, and Jill Hupp itemize particular questions that may be translated, in whole or part, into research designs for specific communities (Tarlow 2002; Van Bueren and Hupp 2000; Van Bueren and Tarlow 2006). Among their basic questions, perhaps the most widely applicable themes include: How did the colony's vision and environmental factors work together to structure a community's material world, in terms of physical layout, architectural plans, and public and private spaces? Was there competence in building abilities and adequate resources to execute building plans as envisioned? How was labor collectivized? How was access to goods distributed among colonists? Which goods were brought from outside sources, and who had access to them? What was the intended and real balance between communal and individual property? What aspects of daily life were informed by mainstream values rather than colony ideals? This last question can be especially significant in communities where members came from diverse backgrounds to join what was often intended to be a materially egalitarian society. Old habits from life before the community could often be maintained in the spaces between community objectives, exposing old social and economic tensions between members. In some limited situations, members were born and died within the embrace of a single intentional community. More frequently, however, each member's experience was a single chapter in her or his life course, which may have seen involvement with other intentional communities as well as participation in the mainstream.

Worthy Challenges

Of course, archaeological methods, while often illuminating, do not provide us with the one clear, undistorted window into communities of the past. Indeed, sometimes the methodological discrepancies between documentary and material histories can compound our frustrations. Geoffrey Hewitt's investigation into the archaeology of the Herrnhut Commune, a Moravian outpost in western Victoria, Australia, from 1853 to 1889, began with a desire to connect the material remains of the communal occupation with the group's ideology and social action. Hewitt's research experience included a program of remote sensing that was troubled by "buckshot soil and igneous geology" (2007:109), documentary evidence confirming postcommunal reoccupation at the site, and a politically tangled written record, exposing problems not so much in the archaeology of intentional communities specifically but in historical archaeology in general. Added to this problem was the peculiar opacity of the Herrnhut community's ideological framework, which hindered Hewitt's clear exploration of the physical expression of their belief and potential contradictions within it. Interestingly, Hewitt remained optimistic that study of the landscape and remains of the built environment using images generated by aerial kite photography may still offer insight into the Herrnhut community's shared beliefs and intentions, providing evidence that is not available in written form (2007:111). Herrnhut's deficiency of documents may be an example to those of us blessed with ample documentary records. How would we interpret the landscape of a communal settlement without the benefit of preconceived expectations or knowledge about the builders' philosophy?

As a self-contained unit intended to be institutionally complete, intentional communities are attractive subjects for archaeological study of time periods in which the boundaries of household, neighborhood, and town can sometimes seem indistinct. In their study of the Llano del Rio Cooperative Company, Van Bueren and Hupp note that a colony like Llano del Rio is "one of the largest social units that may be readily amenable to archaeological analysis" (2000:29). We can feel secure in viewing an intentional community as a discrete example—a data universe within which we can make comparisons between smaller units in space and time based on our knowledge of the group's ideals. Later researchers at Llano del Rio also show, paradoxically, how this very aspect of intentional communities can cause anxiety about accessing the community thoroughly enough to understand the relationships of its many working parts. In their 2009 report for the Society for California Archaeology, John M. Foster and Alex Kirkish show their discomfort with the anomalous nature of the site and limited ability for in-depth archaeological study. Of their methodological approach they write:

> The principal goal of this investigation was to make meaningful interpretations of a small cross-section of a very large historical archaeological site. This method inherently limits the degree of confidence in making generalizations and coming to terms with the amount of variation in the larger site universe. Archaeologists like to move from specifics to generalities that would encompass similar situations, environments, and cultural contexts. Notwithstanding these broader scientific goals, this work can be seen as a progression of building blocks that eventually will contribute to the patterns that we are trying to discern. (Foster and Kirkish 2009:4)

This intellectual discomfort with the relatively small sample size highlights a quality of intentional communities that might set them apart from other archaeological examples. We are always limited in our ability to consider a data universe, as most of our efforts address only a small part of a larger social whole—whether it's a single house lot in a city or a linear right-of-way through a complex rural landscape. The difference comes in our desire to view and interpret an intentional community as a whole. It may be difficult for us to feel secure in our interpretations of debris from individual structures and households from the past when we know that the people who left those remains saw themselves as an intentional part of a larger, more or less cohesive unit that expands beyond our research scope. This will continue to be a challenge for archaeologists, as most of us work with limited time frames, budgets, and spatial extents in our studies, whether based in academic research or legislative compliance. If we are careful to delineate our research questions to scales appropriate to the data we can reasonably expect to recover, our projects can act as building blocks toward greater understanding.

Scales of Understanding

The following three chapters discuss archaeological approaches to intentional community according to scales of focus, from the broadest view of the culturally constructed and interpreted landscape; to the built environment of villages, workshops, and industries; to the narrowest view at the level of artifacts. These stops along the continuum of scale are somewhat artificial, as artifacts, buildings, and spaces all interact in concert along a continuum of scales. The value in making distinctions is to demonstrate how different scales of evidence can lead to different answers to our questions about intentional communities, such as when exploring communalism and egalitarianism among the Doukhobors' settlement pattern and village layouts, discussed below; or the tension between individuality and cooperation in the Llano del Rio colony's plans for urban design and architecture, discussed in chapters 3 and 5.

Archaeologists base our interest in space—the landscape and built environment—on the assumption that not only are material objects culturally constructed, but the ways that people use and inhabit space are culturally defined. Built environments are realms of discursive practice for those wishing to structure their own lives and communicate their ideals. Within and around intentional communities, the organization of space and the built environment helped to separate members from mainstream society and facilitate internal cohesiveness. Our perspective as researchers is often one of heightened awareness—a kind of documentary omnipresence that was not enjoyed by most community members. Shaker sisters and brothers did not read each other's diaries, the multiple iterations of the Millennial Laws were not widely printed and disseminated, and Isaac Young's ca. 1835 maps of western Shaker villages were not available for all to see in the comparative way we may now view them. Shaker villagers would have learned about doctrine and devotion, in part, by living within the built environment of only their own community, and continuing to build that environment according to the direct instructions of their Elders and Eldresses. So what did the built environment tell these workaday brothers and sisters, who had varying levels of familiarity with church doctrine, about what it meant to be a Shaker?

The spaces inside of intentional communities represented, restructured, and reproduced members' senses of identity and acceptable conduct. In their definitive article outlining the value of archaeological studies of intentional and utopian communities, Thad Van Bueren and Sarah Tarlow write:

> Utopian groups focused great energy on defining and portraying their worldviews. The architecture of each community was often highly symbolic and related directly to the way community values were defined. For example, group housing and circular community designs were frequently used to convey principles of shared life, cooperation, and equality. It was common to equate utopian settlements with an earthly Eden, and exalted settings were often chosen. (2006:4)

The spaces within which intentional communities built their ideal worlds were usually envisioned in greater completion and perfection than could ever be realistically attained. Generalizing about communal societies' building efforts, but with specific reference to Brook Farm's eclectic collection of inherited and purpose-built structures, Robert Preucel writes that most communities were limited in their ability to realize the full planning and architectural aspects of their ideal settlements by financial constraints. Rather, "they tended to create vernacular expressions composed of a variety of architectural styles. This variety, however, was not a random choice of available styles, but rather a conscious selection that usually involved specific modifications for appropriate community needs" (Preucel 2006:178).

Exalted settings could be created at a smaller scale within communities, as in the case of ornamental gardens planted at the Harmonists' town of Economy, Pennsylvania, and the Separatists' settlement at Zoar, Ohio. Though less visually evocative, Shaker and Amana Inspirationist pathways between buildings and work areas concretely and metaphorically guided followers' footsteps through shared spaces for the work and play of community life.

Thinking of how colonists moved through their community environments, we remember that building and occupying space involve ongoing and intertwined processes that expand across time as well as space. The Amana Inspirationists began building on land purchased by the colony in the summer of 1855, moving families gradually from their first settlement at Ebenezer, New York. Members managed their villages and operated their farms and industries, which were dominated by large woolen mills, communally until 1932 when economic and social pressures forced their reorganization into a joint stock corporation. Remaining members were given the option of buying their formerly community-owned homes, and formed the Amana Church Society as their shared religious body. In reflecting on an early 1980s battle over designation of a special zoning district in Amana, Iowa, within which aspects of the nineteenth-century Inspirationist community's historic built environment would be considered before issuing new building or renovation permits, Jonathan Andelson writes:

> Since 1855, Amanans have shaped their built environment jointly, and it has shaped them: their behavior, their attitudes, and their dealings with the world outside the villages. The built environment was malleable and could be changed to express new meanings, but it also possessed inertia—it could not be totally and quickly re-formed— and for that reason it was a backdrop against which Amanans measured the meaning of their behavior and the character of their community. The process has always been interactive. (1986:58)

Part of this interactive process has also been a variability in how members from different backgrounds experience their community's built environment. In discussing the cultural landscapes of Utah Mormon villages, architectural historian Dell Upton suggests that though a Mormon village might seem, to us, to be an unremarkable environment in which to transform residents into the new people their adopted religion would hope for them to become, "the degree to which the Mormon built environment could promote the development of new men and women may have depended upon the convert's starting point and thus on the degree to which the Great Basin setting was novel" (2005:26). Upton's specific examples suppose that new members from Tennessee and Kentucky would find it very different from their rural homes with isolated dwellings, whereas a Norwegian with a background in tightly spaced agricultural villages would be more immediately comfortable. Even in the midst of community, the search for paradise can be an individual one.

Focusing more closely within community settlements at the level of the residence, intentional communities' domestic arrangements remind us that our basic definition of "household" need not automatically coincide with the idea of the biologically related nuclear or even extended family. Shaker families, Moravian choirs, and Oneida's complex marriages all illuminate the potentially very broad connotation of the word "family" as it refers to a group of people who live together in a residential building. It is true that there do exist many examples of temporary, situational households that diverge from North Americans' assumptions about the nuclear family. Groups of women living together in a brothel, occupants of a military barracks, or tents full of young male forestry workers in the Sierra Nevada range can all be viewed as challenging alternatives to the comfortable image of a family household. But these alternative living situations are also accepted as temporary formations supported, or at least tolerated, within mainstream attitudes about appropriate residential groups. The young loggers will earn the money they seek, and then presumably redistribute themselves appropriately with nuclear families. Young women in prostitution will take on respectable work, become pregnant, or die, only to be replaced by new recruits. The brothel as a whole will continue to function but will likely never challenge broadly held assumptions about appropriate household structures, and instead will usually be seen as a cautionary tale or a necessary evil. Intentional communities' alternative families, on the other hand, can fly in the face of assumed notions about household structure. Shaker families question the very connection between parent and child. Moravian choir dormitories counter the expectation that marriage requires husbands and wives to share a house and bed. The Oneida Perfectionists' family contradicts the belief that childbearing and physical union need occur between only two adults, if not permanently then at least serially. All adults at Oneida were considered married to one another in a system of "complex marriage," within which sexual relations were carefully managed with a mind to the spiritual elevation of younger members through association with older members, controlling births through male continence, and avoiding exclusive partnerships and friendships. Over 100 people joined the community within its first two years. Without specific times set aside for religious worship, daily life became a process of worship and spiritual activity committed to creating their heaven on Earth. Behavioral control was implemented at meetings through "mutual criticism," as individual members would take turns subjecting themselves to the constructive commentary of their peers. Although new converts and visitors were welcomed at the community, the idea of proselytizing or trying to extend settlement to additional communities was not seen as important. Rather, the lived example itself was the goal. Architectural thinker and historian Dolores Hayden writes of the Oneida colonists and their unique Mansion House that they "defined their lives in terms of the perfection of the environment; it is tempting to term their collective home a machine for communal living" (1976:219).

Scholarly awareness that the landscapes and built environments of intentional communities are special cases from which we can learn goes back at least four decades, as evidenced by Hayden's now classic 1976 study, *Seven American Utopias*. Based on what she perceives as the three dilemmas facing ideal communities in their design process—authoritarianism vs. participation; communalism vs. privacy; and unique vs. replicable plans—Hayden discusses the efforts of well-known American intentional communities to achieve their social and religious goals through the built environment and cultural landscape. Nearly 40 years after its publication, Hayden's work, from outside our discipline, still remains one of the most persistent influences for archaeologists studying intentional communities. Her thoughts about Llano del Rio are cited by Thad Van Bueren and Jill Hupp (2000) and John M. Foster (2008, with Alex Kirkish in 2009); on the Shakers, by Andrew Sewell, Roy A. Hampton III, and Rory Krupp (2009a); and in considering domestic reform in the household by Suzanne Spencer-Wood (1999). While Hayden's thoughtful work is abiding in its utility, we should be asking ourselves why historical archaeologists still haven't successfully surpassed or even expanded upon her comprehensive approach.

As will be seen in the following chapters, perhaps the most challenging scale archaeologists encounter when looking at the archaeological remains of intentional communities is that of artifacts and assemblages—the remains of the objects that members made, bought, modified, held, broke, lost, and threw away in their daily lives. Some objects made within community workshops, such as Moravian and Harmonist potters' wares, were distinctive in style and specific to their communities of origin. Many more objects, though, were either so generic in form and function as to be largely the same inside and outside of specific group contexts, such as the simple tobacco pipes from Shaker potteries, or were bought from noncommunity stores or manufacturers. Within studies of the artifacts of intentional communities, mass-produced household and personal items can be among the most ambiguous for archaeologists. These items could be seen as emissaries of the mainstream world, both explicitly and unconsciously, by both community members and modern researchers, that bring the values of individualistic capitalism or worldly godlessness into the very homes of those attempting to reject the trappings of broader society.

Stepping back to consider the ways meaning can be constructed and attached to objects in ideologically charged situations, we can gain some perspective from Victor Buchli's discussion of household objects in the Narkomfin Communal Complex, a Soviet-era apartment building in Moscow, in his 1999 book *An Archaeology of Socialism*. In living according to socialist principles, government workers who were residents of the complex necessarily brought with them many objects made before the adoption of the new political and economic system. Some accommodation needed to be made for "all those stuffed armchairs, potted geraniums, canaries and gramophones" with which residents furnished their now-socialist surroundings. The entire assemblage of household goods could not usefully be labeled petit-bourgeois without making "the social negotiation of the material world utterly hopeless." Eventually the compromise arose such that residents use of the objects, rather than the objects themselves, became social signifiers of petit-bourgeois consciousness (Buchli 1999:59). Household objects confiscated during purges of Narkomfin residents deemed to be class enemies could then be reintegrated into the households of "proper Soviet citizens" without the petit-bourgeois taint, as long as they were appropriately incorporated into the performance of socialism (Buchli 1999:106). Obviously, as with landscape and the built environment, interaction with objects is shaped by social context, but, like buildings and landscapes, objects also shape the social contexts within which they are used. Neither intentional community members nor Soviet citizens could fully strip a household item of its possible meanings just by incorporating it into the performance of a particular ideal.

A key to pursuing productive studies of intentional communities lies in understanding the questions we can ask at different scales of resolution in our evidence. Below is a brief sketch of how different scales of archaeological lens illuminate different aspects of one intentional community's story, the Doukhobor Village of Kirilovka, in Saskatchewan, Canada (see #25 in the Appendix).

A Study in Scales: The Saskatchewan Doukhobors

I began thinking about how different archaeological scales tell different, intertwined stories while writing about the Doukhobor village site of Kirilovka, in Saskatchewan, Canada. I had developed a research interest and had already begun visiting the sites of Doukhobor villages around the province when an unexpected opportunity arose. Road construction crews preparing the right-of-way for dividing the east and west traffic lanes of Highway 16 between Langham and the Borden Bridge uncovered shoes and other artifacts in a cultivated field. The area was known to be the former location of Kirilovka, but project archaeologists had not expected remains to be intact, as no visible trace of the village remained above ground (fig. 2.1). I joined the team to supervise mitigation excavation through August and September of 1996, and spent the next two years immersed in analysis of the material and documentary evidence.

Doukhobors belong to a Russian Christian sect with roots in eighteenth-century schisms from the established Eastern Orthodox Church. Their core beliefs include recognition of an inner divine spirit in each individual, rejection of institutions such as church buildings and written scripture, and refusal to swear oaths to worldly powers. Throughout Russia, members of the sect refused to be conscripted into tsarist military forces and eventually had to flee persecution for their pacifist stance, first congregating in

Figure 2.1. Looking west across the trench that bisected the former location of the Doukhobor village of Kirilovka in Saskatchewan, Canada. No aboveground trace of the village survived, while nearly three dozen buried features remained just beneath the plow zone. Photo by author, 1996.

the Molochnaya (or Milky Waters) River area near the Crimean Peninsula in the mid-nineteenth century, then moving in groups to build villages in Transcaucasia. Their most vocal spiritual leader, Peter Vasileyvich Verigin, was exiled to Siberia in 1887 but continued to communicate instructions to his loyal believers. At midnight on a late June night in 1895, in response to continued pressure through beatings and imprisonment to obey orders to provide military service, groups of Doukhobors threw all of their weapons into bonfires, then stood around the flames, singing psalms. This bold statement of pacifism provoked increased rage from the tsar's soldiers, and violence against Doukhobors' bodies and homes escalated. As Doukhobor representatives sought a new home for their people where they would be free from the demand for military service and persecution for their religious practices, the Canadian government made a generous offer: free rail transportation, a $20,800 special fund grant, and the allowance of communal land tenure not otherwise available under the Dominion Lands Act of 1872 (Tarasoff 1972:4). In exchange, the government expected that the Doukhobor settlers would become law-abiding agricultural producers, helping to populate the Canadian frontier and turn wild prairie into productive farmland. Approximately 270,480 acres of land were reserved for the Doukhobor migrants.

Doukhobor Lands

In 1899, about 7,400 Doukhobors arrived in Canada, and in the next few years they established 61 villages in what was then the Northwest Territories. Their efforts were assisted materially by Leo Tolstoy, a longtime sympathizer who donated all royalties from his 1899 novel, *Resurrection*, to their cause. Quakers in Europe and North America gave vital support, providing logistical assistance and donations of money, food, and clothing. Each village established agricultural fields, built shared barns and bakeries, and operated according to varying levels of communal practice. How groups of families placed these villages on the landscape, how buildings in each village were arranged, and how each household lived within their village were informed by a complex interplay between Russian traditional practice; ever-developing Doukhobor religious tenets codified by their visionary leader, Peter Verigin; Canadian governmental policies; and the exigencies of the concrete, lived landscape. While each of these contributing factors to how Doukhobors lived in the Saskatchewan colonies permeated the scales from settlement pattern to individual household, different factors may be more visible at one scale or another.

At the broadest scale, next to that of their intercontinental migration, is the Doukhobors' settlement pattern in the portion of the Northwest Territories that in 1905 became the province of Saskatchewan. The relative locations of Doukhobor villages and their associated farmland contributed to differences in group insularity and doctrinal adherence in the two decades after their immigration. The 61 Saskatchewan villages were grouped into three colonies called the North Colony, South Colony, and Prince Albert Colony. Villages within the North and South Colonies near Kamsack, Saskatchewan, were relatively close together, surrounded by farmland reserved exclusively for Doukhobor use, and grouped within about 60 miles of what became their leadership center at the town of Veregin. Most of the villages of the Prince Albert Colony, near the towns of Langham and Blaine Lake, Saskatchewan, were more than 250 miles to the northwest of Veregin, and grouped within an easy day's travel of one another but relatively distant from their spiritual brethren in the North and South Colonies (fig. 2.2). Agricultural lands surrounding each village site in the Prince Albert Colony were not in adjacent sections, as in the other colonies, but were instead granted in an alternating patchwork interspersed with railway, school, and Hudson's Bay Company lands. This allowed for non-Doukhobor settlers and services to be established among the Doukhobor lands. Contemporary visitors to the Doukhobor villages noted that, compared to the North and South Colony villages, the Prince Albert Colony villages contained more "independent" members (those who did not follow Verigin's economic and behavioral regulations as strictly).

It was difficult for Doukhobors, who lived in centralized villages and farmed the surrounding lands, to fulfill the Department of the Interior's requirements for attaining title to their dispersed agricultural lands through communal farming. To qualify for title to the 160 acres of land available to each individual farmer under the Dominion Lands Act, an applicant had to at least build a permanent dwelling, reside in it for part of the year, and cultivate 40 acres of the quarter section within the first three years. Initially reassured by their qualification for the "hamlet clause" of the act, which allowed group settlement within a few miles of a resident's quarter sections, the Doukhobors did not build homes on their agricultural fields and concentrated their clearing and cultivation to the sections adjacent to their villages. A 1905 change in leadership at the Department of the Interior, from the sympathetic minister Clifford Sifton to Frank Oliver, who overruled many of his predecessor's concessions to the Doukhobors' landholding requirements, led to detailed government inspection and assessment of what these sectarian settlers had achieved and how much of their land had been "improved." After 1907, much of the group's reserved territory was forfeited due to what government inspectors reported to be insufficient development. Further, as the Doukhobors refused to swear secular oaths, they had not become British subjects, the status held by those born or naturalized in Canada. This was seen by some in the government as an affront to the country that had generously welcomed them. The forfeited land was generally claimed by non-Doukhobor settlers who migrated to the area on the new rail services expanding to reach these areas, and who sought to operate independent farms in the manner preferred by Canada's Department of the

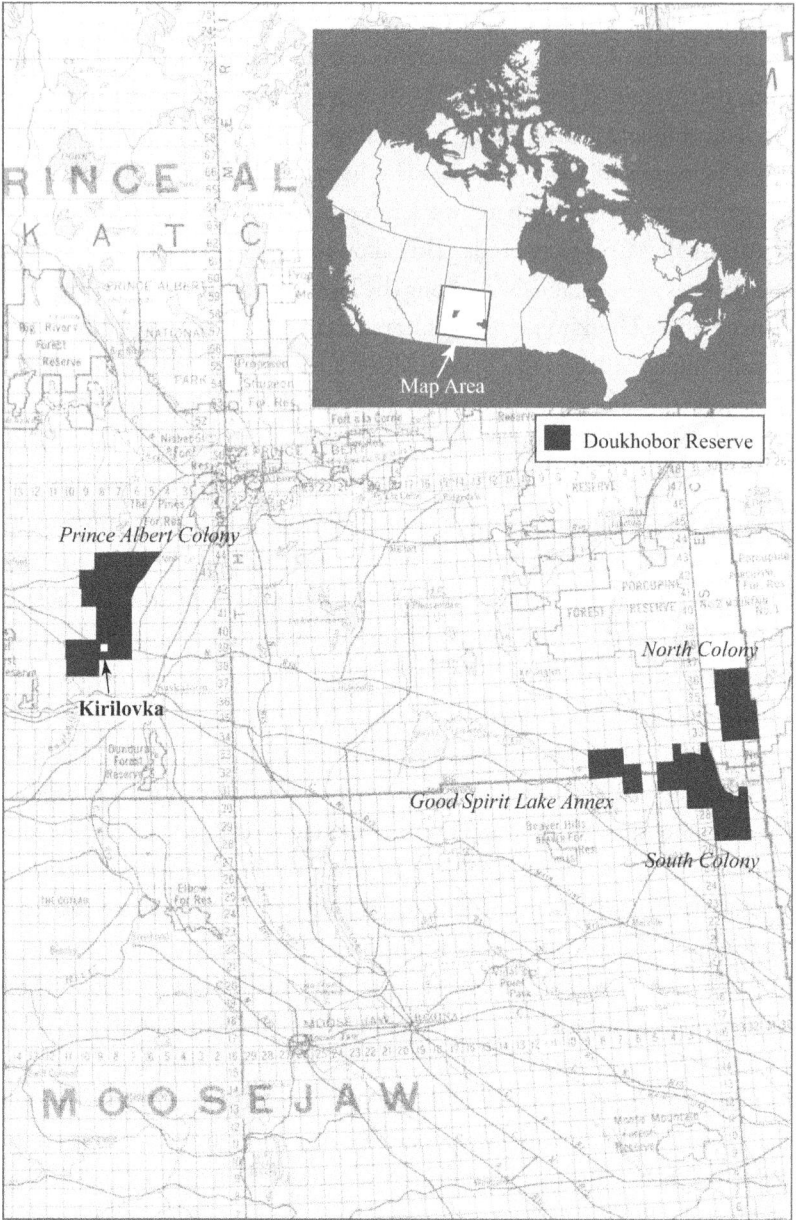

Figure 2.2. Map of Doukhobor land reserves granted by the Canadian government in 1899. The block of lands surrounding Kirilovka and the nine other "Saskatchewan Colony" villages established in the first year is separated by over 200 miles from the blocks of land surrounding the other 47 original villages. Base map is extracted from Index to Townships in Manitoba, Saskatchewan, Alberta, and British Columbia, by the Topographical Survey of Canada, 1929. Public Archives Canada National Map Collection 0043265. Land grant and village locations adapted from Tracie 1996. Compiled by author.

Interior. Unable to support themselves with their shrunken land holdings, between 1908 and 1912 Peter Verigin and thousands of his followers who wished to continue living communally moved to lands purchased in British Columbia, later adding settlements in southern Alberta. In Saskatchewan, through a slow process of dispersion, most remaining Doukhobor families left their villages in order to occupy privately held land. At its height during the first decade of the twentieth century, the village of Kirilovka, in the Prince Albert Colony, was home to about 200 people. By 1912 less than half of these remained, and by 1917 only 22 people still lived in the village (Kozakavich 1998:45).

Many of those who stayed in Saskatchewan continued to embrace Russian ethnic customs and espouse the basic spiritual principles and practices of their faith. Strong Doukhobor descendant communities exist in Saskatchewan today, though none have lived in communal villages for nearly a century. From the perspective of the broad settlement pattern we can see a disjuncture between the ideal of agricultural land use originally envisioned by the Doukhobor settlers and the ideal of agricultural settlement as envisioned by the Canadian government. The resulting split between communally living and independently farming Doukhobor families widened a geographical gap that already created tension within the faith but did not sever the shared connection of religious and ethnic identity.

Doukhobor Homes

Looking at a single example of the Doukhobors' communal villages is the next closest scale of inquiry. At this level of the built environment, the ordering principles of communality and equality are most visible within the scales of Doukhobor life. The ideal layout of Doukhobor villages in Saskatchewan is well documented in photographs, written descriptions, and maps produced between 1907 and 1913 for the Canadian Department of the Interior. This generalized layout was not as influenced by Canada's governmental forces as was the distribution of village locations and farm lands, and thus the Doukhobors themselves drew from their own building expertise and spiritual principles to design their local architectural and spatial surroundings.

Figure 2.3. At left, traces left by the village seen in agricultural fields in a 1944 aerial photo. The standing buildings and objects are part of the Rebalkin farm. At right, the lot and building layout of Kirilovka in 1907 and the 1996 highway construction right-of-way superimposed over the air photo. Air photo excerpted from National Air Photo Library, Natural Resources Canada, Roll A7217 Photo 2. Lot and building locations adapted from Fairchild 1907.

500 feet

1907 building location
1907 lot boundary
1996 construction right-of-way

Intended to be economically communal, each village of approximately 200 people was arranged according to a *strassendorf* plan, drawn from the settlement style of Mennonite villagers living near where Doukhobors co-alesced in the Crimean region in the mid-nineteenth century. According to this plan, two rows of nearly identical houses within deep rectangular yards faced each other across a single main street (fig. 2.3). Houses and lots were equal in size and equally visible from the street, but families main-tained a degree of privacy, as home entrances were oriented to the side of each lot, and fences separated private family yards from public street space. Specialized communal buildings such as the *bania* (bathhouse), granaries, barns, and outdoor bakeries might also be located along the main street, or on a perpendicular street branching from it. Similar village plans were implemented by Molokan settlers, Russian Christian sectarians sharing ethnic and religious roots with the Doukhobors, who established villages near Glendale, Arizona, in 1912 and Park Valley, Utah, in 1914 (Bowen 2006). Like the Doukhobors, Russia's Molokans separated from the East-ern Orthodox Church in the eighteenth century and moved throughout eastern Europe to avoid forced conscription and persecution through the nineteenth century. They are also pacifist and egalitarian, and reject the structured institutions of organized religion. Multiple theories exist for why they are called the "milk drinkers" (the rough translation of the term *"Molokan"*), ranging from their own restrictive dietary habits to their re-fusal to follow Orthodox dietary restrictions, to their origin in the Moloch-naya River region.

Occupied by one extended Doukhobor family, each whitewashed rec-tangular log house was placed with the gable end of the sod roof facing the street and the entrance facing the side of the fenced yard (fig. 2.4). The portion of the home closest to the street contained one private bedroom and one combined living and sleeping room, with a central kitchen area containing a traditional Russian brick oven called a *pech*. The portion of the home toward the back of the lot, not always whitewashed, was an attached utility building that served sometimes as a granary, barn, stable, storage shed, washhouse, chicken house, or some combination of these functions. Each family kept a garden and sometimes a few chickens or other small animals within their own lot.

Figure 2.4. View along the side of a Doukhobor family's house and yard in a Saskatchewan colony village. The whitewashed portion was closest to the main street and contained the sleeping, cooking, and sitting areas of the house. The rear portion with unpainted mud plaster would have been used for storage or livestock. Photo LH-2678, Saskatoon Public Library—Local History.

Most large livestock and farming equipment at Kirilovka, as at other Doukhobor villages, was owned communally. In 1905, this consisted of 50 horses, 50 sheep, 120 head of cattle, 5 binders, 9 mowers, 11 sets of harrows, 11 sleighs, 3 rollers, 3 rakes, 18 plows, 1 disk, 22 wagons, and 2 disc seeders (Kirilovka Village File). Though committed to producing as much of their own food and material goods as possible, the Doukhobors were not averse to technological advancement. Contemporary observers remarked at the adoption of up-to-date steam-powered farm machinery within the first few years of Doukhobor settlement (Kozakavich 1998:55–56).

When archaeologists began working at Kirilovka, the village had long been dismantled and replaced by grain fields. No visible trace of the houses, barns, or fences remained at eye level or on modern satellite photos. Only one Doukhobor settlement had previously been investigated by archaeologists. The site of *Bozhiya Milost*, in the Cowley-Lundbreck region of southern Alberta, Canada, was the focus of cultural resource management mitigation excavations as part of the Oldman River Dam project in the mid-1980s (Kennedy and Reeves 1986) (see #29 in the Appendix).

Only a few features found at this site—a root cellar, privy, and dump—contained artifacts dating to the ca. 1915–1937 Doukhobor village. Continuous twentieth-century occupation and cultivation had disturbed any other evidence (Balcom 1991:22). Remains of the Doukhobor occupation at Kirilovka only became clearly visible when construction crews working on twinning Highway 16 cut away the plow zone and up to a 3.5-foot-deep, 200-foot-wide strip of soil across the site, exposing 33 buried features. These cellars, privies, and buried trash deposits were all that remained of the houses aligned along the main street of Kirilovka, which ran just slightly northwest–southeast overlooking the North Saskatchewan River valley. Combining information from a 1909 Department of the Interior surveyor's map showing 38 buildings and 33 lots, and a 1944 aerial photo showing a ghost of the village's layout in the cultivated field, we were able to interpret the grouped features as representing the remains of roughly four households, with two groupings on either side of a featureless north–south strip, which was the location of the main street. After the village was gradually abandoned, the Rebalkin family stayed on and received patent for the land occupied by the former village site. The 1944 aerial photo shows their "new" house at the center of the south end of the main street, overlooking the empty lots of their former neighbors. Plowing the village under in the interest of planted fields could have been an economic decision made by the Rebalkins, as well as an effort to erase the past communal, egalitarian landscape from view. The family's home stood until the 1980s when the land was sold out of the family.

Artifacts from Kirilovka illuminate our understanding of daily life for Doukhobor families whose households comprised the village. Materials were collected by hand excavation and backhoe testing of the 33 subsurface features exposed during highway construction, including 11 privies, six possible cellars, five trench-shaped middens, and 12 unidentified feature types. In all, nearly 16,000 artifacts were collected, representing a wide range of household activities. A Russian-made iron cooking pot of the style used in traditional brick ovens was found alongside British- and North American–made transfer-decorated, painted, molded, and plain whiteware tablewares of many different patterns. In one feature quadrant, 11 different transfer-print designs are present in a collection of 17 transfer-print fragments, in addition to four distinct banded patterns (Kozakavich 1998:162).

Doukhobors were buying, or otherwise acquiring, table and serving vessels in similar styles to those of their English-speaking neighbors but appeared to be making no effort to assemble matched table settings. Scraps of wool, cotton, and silk textile remains from clothing and household linens included both Doukhobor-made and commercially produced items. Hand-nailed and hand-stitched shoe fragments were found, as were machine-turned and mechanically pegged shoe fragments. The mud-plastered log homes were furnished with factory-made cast-iron heating stoves that augmented the heat from traditional brick ovens, and linoleum partially covered the traditionally dirt floors (Kozakavich 1998:179) (fig. 2.5).

We archaeologists were far from the first to notice this juxtaposition of Russian folk goods and modern North American material culture. A visitor in 1900 noted the existence of Russian traditional items such as a wooden spinning wheel alongside a modern alarm clock and cast-iron stove inside a Doukhobor home (Rhoads 1900:11). The assemblage of household and personal goods from Kirilovka paints a picture of the ways Doukhobor residents could be simultaneously North American consumers of some items to meet their basic needs, and self-sufficient producers of others. Even when they were consuming mass-produced goods, though, the Doukhobors were making choices according to different priorities than we may expect for English-speaking Canadians of the time, and the materials they used and left behind may have had different meanings in the context of their belief structure.

Among the remains at Kirilovka were some artifacts that spurred questions about the changing nature of Doukhobor practice and identity. Beginning in the 1890s, Doukhobor leaders instructed their followers to expand their pacifism to include all living creatures, and devout members became vegetarians to avoid taking the lives of animals. The bones of cows, chickens and other fowl, rabbits, and at least one sheep and one pig were found in small amounts in each of the different feature groupings of Kirilovka, some with clear butchering marks. It is entirely probable that the chickens were relied upon for eggs, the cows for milk, and the sheep for wool. But it is also very possible that Doukhobor residents occasionally shared the meat from these animals in their families' meals. Also in the years immediately before migration to Canada, Doukhobor leaders admonished their congregations to abstain from using tobacco and alcohol. A small number of beverage

Figure 2.5. Scraps of linoleum and the molded glass base of a kerosene lamp are remnants of a Kirilovka family's household furnishing choices in Canada. Photos by author, 1997.

bottles dating from the period of Doukhobor occupation, including whiskey, wine, beer, and gin, were present in each feature grouping at Kirilovka. Though it is entirely possible that each of these bottles represented Doukhobor reuse of a bottle discarded by a non-Doukhobor neighbor, it is just as possible that some of Kirilovka's residents occasionally drank spirits. Australian archaeologist Geoff Hewitt accuses archaeologists (including myself) of "scarcely bridled optimism" in interpreting commercial product containers as being used primarily for their labeled contents at the time of sale (2007:108), and although this admonition could be fairly leveled at any archaeologist who encounters the remains of factory-made goods, it is especially applicable to those among us for whom the discovery of a whiskey bottle might mean the difference between past adherence to or defiance of community restrictions. Further, some modern Saskatchewan Doukhobors descended from the 1899 immigrants have been critical of interpretations suggesting that Doukhobor ancestors engaged in behaviors that were prohibited by their spiritual leaders (Brooks 2005:35). In the case of the Doukhobors of Kirilovka, as with any intentional community, we need to fully consider our evidence, and acknowledge multiple possible interpretations, before publishing such potentially controversial conclusions.

Although the tenets of vegetarianism and abstention from tobacco and alcohol were popularly professed among succeeding generations of descendants and scholars as essential to Doukhobor identity in Canada, these behavioral restrictions were part of Peter Verigin's new principles of Doukhoborism introduced less than 10 years before his followers migrated to Canada from Russia. They were among the distinguishing characteristics that demonstrated Doukhobor settlers' seriousness and pacifism in a cultural landscape within which they faced discrimination as a Russian-speaking minority with distinct religious practices. However, after they were introduced, Verigin's behavioral restrictions led to factionalization within Doukhobor communities in both Russia and Canada (Tarasoff 1977). Perhaps most notably, in 1907 a Department of the Interior inspector observed that meat-eating and vegetarian Doukhobors could be found together in the same villages (Johnson 1907). Meat eating and alcohol consumption were not necessarily indicators of assimilation to Canadian ways but instead demonstrated the heterogeneity of interpretations about living according to Doukhobor faith that existed before their move to the Canadian prairies. Though they became well-known elements in the cultural identity of later twentieth-century Saskatchewan Doukhobors, vegetarianism and abstinence were not consistently as central to the faith as were a commitment to equality, recognition of the inner guiding spirit, communal worship, and spiritual teaching through song and the spoken word. These aspects of practice, along with some Russian-based traditions such as the *bania*, lived on in those families that ate meat, drank spirits, and moved away from the village to privately owned family farms while still maintaining their identity as Doukhobors.

Each scale of archaeological inquiry into the lives of Saskatchewan Doukhobors offers the potential to explore different aspects of this complex group's communal and spiritual efforts. Settlement and migration patterns show the tension that existed between Doukhobor settlers, who sought to live according to their faith and farm in communal villages, and the Canadian government, whose goal was to fully settle and exploit western agricultural lands. The village built environment was structured according to principles of equality and cooperation, and in turn reinforced these values to residents as they shared communal facilities and visited one another's nearly identical homes. Within the household, families practiced a degree of autonomy in furnishing their space, preparing meals, and populating their daily lives with purchased material goods. Artifacts found in the features left behind by Kirilovka's Doukhobor households show varying ways that residents lived according to their faith and custom within a new world of goods and challenges.

What follows in the next three chapters is an overview of historical archaeological approaches taken by many different researchers to different North American intentional communities, from the eighteenth-century Ephrata Cloister of Pennsylvania through to the 1960s Chosen Family at Olompali, California. This discussion of archaeological work at intentional community sites is organized by the scale of view taken by researchers, from the settlement pattern and cultural landscape at the broadest scale in chapter 3; narrowing through the built environment and architecture in chapter 4; to the smallest, artifact level of analysis in chapter 5. This means that some groups or communities, such as the Shakers, resurface multiple times through the chapters, while others for whom limited studies have been conducted are touched upon only once. This isn't intended to confuse readers about the particular philosophical bent or time period at hand but rather to avoid compartmentalizing archaeological approaches to specific communities. Scalar views will show how our research questions and our potential for understanding the lives of past radicals can be more or less effective at different resolutions.

3

---★---

MAPS OF IDEALISM

Intentional Community Landscapes

The culturally constructed landscapes of intentional communities were often consciously designed with the belief that a properly shaped environment could mold its inhabitants according to shared social or spiritual goals. Examples discussed in this chapter demonstrate how ideology was built into the physical world of community members to, for example, connect them to a European Christian philosophical history, as in the case of the Harmonists' garden at Economy, Pennsylvania; or to ensure predictability and order in neighborhoods, as in the Mormons' Plat of the City of Zion. As the Shakers had the greatest geographical breadth and most extensive lasting impact on the American landscape of the groups discussed here, I begin my discussion with their fenced and finite village complexes.

Ordered Shaker Landscapes

The United Society of Believers in Christ's Second Appearance, more popularly known as the Shakers, were among the longest lived and most successful of North America's intentional community movements. The broad distribution of archaeological projects at Shaker sites highlights their geographical spread, as members of the group built 20 villages in nine states, including Maine, New Hampshire, Massachusetts, Connecticut, New York, Ohio, Indiana, Kentucky, and Florida. Converts expanded the group's population to include more than 6,000 members at the height of their growth in the 1850s. This abundance of Shaker community sites has provided inspiration and opportunities to a plethora of research teams, each with their own focus and approach. Since the 1980s, Plymouth State University anthropology professor David R. Starbuck has engaged with the buried past at Canterbury, New Hampshire, near the northeastern extent of the Shaker domain (see #7 in the Appendix). He continues to be active in researching Shaker sites in this state. In 2015, Starbuck coordinated with the Enfield Shaker Museum to supervise as Plymouth State University field school students excavated remains of the Church Family Trustees Office at Enfield, New Hampshire (O'Connor 2015) (see #6 in the Appendix). In 2005, an Ohio Department of Transportation highway project brought Bruce Aument, Andrew Sewell, and their colleagues to the North Family Lot of Union Village, Ohio, for fieldwork. Their ensuing extensive cultural resource management project report highlights the geographic spread of the Shakers outside of New England, into what was at the time the western frontier of a relatively new nation. Farther to the southwest into Kentucky, archaeologists Don Janzen (1981), Mark Leone (1981), and Kim McBride (1995, 2010) have taken varied approaches to the ca. 1810–1923 village of Pleasant Hill. With a population of nearly 500 people at the mid-nineteenth-century height of its growth, Pleasant Hill was, for a time, the third-largest Shaker village in the United States (McBride and McBride 2008:1013). The slightly smaller Kentucky village of South Union had up to 350 members at its height and used more than 200 buildings between 1807 and 1922. Archaeological inquiry at South Union since the early 1990s has begun to contribute to public interpretation of this southwestern extent of the Shaker expanse (Fiegel 1995; Tallent 2009).

The broadest scale of interaction with the landscape that most individual Shakers and their families contributed to and experienced was at the level of their village. At this level, Shakers constructed their world according to the instructions of their elders, and within the constraints of the physical environment and existing settlement. Their modifications to the landscape were extensive, with systems of mill ponds and races, collections of buildings, earth leveling, gardens, orchards and fields, and encompassing lines of fences that separated believers from worldly people and from uncontrolled nature. What set the Shakers' landscapes apart from the farms and the villages from which members came, and which surrounded their settlements, was the intentionality of their form. Every building was placed thoughtfully, every path was planned, and every participant in construction took part in shaping the environment that shaped brothers' (the male members) and sisters' (the female members) daily activities. The most basic archaeological approach to interpreting Shaker landscapes at the village scale has been to undertake detailed mapping of buildings, structures, and infrastructure to document the nature and extent of Shaker-era development. Fitting to its hosting publication, the *Journal of the Society for Industrial Archaeology*, David Starbuck's 1986 view of the mill system at Canterbury, New Hampshire, seeks to enlighten readers about the extensive industrial systems put in place by Shakers. While they are often popularly remembered as a group of quaint agrarian tinkerers, whose innovations were limited to labor-saving household tools, the Shakers in the context of the time were technologically ambitious. Lacking a nearby natural water source, the Shakers at Canterbury built an extensive system of ditches and ponds to provide water power to a grist mill, turning mill, and other industries. The work began in 1800 and expanded to eventually power nine different mills by 1850 (Starbuck 1986:22). Starbuck's focus on the industrial landscape of Shaker industry is indebted to Don Janzen's earlier work on the Shaker mill system at Pleasant Hill, Kentucky (1981), which documented remains of the water system supplying power to a grist mill and sawmill on Shawnee Run. Starbuck's 2004 report on the Shaker Mapping Project, published as a portion of his volume *Neither Plain nor Simple: New Perspectives on the Canterbury Shakers*, is a thorough documentation of the remaining elements of the Canterbury Shakers' built environment as mapped between 1978 and 1982, and consists of an account of each building, structure, and feature recorded, followed by over 60 1:500 scale maps of 600 acres of the Shakers' land holdings.

Starbuck and his team's extensive and systematic approach to recording at Canterbury is impressive, and creates an invaluable resource for further study. It may be possible, however, to argue with his observation that "clearly, the Shakers tended to cluster buildings within 'sacred' and 'secular' zones, keeping church and ministry buildings apart from dwellings and workshops, and these, in turn, apart from agricultural and service buildings" (Starbuck 1988:19). This assertion shows a moment of forgetting that, within Shaker daily practice, there was little distinction between the sacred and the secular. Shaker builders considered the idea for the design of the unique round stone barn at Hancock, Massachusetts, to be a gift from God, providing testament to their sense of the connection between the practical and the divine (Hayden 1976:92). In the Shaker context, "Hands to work" was just as sacred as "Hearts to God."

Expanding Order in Shaker Villages: Positions and Pathways

Archaeologists working at Pleasant Hill, Kentucky, and Union Village, Ohio, have more deeply considered how developments in Shaker belief and practice structured and were structured by the built environment and cultural landscape. To best understand the way Shaker villages were planned, we must consider the powerful role that faith leaders and elders had in organizing members' daily lives. In the years following Mother Ann Lee's death in 1784, under successors Joseph Meacham and Lucy Wright, the Shaker faith community continued in its growth and heightened its commitment to communalism. The design of the Shaker's spiritual, social, and spatial world was divided into a tightly ordered hierarchy, both within villages and across the Shaker domain. Distinct levels of commitment between different individuals and families of the faith's followers were expressed and codified in clearly defined differentiations in status and influence. This Gospel Order, as it was called, comprised from two to seven distinct and physically separated groups of members and their residential and work buildings in each village. These included the Novitiate, or Gathering Order, sometimes called Young Believers, who were new to the community and not yet fully committed; the Second Order, encompassing other families of committed members, who were sometimes named for particular directions (East Family) in relation to the Church Order lot, or to the landform of their own home (Hill Family); and the central Church Order of senior members. The covenanted members of the central Church Order had donated all of their personal property to the community, and they lived and worked separately from the junior and gathering orders. Members of the outer orders in each village may have retained some personal property and outside connections (Sewell, Hampton, and Krupp 2009b:8). Each family group consisted of both male and female members, adults and children, and ranged in size between 30 and 150 people. Each operated as a residential and working family under the spiritual management of male and female family elders who deferred to the Church Family at their village, and ultimately to the centralized Shaker leadership in the New York villages of New Lebanon and Watervliet (Savulis 1992:196). Economically, each family operated relatively independently according to its needs and abilities under the management of local deacons and trustees.

New villages were usually formed when local landowning families converted to the faith and chose to give over their property to the community. At Canterbury, New Hampshire, for example, the Whitcher farm and its buildings became the center of settlement for the Church Order, the most senior members of the community, in 1792. As more converts streamed in, it became necessary to acquire neighboring farms to accommodate the community's expansion into the multiple families of the Gospel Order (Starbuck 1988:4). The ideal intended structure of a Shaker community consisted of a nucleated group settlement, with the residences and workplaces of farmers and craftspeople surrounded, and indeed buffered, by agricultural lands on all sides, with four routes of entrance and exit corresponding to the cardinal directions (Aument and Sewell 2009:61, 183–184). This arrangement was designed to reflect the layout of the Temple of Solomon, in which a central temple, corresponding in Shaker life to the Church Order and meeting hall, was surrounded by courtyards and a gated outer wall. Any visitor to such a Shaker village would need to pass through a gated fence surrounding the entirety of the Shakers' land holdings and cross a stretch of agricultural field or woodland before arriving at one of the outer family lots. At this node of settlement there might be a communal house, kitchen, and craft shops where members of that family lived and worked. Stone fences segregated spaces inside and outside each family lot, and walkways connected buildings and work areas. Passing through this cluster of buildings and people, the visitor would cross another open expanse before arriving at the central Church Order lot, with its communal house, kitchen, craft shops, and meetinghouse (fig. 3.1). Continuing out of the Shaker settlement, in any of the four directions, would involve passing through another family lot, fields or woodlands, and gate.

At Pleasant Hill, Kentucky, Kim McBride brings the concept of *order* in space and behavior into her view of a village that abounds with examples

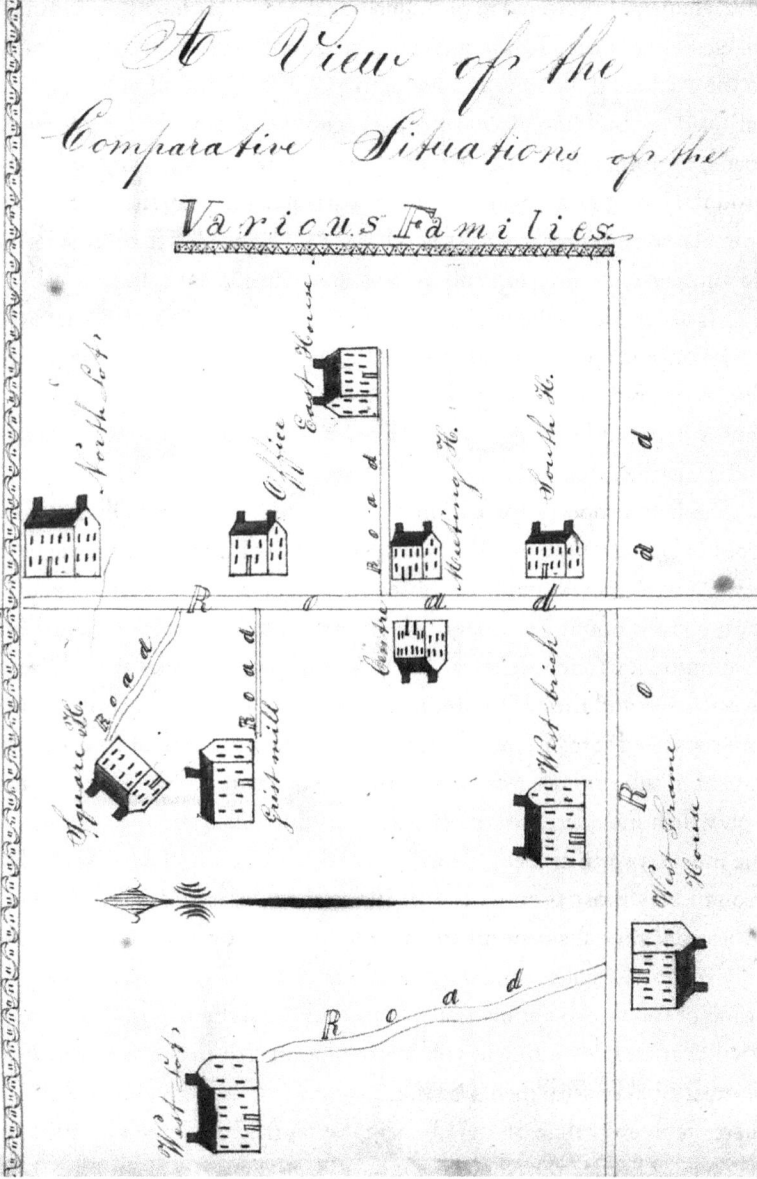

Figure 3.1. "A View of the Comparative Situations of the Various Families" at Union Village, Ohio, showing the Center Family house and meetinghouse bounded by the North Lot, East House, South House, and West Lot. By Isaac Youngs and George Kendall, 1835. Library of Congress, Geography and Map Division.

where order was reflected in and enforced by the Shakers' built world. She sees three types of "order" prevalent in Shaker life: the orders of membership from Novitiate to Church Order; order from spiritual forces, the basis of religious belief; and the order and regularity of daily life and the built environment (McBride 1995:394, 2010:254–255). Landscape and architectural elements connected to order include the long-lasting use of symmetrical elements of the Georgian architectural style; the orientation of villages to the cardinal directions and maintenance of a regular (if not mathematical) grid for building placement; parallel rows of buildings bordering the roads; a proliferation of single-purpose structures separating tasks, their products, and practitioners; separate structures for different types of stock animals; stone fences in excess of what would be needed to contain domestic animals enclosing and subdividing space inside the village; leveling of rolling areas within the village to create artificially flat surfaces; disposal of trash concentrated in abandoned buildings' foundations and cellars, rather than scattered in surface middens; and stone walks mandating walking routes between buildings and barns (McBride 1995:396–404; McBride and McBride 2008:1013).

The first property for Union Village in southwestern Ohio's Warren County was acquired in 1805 by a small group of Shakers from the northeastern settlements, and over subsequent years more Eastern Shakers and local converts built the village. The North Family Lot was established to accommodate Young Believers in 1815. Fencing and walkway building between 1838 and the 1850s seems to have solidified the North Lot's layout and separated it from the road. Throughout the duration of its occupation it held a "subservient" position to the "devout core" of the Center Family Lot, which included the community's meetinghouse and the residences of the most senior members (Aument and Sewell 2009:30, 90). The village's growth was most pronounced in the first two decades of settlement as Protestant revivalism swept the nation, followed by a second surge of energy with Spiritualism and millenarianism in the 1840s–1850s. The population of the North Family Lot was around 80 in the 1850s. Following the Civil War, a slow decline in village populations led to the eventual closure of most Shaker settlements by the turn of the twentieth century. By 1880 there were fewer than 50 members in the North Family, and by 1900 only 43 Shakers lived in the whole of Union Village (Sewell et al. 2009b:23–28).

Twentieth-century owners razed the remaining buildings by the 1960s and filled in the remaining cellars. By 2004, when archaeological field crews came to study the site in advance of highway realignment construction, the North Family Lot had become a grassy field. Combined geophysical and archival information led researchers to the foundation and cellar remains of four brick buildings that were not depicted on extant Shaker maps (as maps' synchronic focus captures one short period of time in an ever-changing built environment), and helped also to identify ancillary structures such as wells, fences, paths, and utility lines. With placement guided by these survey results, excavators opened a total of 106 units across the site, exposing 107 features including foundations, walls, chimney bases, drain pipes, paths, pits, modern fence posts, historic post molds, builder's trenches, metal pipes, cellar entrances, trash deposits, brick post bases, brick piers, floors, cisterns, and wells (Aument and Sewell 2009:145–154). Using the archaeological data from geophysical exploration and excavation in concert with archival maps and journal entries, the authors constructed a map of the North Family Lot buildings and a few small sections of pathways within the project area. Researchers superimposed grids of varying units and scales over their mapped information to help determine if these buildings, most of which were aligned longitudinally north–south, were planned according to a regular grid with an identifiable unit of measurement. While 25 feet seems to have fit best (Sewell et al. 2009a:2, 2009b:160), it isn't a standard for Union Village, let alone the Western Shakers as a whole. It might be safer and perhaps more meaningful to say that the buildings at the North Family Lot displayed a strong sense of order and regularity in their spacing and alignment along parallel and perpendicular lines (fig. 3.2).

Though carefully ordered, Shaker village landscapes were not static. At Canterbury, New Hampshire, for example, the West Family buildings were established soon after the village was founded in 1792, and were then moved or torn down within the community's first three decades to meet changing needs (Starbuck 1988:7). Researchers at the North Lot of Union Village, Ohio, also found documentary evidence that buildings were frequently moved within and between the village's different family lots in response to changing internal residential patterns or production needs (Sewell et al. 2009a:43).

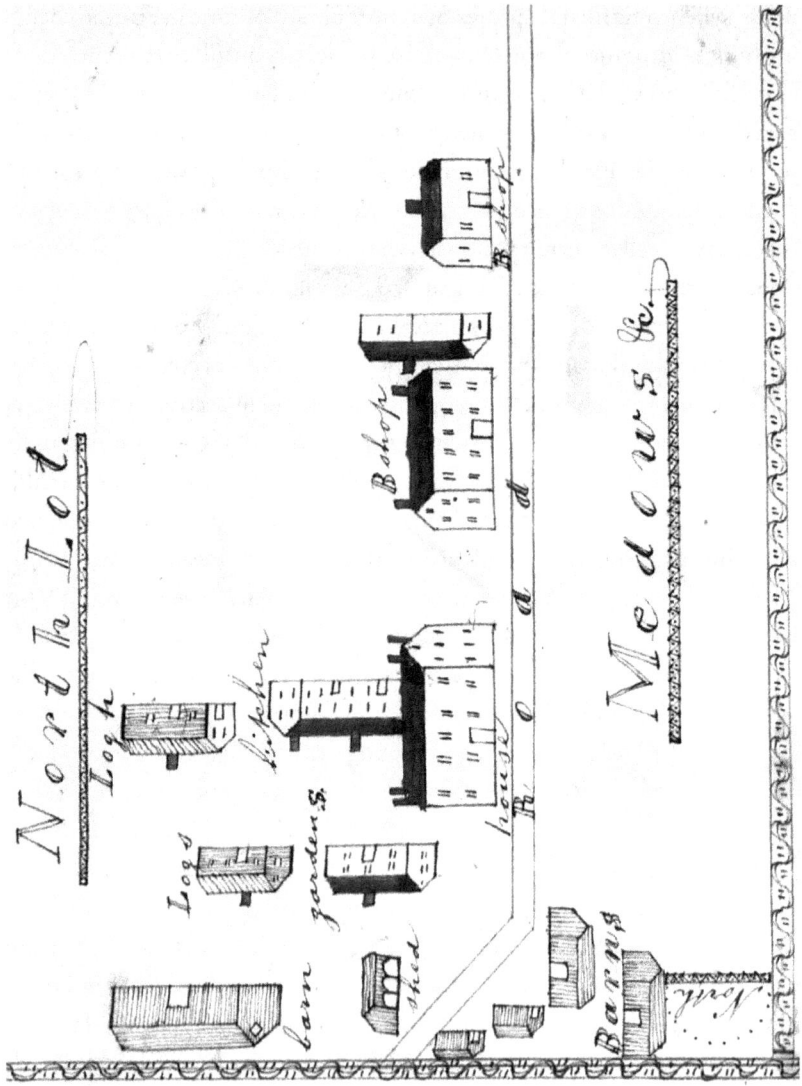

Figure 3.2. A schematic drawing of the North Lot of Union Village, showing a regular, rectilinear arrangement of buildings and alignment to the cardinal directions. By Isaac Youngs and George Kendall, 1835. Library of Congress, Geography and Map Division.

Ordering Brothers and Sisters

The mid-nineteenth-century Shaker Millennial Laws were guidelines issued by the central authority at New Lebanon, New York, to formalize and codify what were considered to be acceptable and prohibited Shaker behaviors and activities, and to provide guidelines for such a wide array of issues as minimizing contact between brothers and sisters, regulating trash and ash disposal, and mitigating the impacts of contact with worldly (non-Shaker) people. Though not widely printed and circulated among Shakers themselves, editions from 1828 and 1845 were transcribed in documents that today's archaeologists consult to aid in the interpretation of Shaker cultural materials. An 1845 rule from that year's version of the Millennial Laws encouraged pedestrians to keep to walkways as "it is not orderly to cut up the dooryards into little cross paths, and by roads" (Sewell et al. 2009a:155). While the interpretation of this admonition varies—Dolores Hayden took the meaning as prohibiting diagonal pathways (1976:69), while Sewell, Hampton, and Krupp (2009a) assume the statement's goal is to limit unofficial paths of any alignment—the essential spirit of it is the maintenance of collective order and adherence to common routes of movement. Its goal was the suppression of individual choice in moving through space so as to maintain a visually ordered landscape.

Kim McBride provides an excellent example of the proliferation of sanctioned walkways in a Pleasant Hill, Kentucky, Shaker village with an East Family journal entry reporting construction of "a stone walk to the sister's new shop, a branch of it to the new cellar door, and thence to the pump, and also to the woodshed, and one from the new shop door to the old loom house" (1995:403). It seems that all potential paths of direct travel between buildings are accounted for, making it easier for workers to keep to the paths than to create their own shortcuts. Paths were significant, also, in the Amana Inspirationist villages of Iowa. In each of the Amana villages, the two-story family houses were aligned regularly along the wide main streets, so visitors passing through town would see a quiet stretch of facades with a uniform appearance, while most residents' daily activity occurred out of view to nonresidents within the blocks behind the rows of homes. Networks of pedestrian paths connected the gardens, services, and work buildings inside each block and concentrated daily activities in these areas (Hayden 1976:238).

Christine Gorby's perspective as an architectural historian contributes to her way of communicating about Shaker spaces. Describing an ideal village, she writes that the "translation of this sacred doctrine into the physical landscape can be seen everywhere in Shaker landscapes from their architecture which is built orthogonally with entry paths, sidewalks and main thoroughfares, fencing and trees at right angles with fields and barns, and cultivated fields and pastures organized in endless geometric square forms" (Gorby 2005:164). Gorby's influence from fellow architectural historian Dolores Hayden is evident. The latter saw the entire Shaker built landscape as an act of conscious construction in which "the 'master builders' specialized in skillful manipulation of their converts' perception of personal space and spheres of movement in order to simulate the experience of the dual spheres" of heavenly and earthly space (Hayden 1976:69).

While it is impossible to know how many Shakers trod off the paths between their homes and workshops against their elders' wishes, archaeologists can find evidence that the yards between buildings were not kept as clear of trash as the Millennial Laws decreed in 1845: "No kind of filthy rubbish, may be left to remain around the dwelling houses or shops, nor in the dooryards, or streets in front of the dwelling houses or shops" (Andrews 1963:280). Archaeologists at the North Family Lot at Union Village found six single-use rubbish pits near buildings being studied for architectural information, and it remains unknown if more undiscovered pits are scattered throughout the lot. While researchers expected to find more evidence that cellars and abandoned buildings were used for concentrating dumped waste, the only excavated cellar feature abandoned during the village's occupation—the Brothers' Shop cellar—doesn't support this idea, as the only artifacts below the architectural debris fill level are those likely dropped during the building's use. Some waste was found in the yard, as was evidence of household waste dumping from the 1820s through the 1850s in the garden areas excavated for building information (Sewell et al. 2009b:56–57). Graduate student Joseph Grygas found a similar result outside the Second Church Family Dwelling House at Watervliet, New York, where the surface survey crew found sheet midden toward one corner of the rear side of the dwelling house. Grygas offers two interpretations: first, that Shakers deposited their garbage on the surface, outside of buildings in the way that many of their non-Shaker neighbors did; and second, that the deposit's location on one side of the building may correlate to the gender-segregated use of the space. Specifically, Grygas thinks that sisters were throwing away more trash (2011:36). Grygas wisely follows in the path of Shaker scholars outside of archaeology who deemphasize the spread of and adherence to the Shaker Millennial Laws' admonitions about proper waste disposal.

As with paths and trash disposal, enforcement of regulations regarding personal space and separation of the sexes varied between villages and across time. Applying the archaeological lens at its broadest, whole-village scale makes it clear that brothers and sisters experienced different levels and types of interaction with the non-Shaker world. Ellen-Rose Savulis writes that, at the turn of the nineteenth century, spaces at Canterbury, New Hampshire, that were closest to the outside world, including the roads connecting to non-Shaker spaces, were inhabited by brothers and dominated by men's more frequently "secular activities" (1992:17). Canterbury's sisters reproduced the sacred values of the family more deeply within the community's protected interior. Savulis sees this Shaker system of gender separation as one that "mirrored the social and economic relationships in the outside world that the Shakers tried to challenge" (1992:200). In Savulis's view, Shaker men controlled the mapped landscape—the layout of buildings and roads—and women were restricted to configuring the interior spaces. Christine Gorby's work supports and expands on this assertion. Gorby's drawn reconstruction of the West Union village Center Family Lot based on "historic Shaker daybooks ... recent archaeological findings, and western Shaker building practices" (2005:170) vividly demonstrates that women's work areas, both workshops and gardens, were clustered around the center of the lot, close to the meetinghouse and dormitory. Sisters were thus protected from the outside world and monitored within their village to protect them from their own baser qualities. She concludes that Shaker men's opportunities for variety and choice in productive work were much greater than women's, even though sisters' work at making the goods produced for sale to the outside world was immensely economically important to villages (Gorby 2005:167–171). This imbalance in the respect accorded to gendered activities is corroborated by a series of Shaker-made maps produced by Isaac Youngs in 1834, which regularly left sisters' workshops unlabeled while brothers' workshops were specified in detail. Savulis writes, "The contrast between male and female visions subverts the unified face conveyed to the public by Shaker society and at Shaker village museums today" (1992:202). We would hope and expect that the spiritual descendants of a powerful woman, Mother Ann Lee, would be inspired to advance the status of their female members past that experienced in broader society. This is not borne out in nineteenth-century representations of Shaker village landscapes. While, as Suzanne Spencer-Wood cautions, we can't assume that all community members came to their radical alternatives having uniformly experienced the "elite Victorian gender ideology" of separate spheres for men and women (1999:162), we still must view Shakers' dual-gendered power structure within the context of the surrounding culture at the time the Shakers were most active (Gorby 1995; Savulis 1992). Shakers' attempt at a structured equality of the sexes was built within the existing early nineteenth-century view of gendered qualities, and while it promoted the importance of women's spiritual strength and earthly usefulness, it also promoted the idea that brothers' capabilities were more important in building the Shakers' physical and economic world. During the spiritual revival period between 1837 and the 1860s, young Shaker women began trying to reclaim influence within their villages by sharing their spiritual visions, which came to be known as "Mothers Work," or the "Era of Manifestations." By this time, however, neither a dramatic surge in religious fervor nor an opportunity for Shaker women to increase their power and influence was enough to slow the trend of population decline. Shaker villages struggled to attract enough new converts to sustain the villages' dwindling workforces.

When we return to the Shakers in discussing the scales of built environment and artifacts, however, the separation and imbalance between Shaker sisters' and brothers' work and spaces seems less clear. The landscapes of Shaker villages provided frameworks to sustain families in their life as believers. They protected residents from the world outside, and guided those residents in their travels, labors, and interactions. Shaker village landscapes were also works in progress, though, and by exploring the finer details of buildings, foundations, and their contents, researchers can better understand the impetus for larger scale changes.

Cultivating the Sublime: Sacred Gardens

George Rapp's elaborate garden at the Harmony Society's village of Economy, Pennsylvania, stands in florid contrast to the Shakers' orderly kitchen, seed, and herb gardens. Economy boasted agricultural infrastructure such as cattle and horse barns, and industrial facilities including a tannery, woolen mill, flour mill, cotton mill, and silk mill. In their Pennsylvania industries, which included weaving, tanning and leather work, and brewing and distilling, the Harmonists embraced technological innovations that would enhance their productivity. Making more than was needed for their own subsistence, Harmonists manufactured goods such as cloth, pork, beef, butter, lard, flour, and whiskey for sale at their own stores, as well as in 22 states and 10 foreign countries. While laboring to produce these goods for the community, most Harmonist Society members had little interaction with non-Harmonist neighbors. Business contacts were limited to a few Harmonist representatives. This isolation led to tension around their communities, which escalated in some cases to acts of violence against the group's members (Strezewski 2013:8–9, 180).

Started when the village was founded in 1824, Rapp's garden was several acres in size and divided into four quadrants around a central pond and pavilion. Each quadrant represented a different theme: the wilderness, the vineyard, the vegetable garden and orchard, and the flower garden (Heberling Associates, 2008:2.3–2.4). Initially under Rapp's own development and care between 1824 and 1835, the garden later became the responsibility of Harmonist community leaders with differing visions for its contents and significance over the years. In its original state, Rapp's garden was a deeply charged and culturally meaningful landscape in its explicit relationship with the "religious, social, economic, and ideological contexts in which Harmony Society culture developed" (De Cunzo et al. 1996:105). Following the Harmony Society's 1905 dissolution, the garden experienced further transformations. The Commonwealth of Pennsylvania acquired the town site in 1916, and massive restoration efforts of the village were undertaken from the late 1930s to the 1960s. The garden that visitors

encounter today has been reinterpreted and restored by generations of local non-Harmonist gardening enthusiasts and historical preservationists,
and now offers only shadows of the former meaning it held for Harmony
Society viewers.

In the late 1980s, University of Delaware historical archaeologist Lu
Ann De Cunzo and her colleagues undertook mapping, documentation,
and archaeological excavations as part of a multidisciplinary study with the
goal of gathering information to better reconstruct and interpret Rapp's
garden at the Old Economy Village public heritage site. Archaeologists
found evidence for the construction sequence of the vineyard mound (including domestic trash dumping episodes before and during its building),
historic pathway materials and locations, and trellis support post holes (De
Cunzo et al. 1996:102–104). Soil samples were taken for flotation and
phytolith analysis to seek more information about Rapp's plant selections.

The structure of the garden reflected and reified the Harmonists' views
of nature, order, and cultural aesthetics. Combining broadly sought documentary sources with the material record in their interpretations, De
Cunzo and her coauthors see in Rapp's garden at Economy the reconstruction of an earthly Eden; the use of quadripartite structures with roots at
least as distant as medieval monasteries; a fountain representing the ancient use of water in ecclesiastical imagery; conifers representing the cedars
of Lebanon; colors and statuary reminiscent of the *Turris Antonia*, a mid-
seventeenth-century Christian mystical painting housed in a small Württemberg church; German heritage in the form of the *Einsiedelei*, a rustic
stone and thatch hut evocative of humble settlers or hermits on its exterior,
and exalted, refined imagery on its interior (fig. 3.3); and in the garden's size
and complexity a marker of Rapp's heightened social and economic status
in relation to his followers' (1996:105–107, 110–111). By looking at mentions of pastoral and agricultural settings in Harmonist hymns, the authors
understand that "paradise prefigured not only in Rapp's garden, but in the
complete agricultural landscape of Economy" (De Cunzo et al. 1996:109).
Rapp's garden was part of a cultivated tableau that represented an earthly
vision of paradise, and acted not only as a location for activity but as a participant in the congregation's worship and music.

The Pennsylvania-based cultural resource management firm Heberling
Associates, Inc. expanded on De Cunzo and her colleagues' work in its

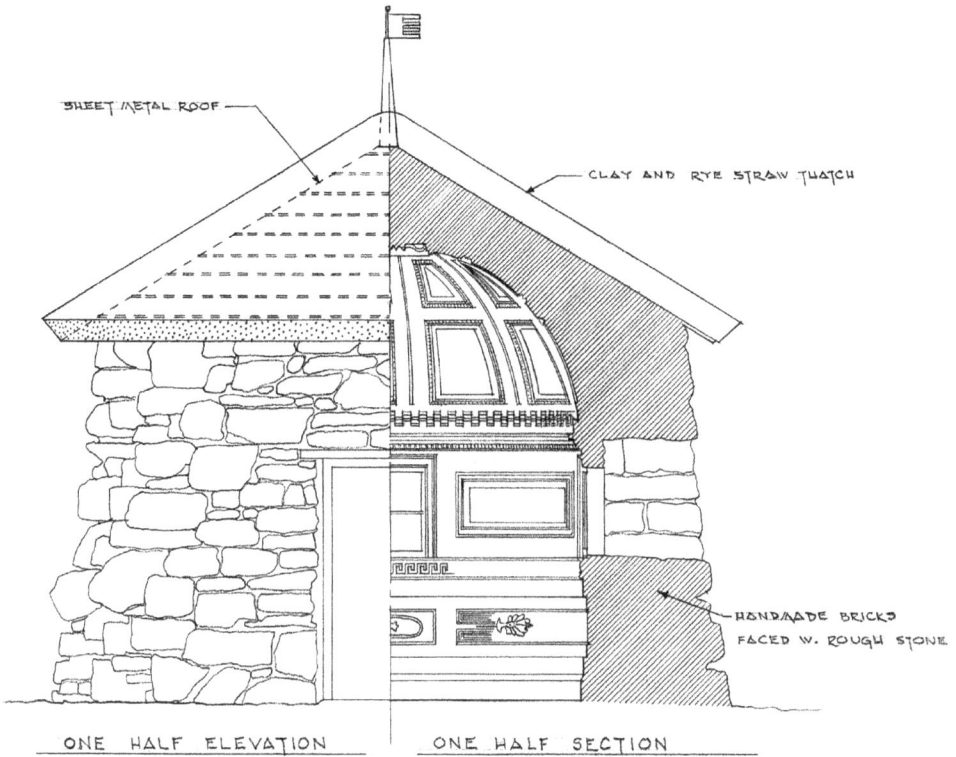

SHEET METAL ROOF

CLAY AND RYE STRAW THATCH

HANDMADE BRICKS FACED W. ROUGH STONE

ONE HALF ELEVATION   ONE HALF SECTION

Figure 3.3. Elevation and section of the Grotto in the Harmonists' Great House Garden at Economy, Pennsylvania, showing the rustic stone and thatch exterior, and classical interior details. Drawn in 1967 by Carlos E. Taylor Jr. of the Carnegie Institute of Technology for the National Park Service Historic American Buildings Survey. Library of Congress HABS PA,4-AMB,1- (sheet 5 of 5).

2007 archaeological and historical studies of Economy's Great House Garden. Conducted as a step in yet another proposed restoration of the garden at the Old Economy Village historic site, this effort was planned to restore the garden to its early nineteenth-century, Harmonist-era appearance. The archaeological program sought to determine the original vineyard row layout, planting locations, path configurations, and location of the greenhouse and other landscape features such as arbors and trellises. The researchers also collected samples for archaeobotanical and phytolith analyses. Unlike De Cunzo and her coauthors' work, these explicitly stated goals aim to inform garden restoration design, rather than to expand our understanding of the way the Harmonists used or envisioned the land as a religious or communal group. However, Rapp's background and beliefs were so interwoven into the structure of the Economy garden that considerations of aesthetics and practicality, symbolism, and changing styles are inevitable.

Through minimal excavation and sensitive stratigraphic analysis at the vineyard mound in the northwestern quadrant of the garden, archaeologists with Heberling Associates, Inc. determined that four different planting patterns with different vine and row spacing and row alignments were employed in the years of the vineyard's use (2008:5.6). Excavators found that the original vineyard configuration was of concentric semicircles, which was reworked into a radiating spoke pattern in the last half of the nineteenth century (Heberling Associates 2008:4.104). Comparing the nineteenth-century concentric row arrangement with recommendations from viticulture and gardening manuals of the time, the authors found that the row spacing was minimally adequate for producing wine grapes. This informs their interpretation that the vineyard at Economy may well have been more important as an aesthetic feature than it was a practical element for supplying Harmonist wine making.

Photographs, particularly an 1891 set from late in the Harmonists' days at the village, helped researchers form an idea of changes made to the garden after Rapp's death. Ultimately, the team identified some features, such as the arbor, path, and pavilion at the central pond, that had not been substantially altered. In the southwestern "wilderness" quadrant, within which the authors suggest the Harmonist landscape consisted primarily of pre-existing mature trees, a systematic shovel testing program identified only three nineteenth-century planting features. This suggests that the area was left largely unmodified during the Harmonist period of use, and was subject to minimal alteration through the twentieth century (Heberling Associates 2008:5.4). Other modifications following Rapp's 1847 death, such as changes in the vineyard planting layout, the addition of a cow barn, and the removal of the vegetable garden, significantly altered the look and function of particular areas of the landscape in the last half of the nineteenth century. Some late Harmonist-era changes were intended to create more typical late-Victorian floral displays than would have been found in the Harmonist leader's original plan, suggesting that the leadership at this time was more influenced by current fashions in garden design than by Rapp's symbolic mysticism (Heberling Associates 2008:4.30). Due to economic constraints, the historic site's landscape restoration plan has not yet been implemented (Heberling, personal communication March 2015).

Joseph Bimeler and his followers at the Society of Separatists of Zoar built a similarly symbolic garden consisting of radial pathways and circles of evergreens in their Ohio village. In their historical travel guide to utopian communities, Gerald and Patricia Gutek suggest that these gardens might have been inspired by the ideas of early seventeenth-century Christian visionary Jakob Boehme, whose ideas influenced Pietist leaders of the nascent Harmonist and Separatist communities in Württemberg, southern Germany (1998:108). Now home to a museum complex interpreting the Separatist society's years there, the National Register–listed Zoar Historic District contains dozens of contributing resources associated with the Separatists' occupation there from 1817 to 1898. Original houses, a bakery, town hall, store, and hotel still stand, and the garden has been restored based on historic records (Sewell 2013:16). Plans for modifications to the nearby Zoar Levee and Diversion Dam have spurred initial cultural resource management studies. On behalf of the U.S. Army Corps of Engineers, Hardlines Design Company of Columbus, Ohio, which also completed the Union Village Shaker investigation a few years earlier, conducted an Archaeological Probability Assessment as well as proposed boundary expansions for the Zoar Historic District (Sewell 2013; U.S. Army Corps of Engineers 2014). Andrew Sewell and colleagues identified several areas throughout the district with high potential for the presence of Separatist-era sites related to residential, religious, educational, commercial, agricultural, and industrial activities. Potential archaeological sites identified, but not yet evaluated, include ruins of the mill race and guard lock from around 1830, a dike from about 1840, the ca. 1850s foundry and slaughterhouse ruins, the late 1870s sawmill ruins, the 1880s kettle house ruins, and other as yet unidentified foundations (2015 Draft National Historic Landmark Nomination, Zoar Historic District). It will be interesting to see how the results of continued archaeological testing conducted at Zoar illuminate the group's ways of imbuing their landscape with meaning, as previous archaeological work there has been minimal (Herson, Pansing, and Pickard 2013).

Inspired in part by Lu Ann De Cunzo's writings on the Harmonist gardens at Economy, Robert J. Austin led a team including Jerome Westphal, Fred Steube, and Anne Yentsch in creating a comprehensive map and historical archaeology management plan for the Koreshan State Historic Site in Florida (Janus Research 1993). Cyrus Teed's follower, Gustav Damkohler, donated land on the Estero River in Florida for the 1894 establishment of the Koreshan Unity settlement based on Teed's spiritual and scientific teachings (Florida Dept. of Environmental Protection 2003:15). The core members of the group were celibate, living nearest the center of the Florida property in separate men's and women's residences and dining communally at separate men's and women's tables. Married couples and families with children resided more peripherally (Baker and Wheeler 2000). Residents established several small businesses and industries to support the community of up to 200, including a bakery and store, vegetable gardens, and citrus groves, as well as decorative concrete manufacturing and boat building. The group's population peaked at around 250 in the early decades of the twentieth century, but a few members still occupied the site several decades after Teed's 1908 death.

With the awareness that the Koreshans living at the Estero community beginning in 1894 had distinct spiritual views about the structure of their physical environment, Austin and his colleagues encourage a comprehensive landscape archaeology program to reconstruct the Koreshans' gardens, paths, and roads, in addition to the locations and dimensions of their buildings (Janus Research 1993:26). One of the centerpieces of this research plan would be to investigate and fully restore what remains of the "Sunken Gardens," an intentionally constructed landscape consisting of mounds and terraces with decorative plants and fruit trees connected by paths and steps. As the Koreshan worldview was based on the idea of a complex universe existing inside of a sphere, examination of the physical landscape at Estero could consider the earthly enactment of Koreshans' scientific and philosophical beliefs.

Mapping Visions: Roads and Fences

Standing in ruins among the desert scrub about 70 miles northeast of Los Angeles, the site of the early twentieth-century Llano del Rio Cooperative

Colony could never have supported the verdant gardens and productive fields that were significant parts of Shaker, Harmonist, Zoar, and Koreshan landscapes. This arid place was nonetheless planned to become a meaningfully designed city with open park spaces interspersed among its homes, schools, and workshops. The colony was run as a joint stock corporation in which members committed to purchase a total of 2,000 shares at $1.00 per share with part of the money up-front—an initial $500 investment—and then once at the colony through labor, which earned a rate of $4.00 per day. Though not explicitly a cooperative colony, one of Llano's goals was to maintain an egalitarian structure. Each member was to hold 2,000 shares, not more or less than any other member.

Llano's community residential plan was an unstable hybrid of individualism and communitarianism, in which organizers aimed to provide affordable housing constructed from the group's own products, including brick and lumber, to be rented and occupied by single, relatively autonomous families. This intentional focus on maintaining private homes was in concert with novelist William Dean Howells's fictional Altruria, "a socialist society that preserved the nuclear family and private home" (Van Bueren 2006:146). Harriman's interest in such a plan may have developed during his family's 1894–1895 association with the Altruria Colony, which formed in an attempt to realize Howells's vision near Santa Rosa in Sonoma County (Foster 2008:15). These colony-built houses designed by self-taught architect Alice Austin were to be built without kitchens, as Austin's plan for food service was to build a communal kitchen that, rather than gathering all colonists in one place to eat together, had a "futuristic underground food-conveyor system" delivering prepared meals to individual homes (Van Bueren and Hupp 2000:30). Other members' visions for the community included more practical communal dining halls where residents shared meals with their neighbors. In reality, many colonists lived in tents during their short stay at the Antelope Valley experiment, while other buildings were made of adobe, wood frame, sheet metal, or mortared cobbles (Foster 2008:53). The cobble structures provide the memorable images in today's landscape of ruins at Llano, with roofless barns and the hotel's cobblestone pillars standing where the rest of the building has deteriorated (fig. 3.4).

A review of Llano del Rio's colony records and the 1916 Great Register

Figure 3.4. The fireplaces and pillars of the Llano del Rio Cooperative Colony's hotel. Photo by author, 2016.

of Voters shows that 389 resident adult members and at least 29 children lived at the colony in that year. More than 60 work departments were designated, with functions as broadly varied as photography, fish hatchery, and steam laundry (Van Bueren and Hupp 2000:19). Perhaps the most useful department to modern researchers was Llano's publication operation, as surviving issues of the *Western Comrade and Llano Colonist* provide us with regular reports of colony building efforts between 1914 and 1917 (Foster 2008:20). Outside of their working hours, residents had access to extensive group-based leisure pursuits, from sports to a Dramatic Club and literary societies.

Two distinct, intentional town plans were developed for Llano del Rio during its occupation. Leonard A. Cooke's 1915 vision was of six identical blocks of houses and services, aligned with one on each side of a hexagonal pathway surrounding the town's civic center (fig. 3.5). The whole would be interwoven with a regular web of paths, streets, and parks (Hayden 1976:298). Alice Constance Austin's 1916 radial plan highlighted a succession of ring roads connecting each spoke and surrounding the city (fig. 3.6). Between the spoke roads, private homes and communal parks and gardens allowed for individual and collective recreation (Hayden 1976:299–300).

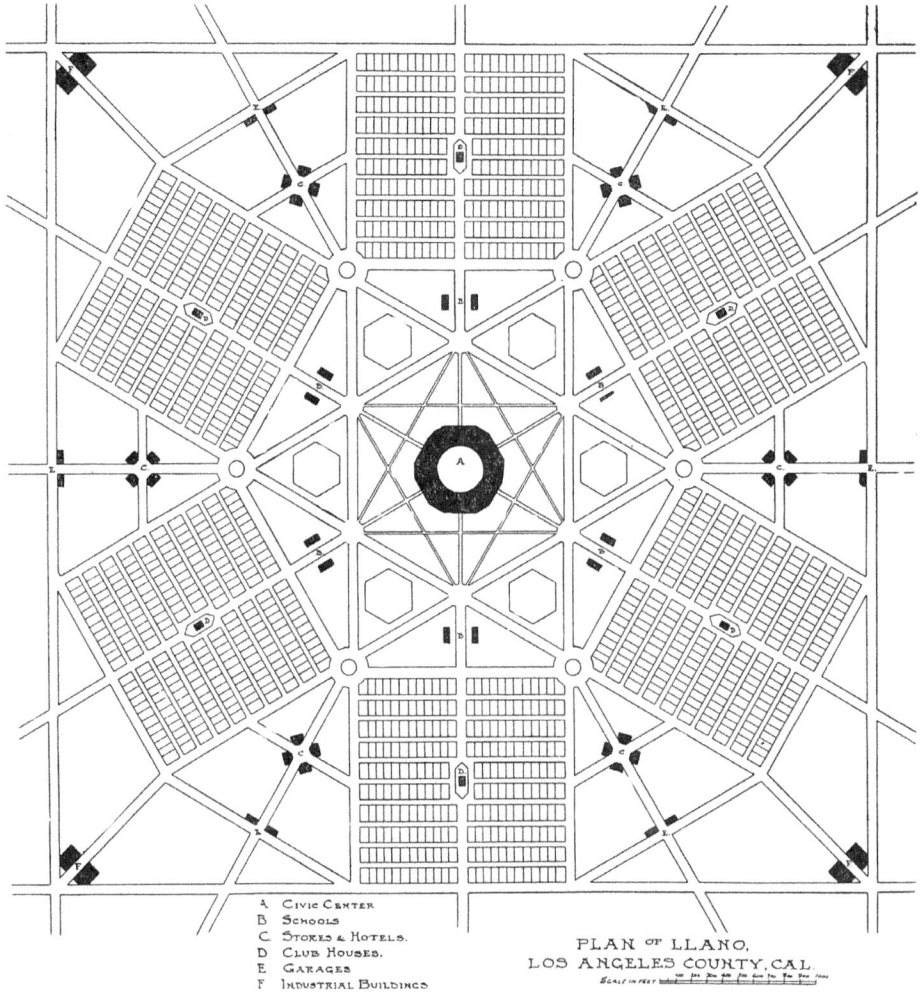

A CIVIC CENTER
B SCHOOLS
C STORES & HOTELS
D CLUB HOUSES.
E GARAGES
F INDUSTRIAL BUILDINGS

PLAN OF LLANO,
LOS ANGELES COUNTY, CAL.
SCALE IN FEET

Figure 3.5. Architect Leonard A. Cooke's plan for Llano del Rio, published in the March 1915 issue of the community's *Western Comrade* (2[11]: 19). The caption includes the description that "the broad streets will be lined with ornamental shade trees and in the narrower streets will be pergolas and vines." Digitized by the California State Library, available as an electronic document at the Internet Archive (archive.org).

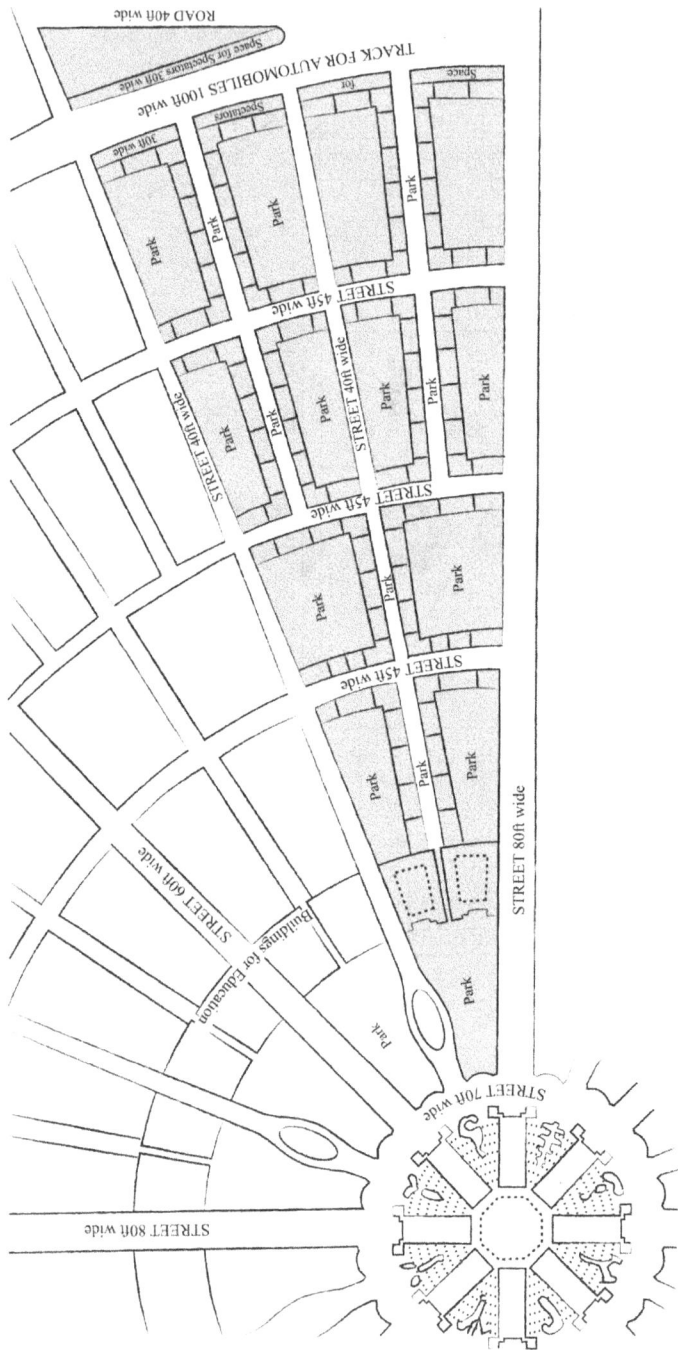

Figure 3.6. Alice Constance Austin's radial plan for Llano del Rio, showing a section that would be repeated around the eight spokes of the city center. Drawn from a version published in the April 1917 issue of the community's *Western Comrade* (4[12]: 16–17). The caption includes "It is aimed for the Llano plan that more persons can be housed with greater privacy and beauty of surroundings than by any other plan yet devised." Note the "Track for Automobiles" and "Space for Spectators" around the circumference of the city plan.

Today's Llano del Rio is a fascinating and relatively rare archaeological example. Though some looting and littering have occurred over the last century, very little occupation or development of the site's 500-acre area occurred after the colonists' departure in 1917. Through a 1999 program of fieldwork and archival study initiated by plans to widen State Route 138 (aka the Pearblossom Highway), which passes through the site, California Department of Transportation archaeologist Thad Van Bueren and architectural historian Jill Hupp conducted a National Register of Historic Places (NRHP) eligibility evaluation for the Llano del Rio Cooperative Colony property. The field strategy involved selective excavation within the proposed project right-of-way, the areas within which road construction would occur, and surface assemblage recordation in other "key areas" of the colony (Van Bueren and Hupp 2000:38). The team recorded 386 features, of which 19 were building ruins (including the hotel, barns, a silo, a creamery, and the men's dormitory), and 173 building pads, as well as numerous water management features, industrial features, and infrastructure remains. Among the most extensive features was a complex of canals and ditches with eight concrete distribution boxes, designed to move water through buried metal pipes into colony cisterns. While it doesn't distinctively represent the colony's ideals in its design or construction, Van Bueren and Hupp see the contributing elements of this large-scale landscape modification as "poignant reminders of the crucial importance of water to the success of the colony" (2000:56). Following these researchers' efforts, the site was determined in 2000 in to be eligible as a "discontinuous district" for the NRHP.

John Foster and colleagues followed Van Bueren and Hupp's initial study with a 2008 report on data recovery from nine building locations and 21 pit features, completed in advance of construction for the proposed highway-widening project. Mapping the site revealed that, for the most part, the town was aligned according to a rectangular north–south grid. However, one row of dwellings seems to have been aligned on a radial line from the village center, as was suggested by Alice Constance Austin's plan (Van Bueren and Hupp 2000:47; Foster 2008:52). While Van Bueren and Hupp withheld speculation before more data recovery could be done, Foster hypothesizes that this alignment of residences may represent the earliest, most idealistically driven stage of colony building (Foster 2008:52).

Van Bueren's earlier surface survey also found wooden stakes planted by colonists in the northeastern quadrant of the settlement during their initial layout of Leonard Cooke's hexagonal colony plan (Van Bueren 2006:145). Thus, it's clear that three different and incompatible spatial plans were actually attempted by builders at Llano del Rio: Leonard Cooke's hexagonal and Alice Constance Austin's radial plans, as well as a more pragmatic rectangular street grid. It would be interesting to know, though difficult to learn, if building toward these three different visions of colony layout were undertaken by the same group of builders, disqualifying each of the more idealistic plans as the urgent needs to provide housing and work space took priority, or if competing factions simultaneously attempted to impress their ideal vision upon the colony's structure (Van Bueren 2006:145).

Mark Leone's 1973 look at "Mormon Town Plans and Fences" is in its essence a reflective work on the impact and contributions of the New Archaeology, the concern with culture process, and the use of models and analogy in anthropological archaeology at the time of its publication. It also acts as a useful case study in combining historical documentation of ideal town planning with analysis of the built environment. Leone describes how the Mormon settlement pattern in the Great Basin combined the needs of building religious community with response to the physical environment. According to Joseph Smith's idealized town plan, the "Revised Plat of the City of Zion," drawn by Frederick G. Williams in 1833, equally sized rectangular house lots were to be placed according to a regular grid composed of equally sized blocks, imposed over the local topography. Lot frontages would be aligned facing alternating directions from block to block so that residents would enjoy the privacy afforded by facing the sides, rather than the fronts, of their neighbors' lots across the street (fig. 3.7). This alternating direction of lots and fences ensured that all residents in a Mormon village built according to the plat had equality with other residents and household privacy while they lived closer to their neighbors than most other Anglo-Americans in the western states at that time. In many Great Basin Mormon communities, a pattern of smaller square residential blocks dominated, on which four family households and their gardens each occupied a corner (Hayden 1976:142), a practical application that contrasts with Smith's more densely settled blocks of 20 lots. According to the 1833 ideal plan, each city was to farm the lands surrounding it, and to be replicated in an

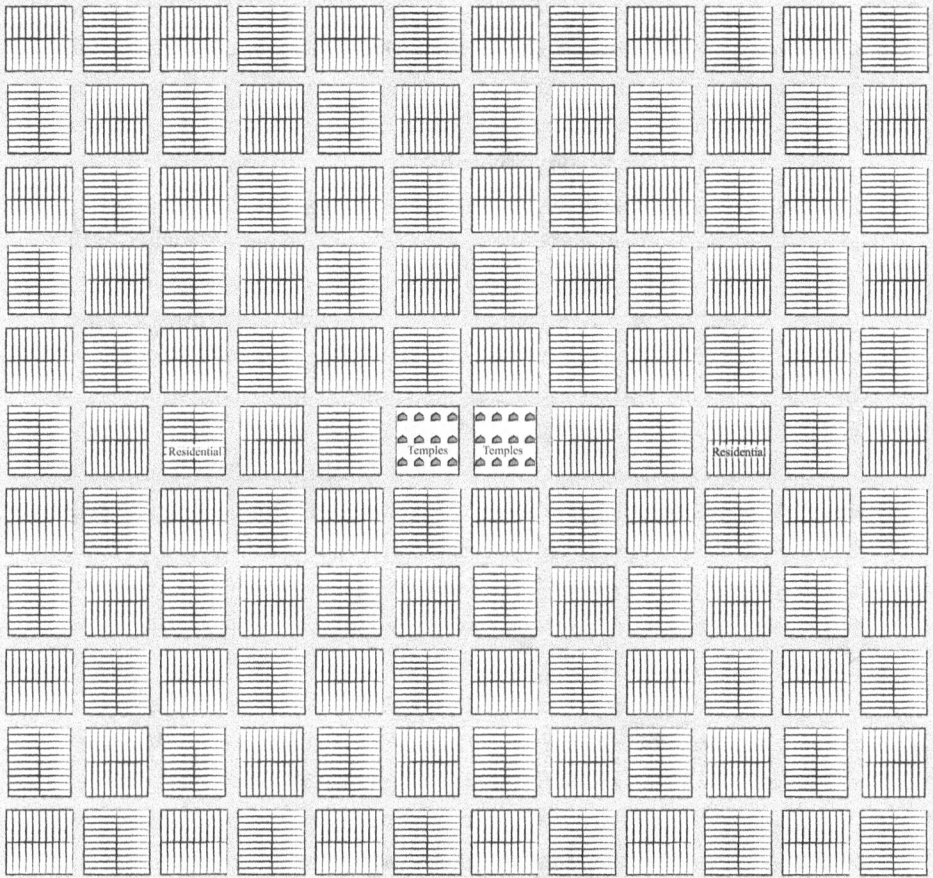

Figure 3.7. The town plan of Frederick G. Williams's 1833 Revised Plat of the City of Zion. Each of the 130 residential blocks contains 20 single-family lots. The two central blocks contain 12 temples each. Drawn by the author based on digital item ID#3505 of the Joseph Smith Papers, www.josephsmithpapers.org.

expanding series of identical cities across the surrounding territory as each city's blocks were filled with devout residents. Within subdivided blocks, fences acted as a "passive product of Mormon culture" and also a "causative agent" (Leone 1973:143) that enabled Mormon farmers to create niches for grazing animals, poultry, gardens, and orchards in each relatively small town lot within an arid environment, keeping competitive species sepa-rate and mitigating the effects of wind erosion and deposition. As social mechanisms, fences allowed households to be closely spaced but maintain individual property boundaries and a degree of privacy. They also, Leone speculates, may have had a cognitive effect on residents by encouraging the ability to compartmentalize distinct and possibly disparate ideas, such as those of faith in the supernatural and empirical observation of the concrete world (1973:147). In an echo of these highly individual (but equal) household lots in the idealized town plan, Leone writes that the Washington, D.C., Mormon Temple individualizes the religious experience with small rooms and passageways that highlight a single member's passage through rituals. In contrast to meetinghouses of truly communal religious groups, which dissolve the family unit and promote membership in a larger whole, the temple isolates and reconnects an individual strongly to his or her own family lineage across time (Leone 1977a:47).

The comparatively modest town of Lower Goshen, Utah, provided a focus for Brigham Young University archaeologist Dale Berge to study early Mormon history as it was lived, as well as how it was planned (1983, 1990). Established in 1860, Lower Goshen was designed with a grid system of 40 residential blocks intended to accommodate 160 families in a variation of the "Revised Plat of the City of Zion." Settlers soon discovered that the alkaline clay soil was inappropriate for agriculture, so residents abandoned the village after only eight years. The location was then relatively undisturbed for 120 years. In 1979, using aerial photos and surface survey, archaeologists mapped 121 components indicated by vegetation patterns and visible stone features. Berge and his colleagues concluded that, although the town was planned to include 40 residential blocks, only 20–25 blocks were occupied during the eight years of its settlement. These results contrast the imagined ideal Mormon community, described by Leone's speculative exploration, with but one example of a real-world attempt to build according to Joseph Smith's vision in an environment that ultimately couldn't support dense settlement. The physical reality of soil conditions intruded upon the vision of the ideal.

Architectural historian Dell Upton offers an updated view of the Great Basin Mormon cultural landscape in a 2005 article published in the *Journal of Mormon History*. Observing the variable house styles present in Mormon communities across the western states, Upton asks how the lack of visual uniformity impacted the experience of being Mormon, then expands his inquiry into an exploration of what promoted communality and what contradicted it (2005:12). He investigates the actual form neighborhoods took when homebuilders attempted to follow the "Plat of the City of Zion," finding that houses' exterior doors were placed on both "fronts" of homes so that they ended up directly facing neighbors rather than away from them as the plat originally intended. He suggests that, as built, the form of residential blocks "undercuts any argument that the arrangement of houses was meant to create a sense of privacy in the Mormon city or town. Rather, the common town plan in Utah seems to have made it difficult to isolate oneself" (Upton 2005:17). Divergences between the real and ideal, so common in our observations of intentional communities, serve to illustrate the cultural landscape as a process of building and being-in, as Upton brings himself around to conclude that

> In asking our initial question about the ways the landscape shaped living as a Mormon, we would do better to see the landscape as the product of a process of working it out—not completely, not consistently, not uniformly—what it meant to live in Zion day by day. (2005:29)

Whether in the orderly clusters of buildings and paths of a Shaker village or the lush vegetation of Economy's and Zoar's spiritually inspired gardens, in the conflicting radial plans of Llano del Rio or the tight fenced-in yards of Mormon villages, intentional communities build their goals for improvement into the landscapes they inhabit. Archaeological perspectives on these landscapes show us where there was still room for improvement in communities' efforts. The Union Village and Watervliet Shakers' trash pits and scatters show how constantly believers struggled with bits of chaos within their ordered lives, and how that struggle leaves visible marks on the ground. Traces of Llano del Rio's overlapping city designs show that members of the community may have all shared a commitment to labor equality but did not all share a consistent view of the shape their egalitarian city should or could take. Looking at the remnants of community landscapes can also show us where we have misunderstood past groups in our popular memory. Don Janzen and David Starbuck stress the significance of industrial technology to the lasting success of Shaker villages, counter to our vision of them as agrarian retreats. Lu Ann De Cunzo and Heberling Associates, Inc. peeled back layers of aesthetic changes to the Harmony

Society's garden at Economy, Pennsylvania, to show the initial Pietist vision built into its composition.

In the next chapter, I focus the lens closer, moving from an analysis of the overall village site and the relationship between buildings, gardens, paths, and other outdoor spaces toward an examination of the structure of the buildings themselves. At this scale, I am interested in the buildings that members constructed as part of their envisioned landscapes of improvement, and which they occupied while attempting to live according to their shared principles. This slightly finer scale casts light on some of the changes in belief over time and the continuing tensions between precepts and practice.

4

———★———

AT HOME, WORK, AND WORSHIP

Community Built Environments

Communities, as we consider them archaeologically and architecturally, are easily abstracted into collections of ideas and practices seeking to be made real. Yet communities are nothing without the households and families who share, live within, build into materiality, and rail against the ideas that give structure to the culturally constituted physical world. The domestic and work spaces inhabited by past intentional community members hold traces of their family structures and can provide evidence of the dynamic nature of community building. As discussed in the following pages, repairs to the Ephrata Cloister's Kedar and a remnant abandoned arch in a Shaker basement are two examples of buildings as processes of negotiation and inhabitation that were physically changed as their builders' needs, abilities, and expectations changed. And as they were inhabited, buildings worked upon their residents to reinforce behaviors central to community belief, from the separating brothers' and sisters' staircases of Shaker family houses to the gathering rooms of the Oneida Mansion House. In providing examples from archaeological and architectural history approaches to intentional communities' built environments, this chapter demonstrates the strength of this scale in accessing family structures and identifying built responses to members' long- and short-term visions and goals.

Families of the Faithful

With several original wood frame buildings standing alongside archaeo-logically informed reconstructions, the Ephrata Cloister in Pennsylvania offers visitors and scholars a view into eighteenth-century construction techniques and architectural styles as well as into the builders' philoso-phies. The Ephrata Cloister was home to a religious community founded by former master baker and Pietist religious dissident Conrad Beissel, who came to the United States from Germany in 1720. After seeking for the hermitage of the Society of the Woman in the Wilderness and finding it diminished, he visited the ascetic Labadist commune at Bohemia Manor in Maryland, before finally establishing himself as a hermit in what later became Lancaster County, Pennsylvania. Beissel's Camp of the Solitary, es-tablished in 1732, became less and less solitary as more German Americans were drawn to his experiment and the group adopted monastic principles of ascetic self-denial, celibacy, and prayer. By 1750 about 300 people lived at Ephrata. Of these, the majority were "householders"—families who did not join the celibate brothers' and sisters' orders but shared their beliefs, and who lived in houses near the periphery of the settlement surrounding the cloisters. Beissel died in 1768, and after a slow decline in membership, the remaining householders reorganized in 1814 to become the Seventh Day Baptist Society of Ephrata (Mohn 2001).

Archaeology of the Ephrata Cloister began in 1963 with a few field sea-sons led by Pennsylvania state archaeologist John Witthoft (Biever 1968). Stephen G. Warfel, as curator of archaeology with the State Museum of Pennsylvania, later renewed these archaeological efforts and directed a de-cade-long field research program at the site between 1993 and 2003, which also operated as an Elizabethtown College field school. Warfel and his stu-dents devoted five seasons of fieldwork to exploring buried remains of the Kedar, the first communal building erected by Ephrata's members in 1735. The building's three stories initially accommodated celibate brothers on the ground floor, celibate sisters on the third floor, and meeting spaces between these on the second floor. Later, as members erected new buildings for the brothers and for community meetings, the Kedar became exclusively the territory of the sisters, the "Order of Spiritual Virgins" (Gutek and Gutek 1998:12). With its footprint dimensions of 30 feet by 84 feet determined during the 1998 field season, Warfel believes that the Kedar was likely one of the largest post-in-ground, or earthfast, structures made in colonial America (Warfel 1999:2). This construction method uses wooden support posts sunk directly into post-holes dug into the ground as support for a building's frame. It was commonly used in expediently made vernacular buildings during the seventeenth and eighteenth centuries, and though some earthfast structures of the colonial era still stand today, they were susceptible to damage from rot and shifting earth. Warfel offers the interpretation that such an impermanent method of construction makes absolute sense for a religious order that was actively awaiting an imminent Second Coming of Christ. Members who joined and built the Ephrata community were not planning for a long earthly existence. Archaeologists found evidence of support and repair posts along the wall lines of the Kedar, showing that the building needed to be repeatedly reinforced during its more than 70 years of use. This, in Warfel's opinion, is much longer than the intended use-life of an earthfast structure (1999:29). Subsequent buildings, such as the Mount Zion brothers' dormitory, which was built in 1738 (and investigated archaeologically during both the 1960s and 1990s), had half-timber construction and stone-lined storage cellars. These sturdier structures were more labor-intensive to build but also more durable, suggesting that the residents expected their divine departure to be less than imminent. By the later 1730s, then, Ephrata colonists' religious views had shifted to accommodate the possibility of a longer-term future than they had originally anticipated (Warfel 2009:146, 2000:2).

While Ephrata's ascetic members built their Kedar in the expectation of Christ's imminent Second Coming, Shakers constructed their villages to be heavens on Earth. For these members of the United Society of Believers in Christ's Second Appearing, the Second Coming had already happened in the form of Mother Ann Lee. Lee and her successors, Lucy Wright and Joseph Meacham, admonished followers to avoid adorning their work with decoration, so although Shaker buildings are distinctive to modern viewers in their formal simplicity, nineteenth-century visitors frequently found them to be neat and inoffensive, though a bit architecturally and aesthetically drab (Martineau 1837 and Nordhoff 1875 quoted in Hayden 1976:100; Stein 1992:46). Adult members generally lived in plain, rectangular, relatively symmetrical two-story boxes with gabled roofs and few, if any, decorative elements. Shakers deliberately eschewed architecture as an aesthetic pursuit as part of their belief that beauty should not be sought in this world but was reserved for heaven.

Simplicity was called for by their ideological beliefs, but in Shakers' flexibility and focus on utility they avoided the dogmatic approach to architecture that led other intentional communities to embrace specific ideal buildings types, like that of the unrealizable Fourierist phalanx or Austin's hopeful vision for Llano del Rio family homes. Shaker builders focused more on designing order and utility into their communities than on adhering to particular styles or forms in building. This allowed the flexibility to adapt to local environments while maintaining fundamental Shaker principles. In some regions, such as southern Kentucky, brick and/ or stone architecture was the norm, while in others wood frame or log with plank siding was more practical. At West Union, Indiana, some original log buildings were later covered with clapboard, which increased their resemblance to the clapboard buildings of the Eastern Shaker settlements, but strict architectural standardization was not required by Shaker leadership. Buildings that once stood at Union Village, Ohio, combined Shakers' regional flexibility with their relative immunity to changing architectural fashions. This village's houses featured the Georgian symmetry characteristic of the earliest Eastern Shaker buildings, in addition to some simple Federal style details that were widespread in the early nineteenth century. Overall, the buildings displayed the simplicity desired by Shaker thought-leaders while being constructed from local building materials. The 1937 Historic American Buildings Survey (HABS) documentation prepared for the 1854 Sisters' Shop, the last standing building at the North Family Lot of Union Village, Ohio, records how it was made in similar form to the earliest buildings at Union Village, and thus shared more characteristics with buildings decades older than with its architectural contemporaries outside the village. In general, photographs and descriptions of the buildings at Union Village show continuous repetition of the side-gabled, evenly bayed brick and timber building styles utilized throughout the community's years of growth (Sewell et al. 2009a:33–34, 105, 161).

Stylistic conservatism shouldn't, however, be confused with technological conservatism. Most discussions of Shaker material culture acknowledge the group's innovations in household, craft, and industrial tools (Stein

1992:303), and this tendency toward practical improvement extended into their building infrastructure as well. Archaeologists Kim McBride and W. Stephen McBride note that the Pleasant Hill, Kentucky, West Lot wash-house was placed to facilitate water intake through an underground lead pipe from a nearby spring and outflow through a limestone drain, and had three furnaces sharing one chimney, potentially for simultaneous work at different crafts (McBride and McBride 2008:1013; Burton 2012:40). Shaker sisters working in the laundry did not have to carry water to their boilers when washing their family's masses of laundry, as they had built-in water access and enough heating capacity to meet the demands of their sizable task. Clearly there was an advantage to being able to draw on a widely skilled membership for collaboration in design and building exper-tise. Simultaneously, the necessity for large-scale operations helped spur Shaker communities to innovate in their infrastructure. Intentional com-munities must respond creatively to the problems of providing adequate services for a population significantly larger than a typical nuclear family grouping, but they may also be able to take advantage of divisions of labor and economies of scale. Providing adequate collective laundry services was laborious and time-consuming for any community before the advent of widespread electric, gas, water, and sewage utility services, and the task became meaning-laden when a group's ideal involved easing the burden of domestic drudgery on its members. Washhouses were significant issues for more than one community's design. Henry Baker and Ryan Wheeler of the Florida Bureau of Archaeological Research present a small archaeological project at the site of the Koreshan Unity's steam laundry building as an example of an attempted technological solution to a problem of domestic labor. They write that "the steam laundry at Koreshan can be seen as a small element in a larger struggle for equality that undoubtedly played a role in creating the Koreshan community" (Baker and Wheeler 2000:15). With the time freed by collectivizing laundry services, individual members could pursue other activities, be they spiritual, intellectual, or practical, without the encumbrances of household drudgery.

In Shaker villages in general, the proliferation of special-use work buildings contrasted sharply with the all-purpose barns and sheds of their non-Shaker neighbors. Kim McBride notes the irony in this, that while Shakers' domestic spaces were economized by communal life, with more adults sharing basic living spaces and amenities than on neighboring farms, true "economy" fell away when considering the abundance of apparently single-use shops and work buildings for everything from pressing clothes to making barrels (2010:257). Documentary and archaeological evidence demonstrates that Shaker shop buildings actually often served multiple purposes at a time, and frequently changed functions through time. David Starbuck's study of the differences between the Second Family and Church Family blacksmith shops suggests that Canterbury, New Hampshire's Shakers were likely both avoiding redundancy of craft activities in the community and using these shop buildings for multiple purposes—in the case of the Second Family, pipe making and tool maintenance and repair, and at the Church Family, shoeing animals, repairing firearms, and making gravestones (2000, 2004:83–84). Documentary records from the North Family Lot of Union Village, Ohio, mentioned use of the Brothers' Shop for wagon making, shoemaking, tailoring, and sisters' silkworm raising, and as a temporary pottery shop during a renovation of the Broom Shop. Archaeological remains within the debris of the demolished building suggest also that stone working, tin working, haberdashery, and medicinal herb preparation may have been practiced there. Artifacts recovered from below the demolition debris included

> a probable hat form made of copper, some bone pottery tools, bone "blanks" that were in the process of being worked into scales for utensil handles, remains of brushes, wooden tubs and casks, stoneware and glass containers, and possible stone-working tools as well as large amounts of pottery, wasters, and saggers. Goods were likely packaged for shipment outside the community at the Brothers' Shop, as well, as this is where a stamp and stencil with trustee Stephen Easton's name were found. (Sewell et al. 2009a:90)

Housing multiple craft activities in single shops could be seen as more significant to Shaker craftspeople than simply reverting to vernacular, rural patterns of the multiuse shed and barn. Working together, even at different vocations, could facilitate exchanges of labor, tools, and materials, while reminding otherwise independent skilled workers that they were part of a larger effort. A single farm family's multiuse barn held the potential for different activities, all enacted by and for the benefit of the property owner or lessee. Shaker brothers and sisters who worked together in a shed or workshop were reminded how their actions, and the actions of their brothers and sisters, contributed not to their own enrichment but to this voluntary family. This idea is similar to John Foster and Alex Kirkish's preliminary interpretation of the centralized industrial complex at the Llano del Rio Cooperative Colony in Southern California (2009:6), and although the secular socialist Llano Colony and the deeply religious Shaker orders diverge widely in terms of motivating ideals and philosophy, they both had to negotiate the practical concerns of structuring the activities and work spaces of groups of people, with an eye toward enacting an idealized society. At both communities, working together provided opportunities for surveillance as well as camaraderie.

In addition to demonstrating that single-purpose built or named workshops often housed multiple crafts, the evidence from Shaker villages also suggests that Shaker men and women were not as rigidly separate in their workplaces as at home and worship. Segregated male and female spaces inside each Shaker village are famously preserved in memory and architecture by dual entrances to meetinghouses and dormitories. Separating males and females in space was the strictest and most noticeable manifestation of Shaker belief expressed through their architecture, and it was achieved through construction of separate entrances to residential buildings and meeting halls, separate sleeping rooms, and sometimes separate men's and women's staircases (fig. 4.1). Male and female children's quarters were kept separate from each other and from the adults' residences until the midteen years. These could be in separate buildings or on the upper floors of shop buildings such as the Green Shop at Union Village, Ohio, where girls of the North Family Lot stayed for a time, and the Brick Shop, where the North Family Lot boys were housed (Sewell et al. 2009a:74).

A commitment to separating men and women in Shaker villages was written into the codified orders and built into the level of the landscape, and it permeated all daily activities. David Starbuck and Paula Dennis (2010) engage us in an intriguing thought-experiment in an attempt to provide an experiential diversion from the standard architectural or archaeological view of statically built unpopulated worlds. They take a moment to imagine the way Shakers actually moved through their constructed space in daily action, rather than focusing primarily on architecture at the layout

Figure 4.1. A view looking beneath the two identical staircases, one each for brothers and sisters, of the Shaker East Family Dwelling House, Pleasant Hill, Kentucky. Even in the state of midrepair captured in this 1963 photo, the symmetry of the doors, staircases, and peg rails conveys the ordered layout of Shaker buildings. Photographed by Jack E. Boucher for the National Park Service Historic American Buildings Survey. Library of Congress HABS KY,84-SHAKT,1—16.

or planning stages. When walking from their dwelling houses to religious meetings, brothers and sisters at Canterbury were

> funneled together side by side along a single granite path, to divide again as they entered gender-specific doors of the Meeting House. Then they marched in circles singing, an ebb and flow of the two genders entwined in spirit—forever joining, forever dividing. As they left the worship, they again divided, exiting through separate doors, to join again on the single stone path, to divide once more as they re-entered their dwelling(s). Throughout the whole, this was a tightly choreographed ballet of the two genders, forever aware of each other's dependency and presence, yet bound never to come into physical contact with each other. (Starbuck and Dennis 2010:236)

Dolores Hayden writes that the strictest enforcement of rules for separation of the sexes was enacted before 1850, and it was rumored that in some communities peepholes in meetinghouse walls and watchtowers on dwelling house roofs prevented infractions. In Hayden's opinion, however, the design of space and its furnishings was a stronger influence in enforcing desired behaviors than any worded rule or human surveillance. She writes that each Shaker was "physically surrounded by the handiwork of other believers. Social control was thus achieved through careful articulation of personal identity, a synthesis quite at odds with modern bureaucratic control and anonymity" (Hayden 1976:71). Each sister and brother sat in chairs and at tables, and walked pathways, made by others whom she or he personally knew and to whom they could consider themselves personally accountable.

Sewell, Hampton, and Krupp (2009b) observe that those North Family Lot buildings at Union Village, Ohio, that were primarily used by women, such as the Green Shop, washhouse, and Sisters' Shop, were placed north of the communal house, while buildings primarily used by men, such as the Brothers' Shop and Pottery/Broom Shop, were south of the communal house. However, archival records recall that a male shoemaker worked in the Green Shop in the 1840s, male hired laborers stayed there after the 1840s, and Union Village sisters raised silkworms in the brothers' workshop cellar in 1848 (Sewell, Hampton, and Krupp 2009b). Archaeology has also helped to blur the gendered line for Shaker work buildings, and to emphasize the daily importance of and innovation devoted to seemingly mundane, "women's" tasks. On the archaeological findings from the Pleasant Hill, Kentucky, West Lot washhouse, Kim McBride writes that "Shaker men put in substantial labor in constructing the washhouse features" including the large furnace, evidence of horse-powered machinery, and water supply and drainage systems (2010:263). Women working in the washhouse were afforded the full benefit of technological innovation and mechanical assistance, and though their work may not have seemed outstanding to contemporary visitors such as Isaac Youngs, the investment made to women's work spaces affirms that their importance was recognized within the community.

As we see in their relocation of buildings within and between family groups, Shakers were agile in their approach to changing social and economic circumstances—even those encountered in the middle of a building project. The archaeologically explored foundations, piers, entrance staircase, window frames, and other structural elements from the house and kitchen addition at the North Family Lot of Union Village, Ohio, provided little information to researchers about how this building may have structured the lives of its residents according to Shaker tenets. The remains do, however, hint at some of the dynamics of North Family Lot's specific history. An incomplete brick arch found built into the side wall of the ca. 1829 kitchen cellar is an undocumented remnant, reminding us how the members of communal groups often need to change strategy midstream in their shared projects to keep within the constraints of changing circumstances (fig. 4.2). The arch, which may have been intended to be part of a water containment feature beneath the kitchen, is very possibly a marker of the moment when the building budget for the kitchen was halved from $5,000 to $2,500 in the middle of construction because of the North Family's ongoing financial difficulties (Sewell et al. 2009a:72–73). The Young Believers who originally occupied the North Lot accumulated approximately $2,000 in debts to outside creditors. A partially realized vision had to be halted and redirected. Markers like this are physical reminders of how the scale of communal groups' infrastructure needs to differ from that of individual families. The kitchen addition required a larger investment of time and resources than would a secular family's lean-to kitchen add-on, and it took long enough to build that it was subject to economic fluctuations while it was in progress. The subsequent residents of the Gathering Order were saddled with this financial burden when they moved in later in 1836 (Sewell et al. 2009b:16). Buildings are subject to the economic and social fluctuations that inevitably occur in large groups, and can harbor traces of these moments of unexpected change in their structures.

In contrast to the Shakers' vast spread of settlements across over 1,000 miles between Maine and Kentucky, the Amana Inspirationists' seven concurrently occupied small villages established between 1855 and 1861 were spaced closely together, within 10 miles of one another along the Iowa River, and connected by relatively direct roads. Grinnell College anthropologist Jonathan Andelson sees this as a balance between dispersion and aggregation. Colonists could avoid congregating in a large center where temptation to sinfulness was possible, while allowing all members to be close to leader Christian Metz (Andelson 1986:48). Although not practicing as an archaeologist, Andelson's view of the Amana Colonies embraces

Figure 4.2. Brick arch remnant in the kitchen cellar adjacent to a filled doorway opening, North Family Lot of Union Village, Ohio. Photo by April Popovitch, Hardlines Design Company, 2005. Fig. 45 of Sewell, Hampton and Krupp 2009a. Used with permission of Hardlines Design Company and the Office of Environmental Services, Ohio Department of Transportation.

a perspective on the historical built environment that is extremely useful to our more comprehensive understanding of the different physical expressions of German Pietist intentional communities in the United States.

Buildings in each of the seven Amana villages were characterized by uniformity of material, style, and layout. Andelson describes a typical Amana building as "unadorned, symmetrical, and functional, reminiscent of Georgian architecture stripped of every classical detail" (1986:47) (fig. 4.3). This simplicity extended to the churches, which, despite their central importance in daily life, were architecturally similar to all the other buildings. Always brick or sandstone, churches had larger windows than other buildings and included "at least one wall of windows unbroken by a doorway" (Andelson 1986:47). Separate entrances for men and women at opposite ends of the building enforced separation of the sexes during worship. Simplicity and egalitarianism are also echoed in Amana's cemeteries, where rows of uniform concrete slab headstones are evenly arranged facing

Figure 4.3. The Middle Amana communal kitchen and cooper shop, built in 1863 and last used for preparing communal meals in 1932. The brick construction and architectural simplicity are typical of the Amana Inspirationists' building style. Photo by Peter Merholz, 2005. Used with permission.

east. The uniformity of these burial sites echoes that of the Moravians' "God's Acre" at Salem, North Carolina, where the dead were buried beneath simple, identical headstones next to others belonging to their age, gender, and marital status cohort rather than close to their immediate families (Thomas 1994:19). Unlike the evangelical Moravians, however, Dolores Hayden writes that the original simplicity of the Amana Inspirationists' style reflects the group's de-emphasis on worldly affairs and disinterest in attracting converts. Pure adornment was considered sinful, as reflected in *Werkzeug* (inspired Instrument of the Lord's will), Barbara Heinemann's 1880 admonition to plant only fruit trees, as these would be useful, while others were to be removed for their contribution only to the "pleasures of the eye" (Hayden 1976:231). Daily tasks were not imbued with the spiritual significance with which Shakers approached their vocations—and thus buildings at Amana became "reflections of pragmatic rather than millennial communism, instruments of religious cohesion and control" (Hayden 1976:229).

Member families lived in shared housing, managed and assigned by church elders. Most houses accommodated up to four unrelated families in private apartments with a common entrance. Though Inspirationists were not exclusively celibate, church elders encouraged small family sizes and had the authority to relocate families to different housing at their discretion based on the number of children (Andelson 1986:49). Large families were not rewarded for expanding the community; rather, they could be inconvenienced with frequent moves to less desirable housing. Individual family homes had no kitchens; instead, a few houses in each village operated as kitchen houses with attached wings where teams of women were tasked with preparing meals for assigned families. At mealtimes diners were segregated by age and gender, and were expected to eat quietly and finish expediently to accommodate multiple seatings. Only after the communal structure was abandoned in 1932, and remaining members were given the option to buy their apartments and to renovate and decorate according to their own needs and tastes, did Amana's families become fully responsible for preparing their own meals in their own homes.

Reconstructing Community Households

The Shakers' large membership and number of villages helped to cement, reinforce, and reproduce their family structure of single brothers and sisters living in assigned Gospel Orders with relative stability for a century. Amana's seven villages likewise maintained stability in their balance between family privacy and communal sharing for almost 80 years. Smaller, single village communities, such as the Harmony Society, Brook Farm, and the Oneida Perfectionists, more actively negotiated what it meant to be a family, and what a family's residence consisted of, as they built and changed their settlements.

University of Southern Indiana archaeologist Michael Strezewski's ongoing work at New Harmony, built and occupied by Harmony Society members between 1814 and 1824, is gradually filling out our knowledge of this group's residential building programs. Observers at the time characterized the Harmonists as "extremely hard-working, producing a variety of manufactured goods and agricultural produce," and Strezewski takes the name for his report on a Harmonist kiln site, "An Exceedingly Industrious Race of People," from an 1823 published remark about the group (2013:1). This village was home to between 700 and 900 residents for 10 years, during which they farmed 3,000 acres and constructed 180 buildings arranged in a rectangular street grid. In the first decades of the nineteenth century, broader enthusiasm for religious revivalism had influenced Harmonist thinking, and members began to abstain from tobacco and embrace celibacy, though the latter was not a universal requirement for membership. Historian Donald E. Pitzer comments that the general move toward celibacy enhanced the village's already strong economy, as "many women whose time would have been consumed by the duties of motherhood were freed to weave, garden, and labor in the fields and factories" (Pitzer and Elliott 1979). After only a decade, the Harmonists abandoned their Indiana town to return to Pennsylvania, establishing the village of Economy, northwest of Pittsburgh, in 1824 (see #13 in the Appendix). Shortly after their departure from New Harmony, Welsh social and industrial reformer Robert Owen, of New Lanark, Scotland, notoriety, purchased the town site for his planned colony based on science, education, and social equality. Though the communal aspect of Owen's experiment survived only until 1827, his compatriots' legacy of scientific advancement remains significant to the town's history and public interpretation (Pitzer and Weinzapfel 2001).

Incorporating maps, secondary studies of Harmonist vital statistics, census data, and archaeological remains, Strezewski examines the changing residential arrangements at New Harmony that moved families from private homes into shared dwellings and back again. In the years before 1820, the village's households each consisted of a nuclear family living in a modest log dwelling. Often one or two unrelated single adult members were assigned to share these family residences with a married couple and their children (Strezewski 2015a). Though no formal efforts were made to enforce George Rapp's preference for celibacy among the members at this time, birth rates were low, and in 1820 the proportion of children in the community was dramatically lower than in neighboring non-Harmonist towns. The Harmonists' log homes were intended only to be temporary accommodations while they built larger and more permanent brick houses, but many families still lived in these small dwellings after five or more years. Few families ever moved into larger, newer, single-family brick houses, and among those a high proportion had a household head with a relatively high-status position in the community. Building efforts between 1821 and 1824 were devoted instead to fulfilling the idea of communal housing, with the construction of four new dormitories that each housed 40–50 people at a time (Strezewski 2015b). These dormitories were not for single members; instead, the community's leaders moved individuals and families who had previously occupied single-family log houses into the dormitories at their discretion. Construction of these dormitories, their grounds, and accessory structures displaced at least 20 households from their previously private home lots. In 1825, Rapp moved all of the faithful Harmonists to a newly acquired site at Economy, Pennsylvania, where single-family homes, rather than communal dormitories, were again the norm. Strezewski interprets this sequence of residential arrangements as evidence of the interplay between Rapp's attempts to establish communal, egalitarian living with resistance from members who preferred the relative autonomy of private family dwellings within a larger economic cooperative (2015a:26).

While the Harmonists were reestablishing individual family homes in Pennsylvania, John Humphrey Noyes was developing his concept of Complex Marriage, which would deeply influence the structure of the Oneida Perfectionist's home about 30 miles east of Syracuse, New York. Oneida's residential buildings were deliberately and specifically designed by and for the community. While at first occupying an existing farmhouse, architect Erastus Hamilton helped his fellow community members to design and build their first Mansion House in 1848. This building was designed to accommodate a communal lifestyle, with a shared dining hall and parlors for formal meetings and informal gatherings, as well as a library for quiet study. Externally resembling a large, Victorian country mansion, Dolores Hayden remarks of the first house: "They produced a structure with a conventional bourgeois, exterior form concealing an unusual arrangement of interior spaces suited to their sexual revolution" (1976:190). As there were no marriages, rather a system of Complex Marriage in which all members were united as one family, there were no separate accommodations for couples and their offspring. Adult members slept in two-person compartments divided by curtains on the dormitory-like third floor of the shared house. Children slept and attended school in a house separated from the adults' residence, away from their birth parents, whose exclusive indulgence or favoritism was believed to be damaging to the individual and family.

When the group's size had exceeded the first Mansion House's capacity to accommodate members' needs, the Oneida Community began planning a residential expansion whose design involved many members in discussions at regular evening meetings. This second 1861 Mansion House was a massive Italianate brick edifice different in size and style, but not function, from its wood-frame predecessor. On the upper floor, individual sleeping rooms offered more privacy for community-sanctioned sexual meetings than curtained compartments, but each room still opened into more public sitting areas where members could observe one another's comings and goings (Van Wormer 2006:47). After Noyes introduced his supervised breeding program, called stirpiculture, a children's wing was added in 1869 to the main Mansion House to accommodate the newest young members, and the prior children's house was moved (Van Wormer 2006:49). Anthropologist Heather Van Wormer has turned an archaeological eye to the built environment and material culture of the Oneida Community to explore the "simultaneously constituted and constitutive" role that material culture played in portraying and perpetuating this well-known group's social ideals (2006:39). Their interior designs were distilled from ideas and experience internal to the community, and included carefully devised elements meant to facilitate education and social interaction. Of members' own writings about the evolving Mansion House spaces, Dolores Hayden writes:

> To describe and define the spaces within their Mansion so carefully and precisely, the Perfectionists needed to be extremely aware of the nuances of psychological responses evoked by such stimuli as the size of tables, personal distances in meeting rooms, the warmth of a stove, or the provision of unstructured activities in waiting areas. . . . The Oneidans' skill as environmental psychologists was unexcelled among communitarians. (1976:218)

Van Wormer notes that buildings' forms and locations were regularly changed to better suit the community's growing population, economic needs, and communal ideals. Old buildings were moved to better encourage group activity, and internal partitions were reconfigured to adapt to changing needs (also Hayden 1976:199). The focus of a building's placement and view changed, too, as the community's vision of itself transformed from pastoral to industrial. The initial economic vision of the Oneida Community was agrarian, with the first wood-frame Mansion House placed to overlook the community's expanding gardens (Van Wormer 2006:45). In contrast, the brick 1861 Mansion House was part of an interconnected landscape of industrial buildings whose commercial products supported the growing community. The community began manufacturing steel leg-hold animal traps, based on member Sewell Newhouse's design, eventually producing them in quantities large enough to supply the Hudson's Bay Company for six decades. Building on this economic success, they then expanded production capacity to include the silverware brand still bearing their name. Oneida's manufacturing industry and unique Mansion House have both outlasted the practice of Complex Marriage, as the family struc-ture was abandoned after threats of arrest for statutory rape (the surround-ing community's interpretation of his sexual experiment) forced Noyes to flee to Canada in 1879.

Like Oneida's family, Brook Farm's Transcendentalist members ex-panded their housing stock to accommodate growing membership and changing functional needs. However, their initial focus was more on the individual's experience in the community than on building family unity. Membership in the joint stock company was opened in 1841 at $500 per share, and within a few years 32 members had joined to pursue the ide-als of individual artistic and spiritual expression within a communal living environment (Preucel 2006:183–185). Agriculture and craft production were to be the economic bases at Brook Farm, and resident members were expected to labor daily at tasks that changed every two hours to prevent occupational monotony. All had access to housing, clothing, and food at what was deemed to be their actual cost. Like Oneida's Perfectionists, the first residents adapted an existing farm house to become the center of their community. This shared residence, kitchen, laundry, and dining hall be-came known as the Hive for its busy centrality. Members of the association later built three additional houses—the Eyrie, the Cottage, and the Pilgrim House—to provide more space for living and working. The Eyrie, built in 1842, held the library and was home to founder George Ripley and his wife, as well as acting as lodging for boarding school students. The Cottage was also built in 1842, as a home for member Anna Alvord and three other member tenants, in rooms comprising the four wings of a cross-shaped plan. With ample windows, this was the brightest of the buildings and be-came a temporary hospital during outbreaks of illness. The Pilgrim House was built in 1843 by a prospective member, Ichabod Morton, to accommo-date two families who ultimately decided not to join the community. Under community ownership the building was altered to provide a ballroom, literary office, and member housing. During the early years of their association, individuals and families lived in private rooms or apartments distributed throughout these four structures. Each building also housed workshops and meeting spaces, which acted as public areas where members would gather in small numbers for industry and education.

The philosophical ideals of Brook Farm's founders changed within a few years of its founding. In the early nineteenth century, many reform-minded Americans discovered the writings of Francois Marie Charles Fourier, a French thinker who devised the concept of "passionate attraction" in human temperament, and designed in theory an ideal community within which humans could express their inherent passional personality types while living free from poverty and inequality. Fourier intended that each settlement, or phalanx, possess two representations of each of what he calculated as the 810 possible passional personality types, and thus deemed a population of 1,620 to be most desirable. Residents' homes and workplaces would be concentrated in a single, monumental building called the Phalanstery.

In 1845, the Brook Farm community's decision to embrace Fourierist communalism and commitment to labor led to the start of construction on a larger building called the Phalanstery. With three stories containing 14 separate three-bedroom apartments, a shared kitchen and dining hall, a lecture hall, and two meeting rooms, the Phalanstery was intended to bring together all members under one roof but was destroyed by an 1846 fire before it was ever occupied. In the wake of this loss, and amid the social and ideological tensions of the transforming community, Brook Farm's communal residents abandoned the experiment by the following year.

Today our inquiries are aided by the availability of extensive contemporaneous social and intellectual writings about Brook Farm, as members published their own newsletter, the *Harbinger*, after 1845. In addition, the experiment attracted such celebrated friends as literary notables Nathaniel Hawthorne and Margaret Fuller. However, there are no extant photographs, building plans, or maps of the community. All of the original 1840s buildings are gone, leaving only a few painted depictions of the community from which to extrapolate about the placement and appearance of the various buildings (fig. 4.4). Archaeologists Robert Preucel and Steven

Pendery implemented an archaeological program at Brook Farm between 1990 and 1994, supervising excavation designed to locate and investigate remains of the community's buildings. Their work aimed to test a remaining portion of the burned Phalanstery's cellar, and to more deeply explore the farmhouse referred to by the Brook Farm colonists as the Hive (Preucel 2006; Preucel and Pendery 2006). Preucel's central argument, based on his semiotic perspective, is that the built environment at Brook Farm was not simply a reflection of members' eclectic, individualist Transcendental philosophy but also an active agent in deciding the eventual fate of the attempted Fourierist phalanx. Comparing official bureaucratic descriptions made in 1849 of Brook Farm's buildings with personal recollections from former colonists, Preucel demonstrates that residents viewed each of the houses as representative of different activities, styles, and experiences at the colony. He posits that, while the familiar vernacular styles of these residential buildings "domesticated the radical ideas of the community," colonists also used architecture to "materialize communal beliefs." For example, renovations such as the expansion of the Hive building to accommodate more resident members with additional sleeping rooms and larger shared dining and laundry services were a step toward embodying their communal ideas through the shared, built space (Preucel 2006:195, 204). These renovations were not enough to cement the colony's commitment to full communalism, however. Even though the economic loss of the burned Phalanstery was a major contributor in the group's failure as a Fourierist phalanx, Preucel believes that the four houses themselves, by physically and aesthetically dividing the residents of each, played an active part in perpetuating individual associations over *communitas*. Preucel writes that the "houses of Brook Farm developed their own distinctive personalities due to their unique functions and social associations. This 'house agency' actively thwarted the attempts by Ripley and others to adopt Fourierism and make Brook Farm the leading Phalanx in America" (2006:203).

Picturesque country houses like Brook Farm's Cottage and Eyrie would not have been considered stylistically out of place or radical in the rural Massachusetts landscape of the Transcendentalists' experiment. In rural Tennessee a few decades later, however, the same type of eclectic, erudite, English country cottages built by the hopeful colonists of Rugby, Tennessee, made a different statement to community members and their

Figure 4.4. *Brook Farm with Rainbow*, showing the community's buildings under the arc of a rainbow. *From left to right*: the Pilgrim House, Cottage, Eyrie, workshop, and Hive. Oil on canvas, painted by Josiah Wolcott, 1845. Wolcott painted a later version from a similar perspective, which includes the foundation of the incomplete Phalanx and a sunset rather than a rainbow. Courtesy of the Massachusetts Historical Society.

neighbors. The village of Rugby, in Morgan County, Tennessee, was established in 1880 by an organization called the Board of Aid to Land Ownership, founded in part by Thomas Hughes, author of the 1857 British boarding school novel *Tom Brown's School Days* and activist for "Christian Socialism" (see #21 in the Appendix). Hughes was active in forming labor unions and workers' cooperatives in England before moving to the United States to help develop a gentleman-farmer colony at Rugby for young men who were left landless as "second sons" and jobless during the economic recession of the 1870s (Avery 2001:23). The primary goal of the Rugby community was not communal land ownership and member equality but at most to discourage materialistic striving while allowing private property and enterprise. The colony struggled economically and organizationally from the start, although at its peak it had a membership of more than 400 residents as well as facilities for lawn bowling and croquet. Rugby lasted as a social experiment only a few years after Thomas Hughes's mother, Margaret, whose presence at the colony had been an anchoring factor, died in 1887 (Sweeny-Justice 2001:14).

On the Tennessee plateau, Rugby's cottages expressed an Englishness that contrasted sharply with local rural vernacular styles. As of yet, archaeological projects at Rugby have been limited to Uffington house, a property bought by the colonists, renovated, and named for Thomas Hughes's Oxfordshire birthplace. The house served as a residence for Hughes's mother, Margaret, and niece, Emily, who arrived from England in 1881. The Hughes family occupied the site only until 1887, after which a series of poorly documented temporary occupants lived in the house until the property was transformed into a more modern farming operation until 1958. Paul Gordon Avery, while a graduate student at the University of Tennessee, undertook a program of limited areal excavations and shovel tests to attempt to answer questions about building sequences and feature functions throughout the site's occupation. Unfortunately, the short initial colony-related occupation followed by long-term private farm-family occupation created an archaeological record in which Hughes-period artifacts and features could not be confidently identified within the larger assemblage (Avery 2001). Future archaeological views of the built environment at Rugby could potentially, like Preucel's view of Brook Farm, provide more insight into the active participation of buildings in structuring colony residents' activities and identities.

I have examined the archaeology of intentional communities at the level of the landscape, where the interrelation between buildings, gardens, and pathways acts to manifest community ideals. We have looked closer to see what information can be gathered from the structure of the buildings themselves. From the Ephrata Cloister's choice to build their first Kedar with the expectation of impermanence to the doomed Phalanstery at Brook Farm, communities built their ideals into the structure of the buildings that housed them. The Shakers' and Amana Colonists' separately gendered entrances and the Oneida Mansion House's sleeping alcoves were attempts to reimagine an ideal structure for human relationships, and both acted to codify and shape members' behaviors in concrete ways. Now we will move in closer again, to the level of the artifact. This most finely grained lens offers us perhaps the most opportunities for complicating our view of community members' constant negotiation between the real and the ideal, the individual and the collective.

5

———★———

MATERIAL VISIONS

Artifacts in Community Contexts

When the State of California acquired the land that is now Olompali State Park in 1977, the property included the remains of the Burdell Mansion and its surrounding ranch, a place that was home to the Chosen Family commune between 1967 and 1969. Archaeologist E. Breck Parkman took a special interest in collections from the Marin County mansion, which was partially destroyed by an electrical fire in February 1969 and was enclosed in more recent years by a protective structure to prevent vandalism and looting (Fernandez and Parkman 2011; Parkman 2014). Founded by real-estate developer Don McCoy in 1967 in a rented house at Olompali, Marin County, California, the commune became home to around 60 members at a time, who shared quarters in the 24-room mansion and a small number of additional buildings (see #30 in the Appendix). Founding members included a core group of families who shared social connections and a desire for a communal lifestyle. These families established a "Not School" for members' children as an alternative to traditional education. For the first year, McCoy's personal fortune funded the group, shielding members from the kinds of economic hardships that destroyed other communal experiments. After the leader's family froze his assets in the fall of 1968, the Chosen Family's economic situation predictably worsened (Parkman 2014:434). The community folded after a 1969 fire destroyed their rented mansion.

Materials collected for archaeological analysis from the remains of the Burdell Mansion in 2002 include 93 vinyl records, mostly 33 ⅓ rpm but

Figure 5.1. A partially melted copy of Babatunde Olatunji's *Flaming Drums!*, from the debris of the Chosen Family's burned home in Olompali State Historic Park, California. Courtesy of Breck Parkman.

with some 45 rpm and 78 rpm discs. The 55 records that could be identified were released between 1953 and 1968, and included examples of rock albums typically associated with popular culture of the era in addition to more unexpected examples of classical music, jazz, big band, and Broadway show soundtracks. They found Judy Garland, Burl Ives, and *South Pacific* alongside the psychedelic arrangements of Vanilla Fudge, the Beatles' 1965 *Rubber Soul*, the 1968 Bloomfield, Kooper, and Stills's *Super Session*, and Babatunde Olatunji's 1962 *Flaming Drums!* (fig. 5.1)

Music was central to the lives of Chosen Family residents. The population of the commune swelled into the hundreds during days-long parties that often featured well-known rock musicians. The Grateful Dead visited the commune and used a location at the ranch for the cover photograph of their 1969 album, *Aoxomoxoa*. Parkman writes that members of the Olompali commune favored the acid rock and psychedelic rock musical styles becoming widely popular at the time, and quotes twentieth-century commune historian Timothy Miller's 1991 statement that rock music was far and away the most significant musical style to the hippies (2014:443). He recently found, among the debris at the Burdell Mansion, a burned turn-table with what may very well be the last record members listened to before fire destroyed their home—a 1968 track called "The Kingdom of Heaven (Is Within You)" by the San Francisco–based rock band Mother Earth (Parkman 2015). To explain the varied collection of records recovered from the Chosen Family's home site, Parkman makes two main assertions. First, he notes evidence from documentary sources that commune members were more likely to attend live performances by their favorite contempo-rary bands than they were to buy the artists' records. Second, he reminds us of that all of the members had lives before the commune—that "many of the records were brought to the commune as items of personal cultural baggage" (Parkman 2014:444) by Chosen Family members with different tastes and backgrounds. Some of the records may have been played and en-joyed at the Burdell Mansion, while others may only have sat on shelves as reminders of past times. Challenging the "hippie" stereotype, these records demonstrate that the commune's members' tastes and performed identities were much more diverse than would be attributable to an oversimplified stereotype. Parkman asserts that "a simplistic one-size-fits-all definition of a hippie is not accurate, nor are the popularly held stereotypes that demean the Sixties experience (cf. Miller 1991)" (2014:445).

Artifacts sometimes work to complicate our previously held image of a group's character and interests, and sometimes reaffirm and reinforce those preexisting ideas. The earliest excavations at the eighteenth-century Ephrata Cloister, undertaken between 1963 and 1966, revealed (among other items) a massive amount of printers' type recovered near the south foundation wall remains of Bethania, the 1746 brothers' house. These finds are the most evocative and consistent with what we already know about the group, and affirm the centrality of printed text to the lives of Ephrata's residents (Biever 1968:54–55). Brothers and sisters are historically known to have engaged with text through both their scriptural and hymnal print-ing and their hand illumination. Gutek and Gutek note that visitors to the historical site at Ephrata can visit the print shop to see a still-operating Philadelphia-made press brought to Ephrata in 1804 (1998:18). Also dis-played are many examples of *Frakturshriften*, ornate calligraphic hymnals and other scriptural texts produced by the community's members for their own use and for paying clients outside the Cloister. Some artifact findings from the 1993–2001 field seasons at Ephrata also support an interpretation that members adhered to their community's values of austerity. Numerous pieces of the simple earthenware tableware found associated with communal building remains showed evidence of repair in order to continue use of a cracked vessel (Warfel 2009:146). A handful of examples can offer such comfortably illustrative views of past community life, such as the recovery of art and craft supplies—cups for watercolor paints, a paintbrush holder, paintbrush ferrules, and a palette knife from the grounds of the self-consciously creative Theosophical Society (Van Wormer and Gross 2006:108) and artists' paint brush handles at the Koreshan Unity Founder's House (Austin 1991:22). It is rare, though, for the cultural materials uncovered through archaeological exploration to fit quite so tidily into our expected vision of group members' unique lived experience. Like the Frank Sinatra records at the Chosen Family's house, artifacts left at intentional community sites force us to consider the residents' daily navigation between the requirements of group membership and the encumbrances of individual identity.

Resistance and Accommodation

Divergences from the ideal, or at least what we might expect was the ideal, are David Starbuck's primary concerns in interpreting artifacts from features excavated at Canterbury, New Hampshire. In addition to his team's ambitious mapping project, Starbuck and his crew excavated a large feature at Canterbury they nicknamed "Hog Heaven," the trash-filled root cellar of a hog house that was used from 1817 to the 1840s and was torn down in 1902 (1998:9). Their research questions regarding the artifacts focus on realities of Shaker equality, adherence to the Millennial Laws, deviations from proscribed behavior, and how consumption of non-Shaker-made goods was in line with or at variance from their appreciation of things "plain and simple" (Starbuck 1998:7). Starbuck makes his bias clear: "Admittedly, we were dubious from the start that there was anything 'plain' or 'simple' about the Shakers, and we expected that Shaker dumps would bear this out" (1998:7–9). His enthusiasm for finding evidence of dissent from Shaker belief is also clear. In a brief discussion of small finds, following mention of shoe blacking and hair medication, he parenthesizes:

"The Shakers clearly were concerned about their appearance" (Starbuck 1998:11). He further leverages the trash that filled Hog Heaven to indict the Canterbury Shakers for alcohol use, pork consumption, and wearing jewelry, all activities that, at one time or another in the group's history, were discouraged or forbidden. Starbuck and his colleagues also excavated remains of the Bee House and Garden Barn foundations, and although the laboratory work was not finished at the time of his 2004 publication, the collected materials seemed similar to those from the hog house excavation, containing a plethora of commercial product containers, ranging from grape juice concentrate to disinfectant (Starbuck 2004:51).

To maintain order across widespread Shaker villages, acceptable parameters for behavior and practice were outlined by pronouncements from the elders at New Lebanon and Watervliet, New York, in forms such as the Millennial Laws, printed and revised a number of times between 1821 and 1845. Archaeologists rely on these documentary sources to guide expectations about what they might encounter in Shaker sites and collections, and to interpret findings. The simplest approach to building expectations involves combining written sources, such as the Millennial Laws, with what we know from examples of lasting Shaker material products. The clarity of such interpretations becomes clouded when we think about who lived and worked in Shaker villages. New converts, non-Shaker visitors, and hired hands all brought the potential for the appearance of dissent from Shaker standards in their baskets and pockets. Non-Shaker hired hands at Union Village, Canterbury, and other settlements have been documented as early as the mid-nineteenth century, presenting a difficult interpretive loophole when asking whether Shakers were following the Millennial Laws' restrictions. It seems that as long as there's a hired hand on site, there's an "out" for evidence left by community members who might not have been following the rules. Interpretive dodges aren't limited to archaeologists studying Shaker sites. Archaeologist Therese Adams Muranaka approached the Molokan village of Guadalupe, Mexico, as a test case in migration, ethnicity, and cultural patterns, specifically looking for "material cultural evidence of ethnicity" (1995:121) whose results could ultimately guide prehistoric archaeologists' research designs and interpretations (see #27 in the Appendix). When Muranaka found alcohol bottles in the remains of Molokan household refuse, she proposed that the bottles must have been left by visiting family members from Los Angeles (who would presumably also be of Molokan descent but not from the village being studied) or had been acquired as empties for a nonalcohol reuse (1992:92). After all, in the early years of their Guadalupe settlement, Molokan belief forbade drinking alcohol.

How do we ensure that our interpretations of archaeological findings that diverge from professed group belief are grounded and meaningful? How can we ever insist that Shakers, or members of any intentional community, must have used potentially disruptive artifacts, when there are always other possible explanations? Starbuck approaches this struggle of interpretation by arguing that any activity within a Shaker village, whether done by someone from within the community or by a non-Shaker hired hand, was performed within the context of Shaker belief—a kind of "my roof, my rules" view of the communities (2004:53). Joseph Grygas rather eloquently calls attention to what Starbuck and others have amply demonstrated by excavating at Shaker sites: that we must expect the unexpected in Shaker remains (2011:3), especially when what we expect is formed by overstatements of the group's simplicity.

With the Mother Ann Lee quote "Do all your work as though you had a thousand years to live, and as you would if you knew you must die tomorrow," Ronald W. Deiss ties the use of durable bricks for building at South Union, Kentucky, to Shaker ideals regarding high standards of craftsmanship (1987:91, requoted from a 1985 manuscript by Tommy Hines, then director of the Shaker Museum at South Union, Kentucky). This is a bit of a convenience for Deiss, as the South Union Shakers lacked building timber but had good access to stone and clay. Presumably, Shakers who made wood-frame houses in other parts of the country were not flouting Mother Ann Lee's ideas. Nor did Shaker brick makers necessarily always demonstrate excellence in their products. Bruce Aument and Andrew Sewell bring Shakers' emphasis on product quality into focus when discussing bricks from the North Family Lot of Union Village, Ohio. As Shaker teaching placed high value on excellence in craftsmanship, Aument and Sewell propose that poorly produced items and evidence of high volumes of waste and production failure may indicate tension between the devout core of the community and its craft practitioners. They work from the assumption that archaeological evidence of diversion from high craft standards would "signify an increase in the degree of social tension between and within the Shaker families" living at the North Family Lot (Aument and Sewell 2009:92–93). The best archaeological evidence to address this research question comes from the poorly made bricks produced on-site for the North Family Lot Shaker's residence and craft shops. Overfired and warped bricks were found in each of the main brick buildings investigated at the North Lot. In their discussion of brick-making as part of the ceramic operation at the North Family Village, Patrick Bennett and his colleagues make the analogy between the warped bricks and the internal tensions of a Shaker village:

> The structures themselves may have been uniform and symmetrical, but the bricks used to build them were far from perfect. This disparity may serve as an analogy for the Shakers themselves, who presented an image to the outside world of an orderly, peaceful community living in harmony, which nevertheless had its share of malcontents, scandals, and dissatisfaction, all visible if you look hard enough. (2009:92)

The bricks themselves likely weren't intentional acts of defiance. Bennett and his colleagues suggest that the poor-quality bricks really reflect the limited skill and productivity of the village's brick makers, who could not produce enough bricks to exclude the warped ones from building. Instead, their inclusion in ordered Shaker buildings is evidence of accommodation to daily realities that diverge from the ideal.

Where There's Smoke

Clay smoking pipes offer an excellent example of a single artifact type without a fixed meaning when found in Shaker archaeological contexts. Relatively early in the study of Shaker archaeology, in 1978 James Murphy reported on Shaker-made red and white earthenware pipes from New York and Ohio and their distinction from the stoneware "Shaker" brand pipes made commercially by non-Shakers in a style reminiscent of Shaker pipes. Murphy's study collided with then popularly held notions about Shakers. He writes that "inquiries at the Shaker Historical Society, Shaker Heights, Ohio, brought the response that the Shakers never manufactured tobacco pipes because smoking was forbidden within the sect" (Murphy 1978:48). Despite the existence of a reed-stem clay pipe labeled "Shakers, Pleasant Hill, KY" found in a building at Pleasant Hill, the Pleasant Hill museum director denied the possibility that the pipe was actually made there. Murphy ultimately received validation and assistance from Robert F. W. Meader, director of the Shaker Museum at Old Chatham, New York, who provided comparative pipes from his site's own collections.

While smoking was indeed prohibited in Shaker villages after the mid-nineteenth century, in earlier periods it was practiced widely and even collectively. Shaker smoking meetings were sometimes planned as communal postworship activities at Union Village and other Shaker settlements, and smoking safety was mandated in an 1828 version of the Millennial Laws. An example of an order aimed at fire prevention is that "No one may smoke in their rooms or shops, under an hour previous to leaving them for the night, neither may they empty their pipes in spit boxes, nor go to smoke in uninhabited rooms" (Bennett et al. 2009:63–64). So, at the time Murphy sought information about Shaker-made pipes, documentation of the Shakers' earlier smoking and pipe production activities already existed, but some Shaker researchers were either unfamiliar with it or unwilling to acknowledge this aspect of antebellum Shaker life. In more recent decades archaeologists have flexed their interpretive skills to accommodate and acknowledge evidence for Shaker smoking. In a 1998 article, Starbuck suggests that two pipe bowl fragments "may have been saved as novelties or heirlooms, for no stem fragments were found in the cellar. After all, by the time Hog Heaven was filled, tobacco smoking had already been prohibited for fifty years or more" (1998:10). In his 2004 volume, in his discussion of evidence for Shaker pipe-making in the Second Family blacksmith shop and pipe smoking in the Church Family blacksmith shop at Canterbury, Starbuck is more willing to admit that smoking may have been a more continuous facet of Shaker life (2004:75–82).

Also more than willing to admit to smoking as Shaker practice, Patrick Bennett and his coauthors interpret their view of the 240 molded redware smoking pipes and pipe fragments found in the pottery excavations from Union Village, Ohio, as deeply representative of Shaker industry as a whole: "The Shaker smoking pipe manifests the Shakers' sense of uniformity and practicality, their aggressive entrepreneurial attitude, and their desire to be self-sufficient" (2009:63). The subtext of this statement is that the smoking pipe remains align with popularly held views of Shaker qualities. Indeed, identically molded, fine-quality Shaker-made pipes represented well the ideal of Shakers as a unified, egalitarian whole. These authors expect that Shakers uniformly used Shaker-made pipes, and suggest that hired hands, visitors, or new Shaker recruits might have been the source of "exotic," non-Shaker-made pipes found at the North Family Lot (Bennett et al. 2009:71).

This is the scale, though, where we must be most careful to remember that intentional communities are not fully self-contained units whose decision-making processes are driven purely and consistently by ideological concerns. Each community is, of necessity, a functioning part of the larger mainstream society in which it is embedded, and some choices may reflect compromises or negotiations with that reality. Evidence from pipe making and brick manufacturing supports the idea that Shaker producers and buyers made economic and stylistic decisions based on broader markets for these goods. Director Robert F. W. Meader of the Shaker Museum at Old Chatham, New York, who provided James Murphy with comparative pipes from his site's collections for Murphy's 1978 analysis, was of the opinion that Shaker pipe makers in New York used commercially made, non-Shaker brass molds that led to similarities in form between Shaker-made and non-Shaker-made pipes. Union Village's North Family pipe makers sold their production equipment in 1851 after technological advances made it impossible for them to compete in volume with non-Shaker commercial pipe producers (Bennett et al. 2009:78). And Sewell, Hampton, and Krupp found that when renovating their 1826 broom shop for use as a pottery shop in 1852, the North Family decided to purchase bricks from the nearby village of Red Lion rather than using their own, often warped and overfired bricks (2009a:100). In contrast, the Harmonist residents of Economy, Pennsylvania, employed their own ability to invest in skilled labor and machinery to produce bricks not for their own settlement but for sale in Pittsburgh and other nearby towns (Sewell et al. 2004). Before their company undertook its investigation of the Union Village Shakers, archaeologists Andrew Sewell, Roy Hampton, R. Joe Brandon, and Amy Case of Hardlines Design Company conducted cultural resource management excavations at the remains of a ca. 1890–1901 Harmony Society brickworks in Leetsdale Industrial Park. Between 1999 and 2002, archaeologists cleared away sediment left by the Ohio River's floods, learning that the factory had seven kilns and was similar in design to other (non-Harmonist) brick factories at the time of its operation. Shaker and Harmonist villages may have been physically separated and spatially insulated from their neighbors, but they were not cut off from the economic channels that carried goods, equipment, and ideas in and out.

Together at the Table

A most personal way that community members engage with their ideals, and with each other, is in making and consuming food together. Daily meals nourish laborers' efforts, while eating communally cements group bonds. Food preferences and restrictions were also ways to express and enforce particulars about shared convictions, which might include religious prohibitions on certain foods, or the belief in nonviolence extended to the animal world. Limits to the consumption of meat or meat products regularly arose as part of intentional communities' objectives, whether for ethical, theological, or hygienic reasons. Archaeologists seem to have a habit of finding evidence that residents occasionally defy these limits in communities where meat was discouraged or forbidden. Bones recovered from excavations at the eighteenth-century Ephrata Cloister, representing wild and domestic species, diverge in type and number from what would be expected from the occasional sanctioned "love feast" mutton stew, in a group whose members were otherwise instructed to abstain from meat (Warfel 2009:147). Lamb and beef bones found in the kitchen debris of the 1967–1969 Chosen Family commune in Northern California contradict group founder Don McCoy's 1968 professions of group vegetarianism. Elizabeth R. Fernandez and E. Breck Parkman suggest that rapid growth in resident numbers late in 1968 could have changed the dietary dynamic of the group (2011:8).

An earlier example from California provides insight into possible differences in perception between meat itself and meat derivatives. In 1990, archaeologists tested a 30 m x 15 m refuse dump associated with the Point Loma Theosophists' community as part of a cultural resource management project (Van Wormer and Gross 2006:102). Researchers analyzed more than 4,200 artifacts recovered from the site, comparing their findings with contemporary non-Theosophical sites in Southern California and Arizona to better understand the Theosophists' decisions as consumers. Theosophy drew its philosophies and teachings from multiple world religions, with a specific emphasis on Eastern thought and practice, in combination with ideas from classical Greek antiquity and ancient Egypt. Resident members participated in agricultural production and education in the arts and philosophy. Children lived separately from their parents, who in turn lived in separate male and female dormitories. As testament to the complexity of community founder Madame Katherine Tingley's philosophy of food, archaeological remains analyzed by Van Wormer and Gross contained a predominance of containers from processed meat products, including potted meats and "albumenized food," a milk additive containing cereal and egg albumen that was marketed as an infant formula. The boarding school's diet was intended to be vegetarian, but the Theosophists' interpretation of that ideal was informed by and grounded in their late nineteenth-century milieu. While apparently avoiding the consumption of fresh red meat, Theosophists were clearly following other contemporary thinkers on health and nutrition by seeking protein from these alternative sources (Van Wormer and Gross 2006:112, 115).

Eating pork was sometimes practiced and sometimes prohibited in Shaker villages, a discontinuous restriction that forces archaeologists to speculate about pig bones recovered from Shaker sites. Faunal remains from the North Family Lot of Union Village, Ohio, included pig bones from "individual and communal meat cuts as well as elements typically classified as butchery waste" (Sewell et al. 2009b:Appendix B, 17). Even in deposits from the 1840s and 1850s, when the renewed Millennial Laws had prohibited eating pork and keeping pigs, archaeological evidence suggested to Sewell, Hampton, and Krupp that the North Family Lot Shakers (or their hired hands) were consuming pork (2009b:53–54). David Starbuck reports that, while the hog house was not used for keeping pigs at Canterbury after the late 1840s, a large number of pork bones found in the building's cellar, which was backfilled some time after 1904, indicate that the ban on eating pork was not consistently observed at this village (1998:13).

Starbuck also briefly mentions that "hundreds of tin cans" were found in the cellar of the hog house at Canterbury but offers no further discussion

146 · The Archaeology of Utopian and Intentional Communities

of the possible date range and contents of the cans and how their presence relates to ideas of Shaker self-sufficiency (1998:13, 2004:63). Food cans have long been more interesting to archaeologists than their mundane presence in our cupboards and recycling bins might suggest. For example, at Southern California's ca. 1914–1917 Llano del Rio Cooperative Colony, archaeologists Thad Van Bueren and Jill Hupp found that most residential tent and cabin pads lacked ceramic tableware fragments and evidence of stove use (2000:74). Resident families of these kitchenless homes would presumably have eaten their meals with comrades in the communal dining hall. However, John M. Foster (2008) suggests that numerous food cans found thrown in a shallow seasonal stream channel reveal that some colonists avoided communal dining by eating individually sized, single-can portions. Residents weren't prohibited from providing and preparing their own family meals, as a member's monthly account statement from company stores included lines for "Meat," "Milk," "Cannery," and "Vegetables" in addition to the "Meals, Hotel" line item. Furthermore, the community experienced economic difficulties near the end of 1916, which led to food shortages in the stores, and to hoarding of individual supplies (Van Bueren and Hupp 2000:12, 23). Foster suggests the possibility that throwing empty cans in the channel rather than in more visible shared disposal areas might have been a way that residents with the economic ability to independently buy and stockpile canned food were hiding the evidence of their anticommunal activity (2008:56) (fig. 5.2).

According to the daily routines established by the end of the eighteenth century and the later Millennial Laws, Shakers were required to be present at communal mealtimes in their families' dining halls except in the case of duty or sickness. Nonmembers enjoyed Shaker-made meals when visiting communities, a hospitality that originated as a service to those considering joining the community. By the 1870s, however, these meals had become so popular with tourists that the Shakers moved to recover their costs, and the once-free room and board was offered in exchange for a small fee from those with means (Murray 2012:80). Guests to Shaker villages always ate and drank separately from the Shakers themselves, who observed highly ritualized mealtimes, beginning with a solemn, orderly entry into the dining hall and continuing through silent eating at separate men's and women's tables. As the orders regarding meals in an 1845 revision of the Millennial

Figure 5.2. This photo, printed in the April 1917 issue of Llano del Rio's publication, the *Western Comrade*, was part of an article on the community's growing industries. It has the caption "Truck Load of Cans for the Cannery. Photo taken in busy season. Will be repeated many times this year" (4[12]: 11). Some of these cans may have been used for individualistic food consumption at Llano rather than cooperative dining. Digitized by the California State Library, available as an electronic document at the Internet Archive (archive.org).

Laws state: "All should leave their work, when the signal is given for them to gather in at meal time, and be in their rooms, or the sitting-room in readiness to repair to the dining room, in order and in the fear of God, keeping step together" (Andrews 1963:270). Even though non-Shakers could view religious meetings, the families' mealtimes were sacred space to which only the devout were admitted. Ruth Ann Murray notes that though mealtime attendance was the official regulation, each village interpreted such restrictions differently (2012:86). Kim McBride's findings from Pleasant Hill, Kentucky, can illuminate how villages may have construed which duties justified missing a group meal. Focusing on order, including regularity of behavior, as an organizing principle in Shaker life, she questions where and when this principle was eschewed in favor of work logistics. A dump behind the West Lot washhouse at Pleasant Hill contained a considerable amount of ceramic table and teawares, and a relative paucity of food preparation vessels. McBride wonders if Shaker women working in the washhouse were delivered meals from the communal kitchen, or if they brought tea or snacks with them to eat alone while working. She asks, "Does the recovery of these ceramics from the washhouse suggest that women eating there may have been a bit less ordered in this case?" (2010:263–264). Along these lines, David Starbuck makes an evocative, though unexplored, mention in his 1986 discussion of the Shaker mills at Canterbury that a dining room was added to the North Family sawmill in 1824 (1986:22). Does this mean that workers were "officially" dining at the mill during their hours of labor, when they might miss mealtimes with the rest of their families? In this instance, did the practical necessity of keeping the sawmill running inspire a local reinterpretation of the guidelines around communal eating as handed down by the Millennial Laws?

In addition to being found outside of the official dining area of Pleasant Hill, many of the ceramics McBride and her crew recovered from the West Lot washhouse dump were decorated—which is strikingly at odds with the Pleasant Hill museum's use of plain white dishes in the reconstructed table settings seen by modern visitors. Commercially produced ceramic tablewares recovered from excavations at the North Family Lot at Union Village also provided researchers with a conundrum. Featuring different decorative motifs, including transfer print floral designs and scenes, hand-painted flowers, and molded relief handles, Aument and Sewell found the tableware fragments to be little different from the type of ceramics that researchers might recover among the remains of a "moderately well-off secular family" of the same time period (2009:171) (fig. 5.3). Our assumption that tableware from Pleasant Hill and other Shaker sites should be plain comes from readings of nineteenth-century Shaker documents that communicated instructions between the central authorities in New York and local elders and deacons. Archaeological evidence allows us to crack open the space between centralized precepts and daily lived experience, exposing the impact of individual choices in interpreting those guidelines. At certain times, elders maintained strict control of the aesthetic guidelines for products made in Shaker workshops—for example, restricting which objects should be painted, and what kinds of objects could be purchased for Shaker use. Deacons, who managed day-to-day economic transactions on behalf of their families, were admonished to "purchase that which is plain, as far as you can, even if the meterial [sic] is not quite so good, rather than

Figure 5.3. Examples of ceramic table, serving, and storage vessels recovered from a post-1892 trash deposit in the Brothers' Shop basement, North Family Lot, Union Village, Ohio. Decoration types on tableware fragments include transfer printing, hand painting, and mold relief. Photo by April Popovitch, Hardlines Design Company, 2005. Fig. 81 of Sewell, Hampton, and Krupp 2009a. Used with permission of Hardlines Design Company and the Office of Environmental Services, Ohio Department of Transportation.

to get that which is covered with superfluous flowers and pictures" (Promey 1993:34, 225). Ellen-Rose Savulis notes that, during the Mothers' Work revivalism most active in the 1840s, Shakers removed decorated stoves from their homes and scraped images from snuff boxes (2003:167–168).

Archaeologists studying other intentional communities have considered the possible meanings of ceramic pieces in their particular contexts. English-made ceramic teaware fragments recovered at the Ephrata Cloister in Pennsylvania were manufactured after founder Conrad Beissel's 1768 death, possibly representing an increase in worldliness and aesthetic appreciation that was outside of the group's initially professed values (Warfel 2009:147). As a counterpoint, in her 2013 analysis of ceramics from the Cottage and Eyrie at Brook Farm, the 1840s Transcendentalist community, Samantha Savory found significantly fewer decorated whiteware tableware fragments than in the comparative noncommunity Tremont Street Housing Site collection from nearby West Roxbury, Massachusetts, which was occupied during a similar time period. Her interpretation is that Brook Farm's residents emphasized simplicity in all aspects of their lives, including their consumer purchases (Savory 2013:70). Though consideration of ceramic tablewares at intentional community sites has largely focused on questions of plainness versus decoration, Therese Adams Muranaka's work with twentieth-century remains from the Molokan Village of Guadalupe showed that some specific decorative patterns were considered preferable to others. Molokan informants told Muranaka that Molokan women avoided Chinese and Chinese-inspired motifs such as dragons and pagodas for religious reasons, instead choosing Chinese-style floral designs when purchasing ceramics for their homes (1992:117–118).

Regarding the disjuncture between the Pleasant Hill museum's public presentation of plain table settings and her archaeological findings of decorated sherds, McBride writes, "It is likely that many Shakers had converted to plain whitewares and ironstones later in the nineteenth century, as had most other ceramic consumers. But since at Pleasant Hill the public interpretation is meant to represent the 1840s and 1850s, the display of plain wares suggests a uniqueness in the Shaker material culture that may not have existed at that time" (2010:264). Just as the restrictions on decoration within Shaker homes and dining rooms varied during the nineteenth century, ceramic styles popular in other consumers' homes changed. Plain paneled white table settings became increasingly popular in non-Shaker households in the decades after 1850 (Wall 1991). Contributing to the potential for interpretive confusion is the previously discussed separation between Shakers' shared meals and those of non-Shaker visitors. Guests were served foods made by Shaker hands but dined only with other nonmembers and were sometimes offered richer or more varied foods than were present on the Shakers' own tables. They may also have been served on different dishes that weren't used in brothers' and sisters' table settings. In 1886, visitors to the village of Mount Lebanon, New York, were reportedly served coffee from a silver pot with matching cream pitcher and sugar bowl into "choice china cups" (Murray 2012:62). If one of archaeologists' goals is to demystify the lives of our subjects, as Aument and Sewell suggest in their 2009 report on the North Family Shakers of Union Village, exploring the remains left by intentional communities' food and dining practices sets us on this path. By grounding us in the realities of consumer choices and concessions, what we encounter is more complex than we might previously have imagined.

Separation and Sameness

Utilitarian redware ceramics made in the Shakers' own workshops were plainer than the decorated, commercially produced whitewares that graced some Shaker tables, but they were no more distinctive in style. Patrick Bennett and his colleagues recovered almost 22,000 redware artifacts—over 200 kg of pottery sherds, mostly from kiln wasters—during excavation of the pottery shop at the North Family Lot of Union Village, Ohio. Vessel types included bottles, chamber pots, crocks, pitchers and jugs, lids, mixing and serving bowls, plates, and jars. Although made by Shaker hands in a Shaker pottery shop, these redware vessels and wasters didn't necessarily exhibit stylistic qualities unique to the community. Bennett, Grooms, Sewell, and Aument write, "Perhaps most disappointing is the lack of a distinctive Shaker style for the pottery produced at the Union Village Pottery. Stylistically, the assemblage may represent an amalgam of pottery styles representing the various regions from which the individual artisans received their training" (2009:96).

If a Shaker aesthetic is so recognizable in extant antiques and reproduction furnishings, how is it that the debris found in archaeological contexts so frequently has no recognizably Shaker-specific qualities? This isn't just limited to locally made and commercially produced ceramics, as discussed so far. Of the collections at Pleasant Hill, McBride writes that "with the exception of straight-lined handcrafted iron items from the village's blacksmith shop, most of the material culture recovered to date are varied, numerous, and in many regards indistinguishable from those excavated from other non-Shaker sites of the period and region" (1995:392). David Starbuck's findings at Canterbury were similarly not "Shaker-like." He notes that the dump fill from the hog house root cellar wasn't notably different from any other late nineteenth-century domestic dump, "except for a lessened number of liquor bottles and a dearth of tobacco pipe fragments" (Starbuck 1998:14). Based on this finding, Starbuck argues that "the easiest interpretation may be that the Shakers had evolved into middle-class consumers. This is not to disparage the Shakers but to suggest that they were becoming more like the World's People and less like the Shakers of old" (2004:64). If, however, we connect our view of the changes that occurred in the Shakers' ways of expressing their faith over 200 years to changes happening over the same 200 years just outside the Shakers' fences, the lines tracing the trajectories of Shakers and the world's people seem a little less convergent. Rather, as time passed, Shakers may have continued to partake of mainstream culture in about the same proportions as they had before. Just as Shakers made many of their own household goods and tools in the beginning years of Shakerism around the turn of the nineteenth century, so did non-Shaker neighbors who were living in the surrounding regions. With the nineteenth-century growth of industrial production, both Shakers and the world's people began to take advantage of relatively convenient and affordable commercially available goods. Just like their non-Shaker neighbors, Pleasant Hill's residents ate from decorated tableware, when those decorated tablewares were abundant in the marketplace. The Shakers didn't necessarily become more "worldly"; they continued to engage with the larger world at a similar pace and level. What we see archaeologically is that the world they were interacting with had changed.

A recurring theme in the interpretation of material collections from Shaker, and other communal, egalitarian sites is the surprise in finding individual names printed, written, or engraved on artifacts. A commercially made whiteware cup with the name "Sophia" on the exterior drew David Starbuck's comment that the piece "is nearly unique in that Shaker artifacts were not personalized in any way" (1998:12). The 1845 revision of the Millennial Laws allowed for individual members to mark tools and clothing of personal use with their own initials but forbade marking of one's products to claim pride in craftsmanship (Andrews 1963:273–274). In their analysis of pottery from the North Family compound at Union Village, Bruce Aument and Andrew Sewell noted that no base sherds bore the names of individual potters, as marking one's own work might indicate a potentially dangerous excess of individualism (2009:181). Ron Deiss reports finding a single brick from South Union, Kentucky, that bore the hand-inscribed name of one of the community's founders, Isaac Whyte, in its indented frog (1987:92). Shakers weren't alone among egalitarian community residents in occasionally marking their goods. A prideful brickmaker who manufactured one of the bricks used in building the Harmonists' Wolf House in New Harmony, Indiana, inscribed the message (in German), "Harmonie the 25 May 1823 is a beautiful day. We have made 2400 bricks. Morning has gold in its mouth" and the initials "CH" or "GP" (Strezewski 2014:12). Earthenware vessels from Ephrata marked with initials after firing also hint at expressions of private ownership (Warfel 2009:149). With numerous examples preserved in archaeological contexts of what seem to be exceptions to our expectation that residents of communal groups will avoid expressing claim to personal property, we might need to consider checking our surprise each time this happens. Few groups were so rigid in their attitude toward personal possessions as Oneida, where any individual ownership was forbidden and all objects were to be held in common, from children's toys to adults' watches (Van Wormer 2006:53). It may be productive to see these scratched and painted claims to ownership as opportunities to question how the rules inside each particular group or village included, or failed to include, the smallest items of everyday routine.

Individual Shakers may have been discouraged from writing their names on objects as marks of ownership or pride in craftsmanship, but the practice seems to have been approached differently when a person's or village's name was tied into the Shaker brand. In her 2012 doctoral dissertation, *Through Their Stomachs: Shakers, Food, and Business Practices in the Nineteenth Century*, Boston University's Ruth Ann Murray demonstrates that understanding Shaker food industries is fundamental to understanding Shakers' identity. Even though there were no consistently codified dietary restrictions, the production, sharing, and selling of food and food products were central to Shakers' social relations inside and outside of their villages. She writes that "for all its beauty and iconic appeal, neither the Shaker chair nor signature Shaker oval box represented a significant business endeavor compared to the size and profitability of the food-related industries" (Murray 2012:31). Shaker villages produced and sold a wide variety of raw produce and processed foods, the types of which depended on a village's local resources and member expertise. The New York and New England villages specialized, for example, in dried sweet corn, maple syrup and candies, dried pumpkin, cheese, butter, and apples and apple products such as cider (Murray 2012:31–33). Their cider was widely appreciated, and based on her reading of contemporary reports, Murray believes that the Shakers' consistently high-quality cider was considered superior to that produced outside of their communities because of the group's "cleanliness, order, and attention to detail" (2012:38). Hospitality was a central part of the Shaker "brand" as well, as villages welcomed potential converts and increasing numbers of curious sightseers as the nineteenth century progressed. Visitors between the 1820s and 1840s enjoyed locally brewed honey liquor, beer, and cider as well as meals with beef, ham, turkey, potatoes, squash, corn pudding, apple and pumpkin pies, bread, and cheese (Murray 2012:56–58). The room and board was free at first, but eventually a nominal charge was established in some villages. The real benefit for Shaker villages in welcoming visitors was the chance to, if not add to the family membership, at least add a loyal customer for their store's products. This identification of outsiders as "customers" appears to have impacted Shakers' approach to labeling objects with personal names in at least two cases. Two specific Shakers' names were found on three archaeologically recovered items from the North Family Lot of Union Village, Ohio. Stephen Easton, who served as a trustee and, by extension, outside sales representative for Shaker-made goods, seems to have emblazoned his name on crates and documents with a stencil and stamp found by archaeologists in the Brothers' Shop cellar. During his tenure as trustee, Stephen Easton is documented to have made "numerous trips to Cincinnati and Lebanon to sell and market Shaker goods" (Sewell et al. 2009b:70). Peter Boyd's name was embossed with the title "Agent" on a glass bottle, presumably only one from a production run of unknown quantity, for "Shaker's Cough Syrup" (Aument and Sewell 2009:181). Shaker scholars seem to suffer some internal conflict about how marketing and sale outside of the community was practiced, as Patrick Bennett and his colleagues note that the Pleasant Hill, Kentucky, Shakers' stamped ceramic pipes were "idiosyncratic" and "uncharacteristically independent and worldly" (2009:73). Kim McBride's 2005 exploration into Shaker pipe styles does find that, across many villages, from South Union, Kentucky, to Sabbathday Lake, Maine, Shaker pipe styles were very similar, simple, and uniformly different from commercially produced pipes (see also the mention of South Union pipes in Fiegel 1995:380) but that only examples from Pleasant Hill were stamped with their village name. It may be uncharacteristic in pipe manufacture, but these pipes and other marked objects may make more sense in the broader context of Shaker production and marketing. Even within a community that eschewed personal property as an indication of pridefulness, allowances were made for those individuals who were in some way acting as intermediaries between the Shaker community and the outside world. Investigations at the level of the artifact raise questions about the ways in which members negotiated a balance between individualism and uniformity, as well as casting light on the various communities' approaches to interacting with the larger society.

Community Potters

In addition to the Shakers' well-known industries, intentional communities such as the Harmonists, Inspirationists, Oneida Perfectionists, Moravians, and western Mormons all built productive industries making goods for sale outside of their communities. The potters of New Harmony, Indiana; Bethabara and Salem, North Carolina; and the Little Colorado River Valley of Arizona all made and sold ceramic products whose durability in the archaeological record presents opportunities to better understand these communities' market participation.

The 1999 excavation of the Ephrata Cloister brothers' dormitory on what members called "Mt. Zion" uncovered a number of green-glazed, stubby smoking pipe fragments. These remnants may act as evidence of tobacco use, a practice discouraged under Conrad Beissel's spiritual leadership between 1732 and 1768 but which may not have been entirely stamped out. The fragments may also point to one community's support of another nearby community's industry. These particular pipes are like those made by Moravian potters, possibly offering a material remnant of documented interactions between the Ephrata Cloister and the nearby Moravian settlement of Lititz, just over 8 miles to the west of Ephrata, and established in 1749, during Ephrata's years of growth (Warfel 2000:25).

German-born Harmonist potter Christoph Weber operated his redware workshop at New Harmony, Indiana, between 1815 and 1825, producing vessels for use by fellow Harmonists as well as for sale in surrounding towns. Between 2008 and 2012, Michael Strezewski led University of Southern Indiana archaeological researchers in their study of two locations containing evidence of the operation of Weber's kiln. The low-fired, lead-glazed mugs, jugs, pitchers, plates, serving bowls, and waste bowls were made from local clays, as were the wares of many potters working throughout the American Midwest at this time. Weber's work differed from other potters, though, in his use of a relatively uncommon kiln type. Strezewski writes that "the archaeological work at the site identified the Harmonist kiln as a cross-draft cassel kiln, a type not previously noted in North America, and quite different from redware kilns excavated elsewhere in the Midwest" (2015b:34). Weber's wares were largely undecorated and utilitarian, thin-walled, and with a dark-brown glazing style similar to that used by Shaker potters at Union Village, Ohio (Strezewski 2013:171). A small proportion of serving vessels, such as plates and pie dishes, were decorated with slip trailing (Strezewski 2013:93, 176).

Strezewski notes that the majority of this Harmonist-made redware was used within New Harmony itself, while some was sold in their own store and at stores in nearby Vincennes, Shawneetown, or what was known as the English Settlement. Around 1819, New Harmony's store records noted a drop in locally produced redware purchases by non-Harmonist consumers, who instead increasingly preferred distantly made improved white earthenwares from English and American factories. In response to customer demand, the Harmonists' stores began stocking and selling these whitewares in greater numbers alongside their own self-produced redware ceramics (Strezewski 2013:182). Strezewski expands further on pottery sale and production at New Harmony in his analysis of materials from the ca. 1823 Wolf House, one of several buildings excavated in the mid-1970s (2014). The house cellar deposits contained both Harmonist- and non-Harmonist-produced redware ceramic fragments; ceramic tableware fragments, including shell-edged, transferware, and annular ware; window and container glass; and rusted metal fragments. In its lowest level, the root cellar contained six redware vessels produced, Strezewski argues, by the Harmonists and stored in the cellar at the time of its collapse. Included in the cellar assemblage were decorated earthenwares—including transferware, annular ware, shell-edged, and hand-painted fragments from tablewares and other household ceramics. Strezewski notes that, according to documentary records, Harmonists stocked the shelves of their store with such ceramics for sale to neighbors outside their fold, but archaeological evidence such as this shows that they were also using decorated whitewares in their own homes. He writes: "Though the Harmonists consciously led a fairly simple life, in terms of their clothing, material possessions, and housing arrangements, it would appear that decorated plates and teawares were not deemed overindulgent" (Strezewski 2014:76).

Beneath the stone floor of the warehouse, which was used by Harmonists for receiving and storing goods to be sold in their community store, excavation revealed a small collection of Harmonist-era artifacts likely related to domestic occupation of the location before the warehouse was built (Strezewski 2014:5). In contrast to findings from the Wolf House, the predominance of fragments from Christoph Weber's redware vessels among domestic debris left by the prewarehouse occupants showed that, in this residence, locally made ceramics were preferred over imported white earthenware (Strezewski 2014:98, 105). Though Strezewski does not explicitly link his findings with the Harmonists' broader economic policies, Pitzer and Elliot (1979) note that Harmony's leaders were vocal advocates of domestic manufacturing as a way of protecting the U.S. economy in times of increased availability of imported goods. Rather than considering them too decorative, then, perhaps the objection to the refined whitewares, many of which were made in the potteries of Staffordshire, England, was that they were somehow unpatriotic, and represented a threat to the community's economic success.

Moravian merchants working in the latter decades of the eighteenth century lacked the relatively easy market access to English-made earthenwares enjoyed by later Harmonist and Shaker traders, opening the opportunity for Moravian potters to create a variety of reproductions, in addition to their own redwares, to satisfy local consumer demand. Early Moravian efforts to establish a community near Savannah, Georgia, beginning in 1735 were refocused when members from the Moravian community of Herrnhut, near Dresden, Germany, arrived in Pennsylvania in 1742 and built their first substantial village of Bethlehem. What set these American Moravians apart from the *Unitas Fratrum*'s other missionizing religious communities in the United States was their level of social organization. Land and crop products were held in common. Towns were laid out according to predetermined plans. The immigrant ships, reportedly, were strategically populated with voluntary migrants representing a range of desirable professions (Foley 1965:62). In 1753, Moravian settlers from Bethlehem established their community at Bethabara, North Carolina, and over the following decades built more permanent villages at Bethania and Salem, many traces of which still stand at Historic Bethania and the Old Salem Historic District near the modern city of Winston-Salem.

Stanley South's 1999 *Historical Archaeology in Wachovia: Excavating Eighteenth-Century Bethabara and Moravian Pottery* is a thorough, if belated, reporting of the results of his 1960s excavations at Bethabara (South 1965), with special attention to the pottery produced by Moravian master potters Gottfried Aust and Rudolph Christ. Kiln waster evidence showed that Aust produced wares for use within the Moravian community, as well as a great variety of objects for sale outside the community. Few manufacturers of household vessels—whether pottery, silver, pewter, or tin—operated on North Carolina's mid-eighteenth-century frontier, so Aust's wares fulfilled a wide range of needs that arose well beyond the Moravians' own villages (South 1999:256). The Moravian center of Salem served as an economic hub for the sparsely populated region during the latter decades of the eighteenth century, serving the English-speaking residents of the surrounding area, including the nearby town of Richmond. Brian W. Thomas's thoughtful 1994 examination of Moravian pottery, informed by his discussion of the group's built environment and language practices, focuses on Moravian ceramics recovered from Richmond and Salem, including pieces made by Aust and Christ, the two potters considered in detail by Stanley South (1999). Thomas found a wide difference between the percentage of British-made ceramics found in collections from Richmond (49 percent) and Salem (21 percent), suggesting that local non-Moravian consumers purchased the majority of these tablewares available in the region. Facing an unreliable import market, Moravian potters began producing locally made copies of British ceramics around 1773. Non-Moravian potter William Ellis joined the Salem community in this year to assist in production of an English-style molded cream-colored ware known as Queensware, and Rudolph Christ took over this aspect of their business with great expertise after Ellis left in 1774 (South 1999:271). Thomas maintains that these copies were specifically made for non-Moravian trade partners, rather than Moravians with a taste for British-made ceramics (1994:26), and this assertion is born out subtly in the archaeological results. Nine percent of ceramics from the Richmond collection analyzed were Moravian-made copies, while only 3 percent of the Salem collection were of this type.

Thomas very explicitly presents the Moravians' primary goal as maintaining an autonomous religious community among, and by the good graces of, growing Anglo-American settlements. Within the years of the Revolutionary War, pacifist Moravians were careful to maintain their exemption from military service. They strategically managed relationships with non-Moravian neighbors by engaging in trade while practicing an internal preference for the German language (Thomas 1994:27). Throughout this time, Moravian leaders adopted "a strategy of reinforcing internal conformity and values, while masking or obfuscating some of these exclusionary practices from the outside world" (Thomas 1994:2007). However, the group's immigration to the United States and subsequent settlements were informed as much by missionary ambition as maintenance of a distinct identity. The 2012 National Landmark Registration Form for the Historic Moravian Bethlehem Historic District in Bethlehem, Pennsylvania, states that Moravians "created an international religious community with a network of towns, cities, and communities that stretched across the world." The Moravians "left their home base in Germany, not to escape persecution, but rather to spread their version of Christianity" (Mowers 2012:18). It is not clear how Moravian plans to disseminate their religious teachings and unite Christianity's followers meshes with what Thomas perceives as their desire to culturally exclude without alienating their important Anglo-American economic contacts. As Thomas accurately argues, the Moravians were not isolated and insular but were participants in a larger American economy. This argument could go further, however, in considering how Moravian leaders, and even potters, participated in sending appealing messages to non-Moravians who might one day become acolytes.

Not unlike Harmonist and Moravian earthenwares, Mormon-made pottery has captured the attention of archaeologists for its ability to delineate connections inside and outside of Mormon communities. The 1991 excavation of Wilhelm Frederick Otto Behrman's ca. 1876–1879 pottery workshop and kiln in Brigham City, Arizona, contributed to local researchers' awareness of a distinctive green-glazed redware that is also found in the remains of other United Order villages in the Little Colorado River valley (Ferg 2005b:7) (see #20 in the Appendix).

Although the LDS church did not universally endorse or require communalism in the majority of its settlements, in the settlements established under the church subgroup the United Order, beginning in the mid-1870s, each member contributed property to his or her community, which operated using a form of joint stock structure (Arrington 2005:328). The United Order organization was attempted in some existing towns, such as St. George, Utah, and in more encompassing fashion in new settlements throughout the Great Basin. Among these were towns like Orderville, Utah, and four northern Arizona villages in the Little Colorado River valley named Brigham City, Joseph City, Obed, and Sunset (see #20 in the Appendix). As short-lived experiments in Mormon communal structure, these villages have held the interest of archaeologists and local preservation groups since the late 1970s (Ferg 2005a, 2005c). Brother Behrman's pottery provides an example of the networks of production and exchange that existed between these fortified towns.

Timothy Scarlett and colleagues Robert J. Speakman and Michael D. Glascock go beyond analyzing pastes and stylistic attributes, using instrumental neutron activation analysis (INAA) to trace the products and interactions of individual pottery shops among eight different Mormon potteries in Utah and Arizona, including Behrman's Brigham City workshop (2007:72). Though each shop produced pottery and was operated by Mormons, there were significant differences among them, including the national origin of the founding potter (England, Denmark, Germany, or the United States), the mechanism of establishment (church mandated or owner initiated), the type of labor employed (family, apprentices, or hired hands), and the method of product distribution (local sale, peddling trips, or church redistribution of tithing). These differing operations also produced variable types of wares, including some colors or textures of clay fabrics, decorations, or vessel forms, that can't be confidently attributed to specific potters or their shops. However, trace elements detected by INAA, consisting of 32 elemental variables, form signatures for specific manufacturing locations and processes. Scarlett, Speakman, and Glascock demonstrate that no two potteries produce exactly the same chemistry, and despite visible variations in colors and textures within a shop's output, chemistry is remarkably stable for each producer. Based on these results, the authors hope for further extensive data collection to achieve the next research step of developing GIS-based studies that show the movement of goods (and the people who carried them) across the Mormon Domain, providing insights into trade within and between settlements, kinship connections, church redistribution systems, and competition with global-scale commercial producers.

Artifacts and Individual Idealism

Community potters, Shaker trustees, and Harmonist brick makers were all individuals working within frameworks established by their community to provide the goods used daily by their fellow believers. Although we can't often tie a particular artifact or scatter of artifacts to the specific person who made and used them, investigation at the artifact scale of analysis brings us closest to the level of individual members of an intentional community. At this scale, we can see how members worked to support their community in perhaps unexpected ways, such as when Moravian potter Rudolph Christ made English-style Queensware ceramics for sale to his non-Moravian neighbors to economically support his brethren at Salem, North Carolina, and to help maintain positive ties with the larger community. We can imagine how Shaker sisters at Pleasant Hill, Kentucky, lived within their own village's interpretation of the Millennial Laws, taking some meals at the washhouse rather than the dining hall when their workload was heavy. The level of the individual artifact is where we can expect to see the most tension between group membership and personal identity. This is not to deny, however, the tensions illuminated at the scale of the building or built environment, where group concepts of family are enacted within shared kitchens, private bed chambers, and communal workshops, or at the scale of the cultural landscape, where idealized town plans meet the realities of earth, water, and local governments. Each scale of inquiry exposes examples of compliance and contradiction, and for each community different levels ask and answer different questions. How did the residents of George Rapp's experiment in dormitory housing comprehend the lavish gardens the leader built adjacent to his own home? How did their realization that the Kedar might crumble before the expected Second Coming of Christ influence Ephrata members' approach to other daily necessities? In the following chapter, the single intentional community of the Kaweah Co-operative Commonwealth will be viewed across these three scales of resolution to present one example of archaeological inquiry into how an ideal world is manifested and contested at the differing scales of landscape, building, and artifact.

6

---★---

SEEKING KAWEAH

From first to last about five hundred others joined them, some from almost every State in the Union and many from countries of Europe. This list of membership itself is a curious study. It is the United States in microcosm; among the members are old and young, rich and poor, wise and foolish, educated and ignorant, worker and professional man, united only by the common interest in Kaweah. There were temperance men and their opposites, churchmen and agnostics, freethinkers, Darwinists and spiritualists, bad poets and good musicians, artists, prophets and priests. There were dress-reform cranks and phonetic spelling fanatics, word-purists and vegetarians. It was a mad mad world and being so small its madness was more visible; but in its delirium it did some noble work, and perhaps—perhaps it was not quite a failure after all.

Burnette Haskell, "How Kaweah Fell"

In 1885, amid the sometimes violent labor unrest growing in San Francisco and many other western cities, lawyers Burnette G. Haskell, J. J. Martin, and John Redstone founded a socialist-inspired experiment they called the Co-Operative Land Purchase and Colonization Association of California. Their initial plan was to invest in residential real estate and develop cooperative economic ventures such as the Fish Rock Pottery, a brick and tile manufacturing plant in Mendocino County. Within a short time, however, their goals became more ambitious. The association decided to build a logging, lumber production, and shipping operation based on cooperative labor and member investment, with the residential community supporting this industry acting as a beacon to the world as a living alternative to competition and corporate monopoly.

Burnette Haskell was a journalist and lawyer, and was simultaneously the most charismatic and radical of the association's cofounders. He had helped organize the Pacific Coast International Workingmen's Association

(IWA) in 1882, was active in organizing the Coast Seaman's Union of the Pacific Coast, and advocated socialist ideals and labor organization in his periodical, *Truth* (ca. 1882–1884). Haskell and Martin have been described as "bomb throwing Communists who believed the barricades of capitalism should be stormed with violence," while Redstone and other early association members were apparently "pure socialists" who only hoped to demonstrate the "virtues of communal living" (Doctor 1968:1).

In the autumn of 1885, taking advantage of inexpensive tracts of timberland offered for \$2.50/acre under the United States Timber and Stone Act of 1878, 56 members of the Co-Operative Land Purchase and Colonization Association of California applied individually for title to what amounted to over 8,000 acres of land in the steeply sloped terrain of the Kaweah River drainage of Tulare County, California. The land agent who received the applications in his Visalia office was suspicious of this large number of entrants, believing they were working for a commercial lumber company attempting to illegally acquire land intended for personal use. He suspended the entries indefinitely in early December 1885. Meanwhile, largely unaware of the suspension of their land entries, hopeful communalists took up residence along the North Fork of the Kaweah River and in October 1886 began building a wagon road from the foothills to the Giant Forest timber. In their new home the group took on the name of the nearby river, derived from the language of the Yokuts people who inhabited the valley for centuries before, thus becoming the Kaweah Co-Operative Commonwealth, or Kaweah Colony.

Rather than providing a refuge for those seeking to escape society, the Kaweah Colony aimed to provide an example of how a democratic society (referring more to effective administration by the people than to elected representation) would end poverty and assure each person his or her best contributing role as a worker (Jones 1891:58). Recruitment literature provided a succinct statement of the ideals of the colony:

Its prime mission is to insure its members against want, or fear of want, by providing comfortable homes, ample sustenance, educational and recreative facilities, and to promote and maintain harmonious social relations, on the solid and grand bases of Liberty, Equality and Fraternity. (Haskell 1889:3)

In developing their philosophical approach, colony leaders found their primary inspiration in Laurence Gronlund's 1884 book, *The Cooperative Commonwealth in Its Outlines: An Exposition of Modern Socialism*. Gronlund's work adapted and explained the basic principles of German scientific socialism for English-speaking readers, outlining an ideal plan for the nonviolent administrative, economic, and moral reorganization of society. Haskell, Martin, and Redstone maintained that simply by educating the public about the scientific principles, or truths, of socialism, a new and perfectly democratic society could be built that practiced a balance of labor, study, and recreation.

Initial capitalization for the effort was to come from the $250,000 collected as membership fees from a fixed maximum of 500 members (Jones 1891:55). After learning of the colony through social or professional acquaintances or by reading of it in one of several publications that either criticized or advertised the experiment, interested parties could apply for membership by paying a first $10 of the full $500 fee. After paying $100 in cash toward their membership, approved members could take up residence on the colony's Tulare County grounds. Once working at the colony, resident members would be issued time-checks in exchange for minutes of labor, which they could then exchange for payments on their membership fee or goods and services in camp (fig. 6.1).

Members could also exchange goods needed by the colony for portions of their membership fee. Prospective member George Clark of Los Angeles made collars and harnesses for the Kaweah Colony draft teams in exchange for his membership fee before moving there to live with his comrades (Letter from J. J. Martin to George Clark, 24 May 1890, Kaweah Co-operative Company Colony Records [KCR], Bancroft Library). Barber Adam Forster provided "3 sets of plush seated barber's chairs complete in every respect with all known modern improvements, together with 3 elegant mirrors" and "a stout healthy looking pole with a rubicund countenance and self assuring gilded ball" (*Kaweah Commonwealth* [KC] 3 May 1890) in exchange for his and his family's membership.

To fully develop the industrial and agricultural vision they desired for the fledgling colony, Kaweah required a wide variety and considerable quantity of skilled laborers to join the effort. Nonresident members kept the Kaweah Colony connected to unions and trade associations,

Figure 6.1. A 200-minute denomination time-check from the Kaweah Colony. From the Kaweah Cooperative Colony Company Records, Bancroft Library MSS C-A 303. Courtesy of the Bancroft Library, University of California, Berkeley.

potentially sources of labor, in other geographical areas. Alfred Fuhrman of San Francisco was president of the Federated Trades Council in 1889, and he organized the Brewers' and Maltsters' Union of the Pacific Coast in a number of cities, and the United Brewery Workmen's Union of the Pacific Coast in 1890. James K. Phillips was president of the Trades Assembly around 1883 and was an instrumental member of the San Francisco Typographical Union. Joseph Buchanan edited the *Denver Labor Enquirer* (when that role was not filled by Burnette Haskell himself) and belonged to the Rocky Mountain Region Knights of Labor (Cross 1935). However, attracting laborers to risk their own livelihoods to join the cause in person proved difficult. In November 1888, the colony advertised under the title "Help Wanted" for

> fifty to one hundred sober, intelligent industrious men comprising the following trades . . . Five blacksmiths, ten carpenters, five cabinet makers, ten farmers, one painter, five machinists, two cooks, ten farm hands, two architects, two potters, five brick-makers, five stone-masons, two plasterers, three bricklayers, two engineers, five loggers, one assayer, one metallurgist, two lime burners, one civil engineer and the balance to be handy men. (*Commonwealth* [C] 24 November 1888)

Members experienced in these basic trades would provide the knowledge necessary to build permanent housing and infrastructure, supervise lumber operations, and provide food to the colony. Such skilled prospective members were not forthcoming, and the group was always shorthanded in most of these useful vocations. A compiled listing of resident members between 1887 and 1892, drawn from census records, local directories, colony records, and the colony newspapers, reveals that among 35 men of known occupation, only 6 fit into the extensive list of job skills that colony organizers hoped to secure: two blacksmiths, one plasterer, one cabinetmaker, one carpenter, one farmer. There were also two harness makers, two mechanics, one cooper, an apiarian, one stevedore, one sail maker, one shipmaster, one shipwright, one brass finisher, one barber, one cobbler, one chandelier maker, one watchmaker, one clerk, one photographer, one pharmacist, two merchants, one dentist, two physicians, two professors of music, and three lawyers living and working at the colony. The colonists were lacking in important skills that would be needed to build basic services, and instead had specialists whose chandeliers, music lessons, and sailing expertise could contribute culturally, but not economically, to the growing community.

Whatever the colonists lacked in practical skills, they attempted to make up for in intellectual and political engagement. Many existing members of the Kaweah Colony, both resident and nonresident, enthusiastically joined the Nationalist movement inspired by Edward Bellamy's widely popular 1888 novel, *Looking Backward: 2000–1887* (fig. 6.2). The protagonist of this story awakes after more than a century-long sleep to discover that his home city of Boston, and the nation as a whole, has drastically changed for the better. All services are nationalized, the cash economy has been replaced by equitable trade, and unemployment is unknown. The Nationalist Club at Advance, the Kaweah Colony's largest tent-city, was organized in the autumn of 1889 and met Wednesday evenings in the library tent to discuss matters central to their cause and engage in lively debate. The topic of one such organized debate was: "Resolved that the People of our Country are sufficiently educated to accept and carry out the principles of Nationalism" (KC 1 November 1889). Apparently the affirmative won.

The discussion of whether the general swath of the American people were indeed sufficiently intelligent to emancipate themselves from wage slavery was a broader one in both space and time. Followers of Nationalism

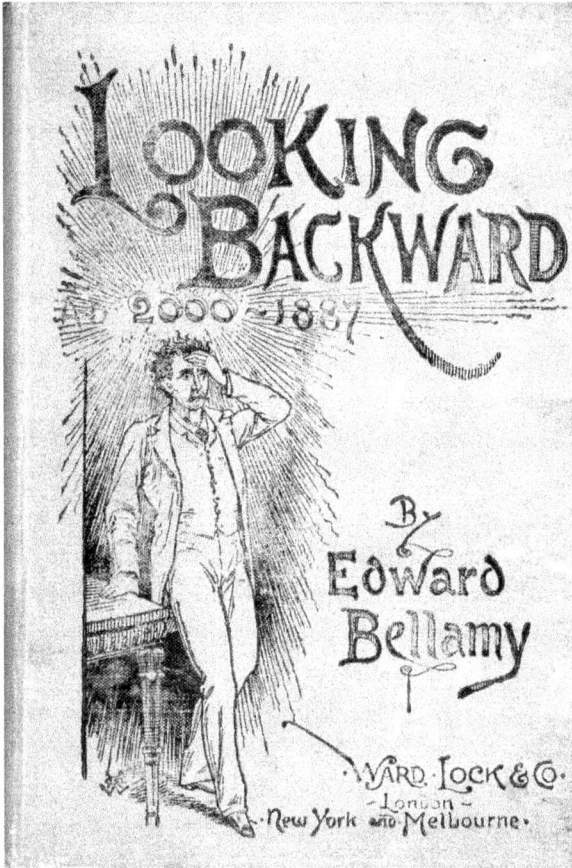

Figure 6.2. Book cover illustration from an 1890 edition of Edward Bellamy's 1888 novel *Looking Backward*. Is Julian West looking in amazement at what he sees in the future of 2000 or back at the harsh reality of 1887? Digitized by the Thomas Fisher Rare Book Library, University of Toronto.

throughout the country—indeed, like the majority of Kaweah colonists—tended to be more highly educated members of the middle class rather than part of the laboring masses whom the movement's proposed reforms were intended to help (Vassault 1890:660; Lipow 1982:131). When working-class members joined cooperative communities, there could be discord between those who had simply read and argued about labor theory and those who had personally felt the changing tides of the wage system in docks, mills, and workshops. Isaac Broome's 1902 retrospective on the ca. 1895–1898 Ruskin Co-Operative Association in Tennessee likened the less-educated community members' responses to stress in the community to that of starved animals unable to learn from their misfortunes (1902:181). In his 1924 review of American communal societies, Ernest

Wooster compared the Georgia-based "Christian Commonwealth's" ad-mission policies, which allowed working-class members with limited edu-cation, to "casting its pearls before swine" (1924:46). A level of intellectual snobbery seemed built into community-minded Nationalist, socialist, and progressive organizations that predisposed them to exclude the very people they purported to liberate.

Combined documentary accounts point to a pattern of regular resident member turnover for a large proportion of the Kaweah Colony population, with short-term members living for several months at a time alongside a small core group of long-term resident families. Overall, the majority of members, 87 percent, participated in the colony for less than three years. Nearly half, 42 percent, spent less than two years committed to the venture. The more permanent families maintained a social focal point at Advance, "presided over by Mrs. Redstone," where the tents of the Christie family (with the treasurer's office inside), the three tents for the Martin family, and the Redstones' tents were clustered together, "commanding a full view of the road" (KC 5 April 1890). In contrast to these settled families, former member Harry Cartwright recalled in a 1930 interview that the men who built the colony's road were primarily single, seafaring men "with strong backs and weak minds" who neither knew much about nor participated in colony business, and whom Haskell had "induced" to come labor at the colony without knowledge of the conditions on the grounds (Ellsworth n.d.). Cartwright's and others' memories did neglect many of the details of these working men's lives recorded in census records, voter lists, and news reports. Some were married, and many worked in trades other than seafar-ing. However, such absences from memory do suggest that members whose stays were brief made little impact on the colony's administrative structure and social goals. Instead, these workers made their contributions in more tangible form on the land as dirt shoveled, rocks blasted, or trees cut.

With several members connected to journalism and the printing trades and access to modern steam-powered printing equipment, the Kaweah colonists produced a vast and varied literature of their own to promote the Kaweah Co-operative Commonwealth and its interests. Their news-papers, the *Commonwealth* and *Kaweah Commonwealth*, were distributed among the resident membership, sent to nonresident members, and sold to nonmember subscribers, including other socialist and communal groups

Figure 6.3. Title illustration from the *Kaweah Commonwealth*, 21 June 1890. From Bancroft Library item xfF868 T8 L41. Courtesy of the Bancroft Library, University of California, Berkeley.

across the United States. Between March 1888 and December 1889, the *Commonwealth* was a multipage monthly published from Burnette G. Haskell's printing office in San Francisco. In December 1890, the printing office moved to a tent at Advance, and the journal became the four-page weekly *Kaweah Commonwealth*, at first coedited by resident-member M. A. Hunter, who donated a steam press in exchange for membership, and Burnette G. Haskell, who continued to write for the paper but was only occasionally on the colony grounds (fig. 6.3). The young women who labored setting type in their canvas printing office and the many anonymous resident writers for the periodical were vital to the colony's efforts to encourage the faithful to uphold their community's bonds in the face of outside opposition and economic hardship. The Colony Job Printing Department also claimed to maintain a busy schedule with other orders in addition to their regular newspaper issues (KC 13 December 1890), producing pamphlets and announcements that were not only communicators of information but were also physical artifacts that played a part in fulfilling the goals of the colony's social and organizational leaders.

Notes and advertisements in the *Commonwealth* and *Kaweah Commonwealth* established and displayed alliances with other intentional communities across the United States and worldwide. When a representative from the Altruist Community of St. Louis sent a copy of his group's own publication, the *Altruist*, to *Kaweah Commonwealth* editors in June 1891, hoping that it might be mentioned in print, he may have known that the colony had already advertised the Altruists'"monthly paper, partly in Phonetic Spelling, and devoted to common property, united labor, Community homes and equal rights to all" as early as 24 June 1889. Other socialist or communitarian publications promoted in the advertising sections of the Kaweah Colony's periodical include five Christian Socialist papers from Australia: the *Australian Herald, Boomerang, Bulletin, Christian Socialist,* and *Worker;* the *Beacon* from San Diego, California; the *Dawn* and the *Nationalist* from Boston; the *Integral Co-Operator* from Grass Valley, California; the *Teachers' Outlook* from Des Moines, Iowa; the *Twentieth Century* and *Workingman's Advocate* from New York; and the *Montague County Independent,* formerly the *Labor Sunbeam* of Bowie, Texas. A list of newspapers that provided reciprocal or paid advertising for the Kaweah Colony has yet to be assembled, but there is evidence that the colony advertised itself outside of the tight realm of socialist intentional communities. A May 1892 receipt was issued to colony secretary J. J. Martin for five lines of advertising printed in four issues, a total of $12.75, in the Funk and Wagnall's Company published prohibitionist newspaper, the *Voice* (KCR). Though their philosophical specifics did not always perfectly align, members of the Kaweah Colony acknowledged their broad connection to and drew inspiration from other socialist and progressive groups across the nation.

After four years of labor devoted to building a road to access timber resources, the yellow pine and redwood of the higher elevations, lumber millers cut the first board of Kaweah lumber on 16 July 1890. This would not be the beginning of a great volume to come but was instead the first drop in an unsteady trickle of productivity. In the fall of 1890, only a few months after the Kaweah Colony road crews had completed the wagon road to reach their lumber mill location and timberlands, the U.S. government created Sequoia National Park and an adjoining forest reservation. In November 1890, four colony trustees were charged with illegal timber cutting on government land, and an expensive and demoralizing legal battle ensued. The colony leased a mill site, Atwell's Mill, outside the protected government land, in the spring of 1891 and continued, optimistically, to cut trees.

Looking beyond their planned lumber business, colony visionaries believed that the Kaweah Colony's lands held abundant natural potential to fuel the settlement's growth into a metropolitan paradise. Haskell and Redstone's writings report plans for fruit, nut, and olive orchards; stocked fish pools; and quarrying. In reality, by the fall of 1891 it was clear that the income from the sale of products from their mill would be unable to cover even the basic costs of labor transportation and animal feed required to produce and ship the lumber. A post-1890 revision to the Kaweah Colony's membership application form demands to know, "Can you pay up your whole $500 in cash? If not, how much of the remaining $400 can you pay in material and what kind of material have you?" This alteration from earlier versions corresponds with the increasing difficulty experienced by colonists in providing for their basic expenses. The lumber mill was not producing enough for sale, and basic provisioning continued to depend on outside funding as membership fees from the existing residents had long been exhausted. By the spring of 1892, the few remaining members who had not sought greater security in their previous homes or moved on to another community enumerated their remaining assets and abandoned the cooperative experiment. A few families remained in the area, operating a stage stop and tour service for visitors along the former colony's road, the only vehicle access route to Sequoia National Park.

Colony Mill Road and the North Fork Valley

The physical landscape of the Kaweah Colony's settlement was as important a character in the story of their efforts as any of the individual members. Approaching landscape archaeologically involves considering the physical environment alongside the "human shaping, perception, and use of that space" (Kryder-Reid 1996:229; also Yamin and Metheny 1996), and an archaeological approach to humans' interaction with the natural landscape and the construction of cultural landscapes is vital to understanding the Kaweah Colony's efforts to develop the North Fork valley. The Kaweah colonists' landscape included the natural world—flora, fauna, topography, and climate—as well as their views of the natural surroundings, cultural modifications, and uses of that environment in the spaces and places of their settlement. The colonists' shaping of the landscape through road construction and camp settlement was suffused with meaning. More than just building a road, they were shaping an imagined future. Their road, in literal terms, was intended to reach trees for their lumber operation. As part of their plan for a new social order it was just the first small step in a much grander plan: "We dream of the time when the Canyon of Kaweah shall be a perpetual exposition greater than this [1899 Paris Exposition] of France; and by Science, harmony, labor, and love we are now toiling to make it come soon. Would you not like to help us in this work?" (C 1 November 1889).

Building the Colony Mill Road to the site of a planned lumber mill was the central project of Kaweah colonists' landscape modification and was a deeply significant practice. From initial survey and blasting to the routines of maintenance and repair, the process of road building was practical and symbolic labor devoted to shared economic and social goals. The members of the Kaweah Colony defined themselves not only by their political and economic views but also by recognition of the practice of labor. The physical activities and time associated with building and maintaining colony infrastructure were rewarded as the basic units of value within Kaweah's socialism, and thus building, working, and producing were practices laden with meaning to individual members and the community. Continuous upward progress of the road, ascending into the forest, was also of paramount importance. The first supervisor of road construction, Charles Keller, was forced out of his position when the General Assembly decided that he wasn't maintaining an acceptable upward grade on the route (Doctor 1968:2). Physical labor on the landscape was intimately connected with social community building. The Colony Mill Road, as a process and a product, was central to the physical, economic, and social landscape of the Kaweah Colony. The ideas of improvement, progress, and ascension were fundamental to the theoretical structure of the colonists' efforts, and were reflected and reinforced in the actions of building a wagon road climbing to the location of a planned sawmill. As the road ascended, so did their hopes for the new social order.

During the four years of road construction between 1886 and 1890, Kaweah Colony road crews and their families established seven tent camps along the North Fork of the Kaweah River as their progress moved from lowest to highest elevation. The names given to the earliest camps along the route echoed the crew's sense of aspiration: Advance, Progress, and Avalon. By late in 1887 imaginative, optimistic titles gave way to sequential numbers or descriptive names like Maple Canyon and Cedar Creek. All residential camps, with the exception of the leased mill away from the North Fork occupied in May 1891, were positioned to support and access the road-building project, and were limited to those few places with level

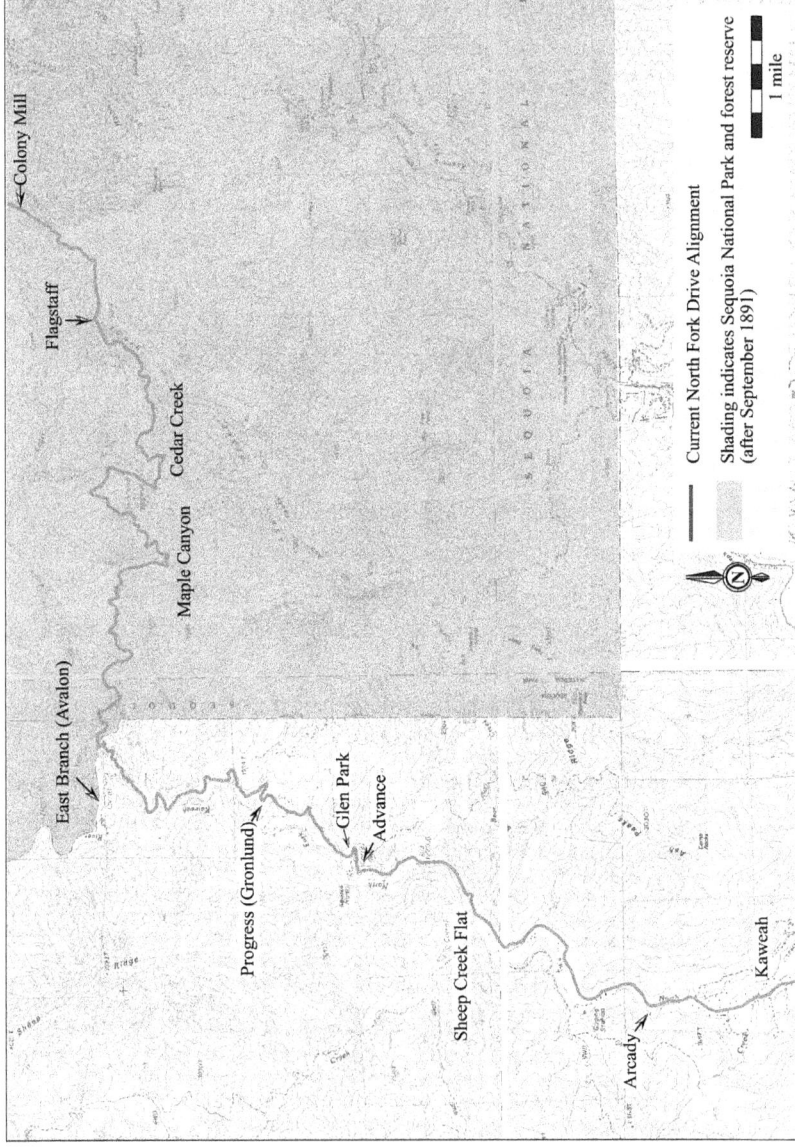

Figure 6.4. Kaweah Colony camp locations along North Fork Drive, much of which was originally built as Colony Mill Road. The shaded area shows the forest preserve and national park established in 1891, within which logging was then prohibited. Base topographic maps excerpted from USGS Shadequarter Mtn. (1993), Giant Forest (1993), Case Mountain (1987), and Kaweah (1986) 1:24000 Quadrangles.

Colony Mill

Flagstaff

Cedar Creek

Maple Canyon

East Branch (Avalon)

Progress (Gronlund)

Glen Park

Advance

Sheep Creek Flat

Arcady

Kaweah

SEQUOIA NATIONAL

——— Current North Fork Drive Alignment

Shading indicates Sequoia National Park and forest reserve (after September 1891)

1 mile

enough ground for a handful of tents (fig. 6.4). As each road camp was created, it was done so with the very skeleton of the previous camp, as the same tents, furniture, and tools were moved upward with the workers. During the whole process of building, there was also consistent movement of tools, materials, machinery, and members between locations on the road, both up and down slope. A few camps—Advance, East Branch, and Kaweah—became longer-term population centers for members working in other supporting tasks for those building the road, including growing food and publishing the newspaper.

Reaching the timber resources planned to be the economic basis of Kaweah's growth was only one goal of road-building. In the vision of colony organizers, pleasure-seekers would also travel the road in their trips to appreciate the natural wonders in the mountains at its highest reaches. By the time it was completed, the road held a monumental significance for colonists, who hailed it as "a mark some twenty miles across the face of nature not as a blemish or defect but as a beauty spot for our successors to point out as the greatest monument ever erected to cooperation by a white civilization" (KC 12 July 1890). As betrayed by this quote, among the project's goals was to employ entirely white labor. This continued what was by this time more than two decades of organized anti-Chinese activism among xenophobic and protectionist trades organizations. Immigrants, and especially Chinese workers, were widely seen as a threat to established laboring groups' identities and expectations. As archaeologist Mark Walker (2004:208) writes, "the language of unionism and craft solidarity was, through the discursive practices of Victorian ideology, married to the language of race and nativism." The "Union-Made" label on manufactured products assured consumers that their purchase was made by white hands as much as it did that the laborers were fairly treated and adequately compensated (see Saxton 1971 for an extensive discussion of the anti-Chinese movement and California's labor activists).

Kaweah's "mountain highway" was to be developed for workers and tourists alike to experience not only relief but also aesthetic pleasure when resting for water at the numerous roadside springs.

It is the intention to put watering troughs at each of these springs which will in future be changed from a wooden trough to a beautiful fountain that will send its sparkling waters into the air dancing for a moment in the bright sunlight glowing with the bright hues of the rainbow to fall into a marble basin for the refreshment of man and beast. (KC 11 October 1890)

Contrasting with this poetic view of the road and its surroundings was the experience of most colony members who actually worked on building the route. These members performed physically demanding labor and were limited to even more Spartan accommodations than those comrades who worked in the shops, offices, dining hall, and school at Advance and Kaweah. Member Philip Winser's description of daily life in the road maintenance camp at Maple Canyon included ants plaguing the cook tent (not an uncommon experience in any part of California) and Comrade Johnson's nightly battles to fight a rat away from his bed with a stick (KC 2 May 1890).

In a social world characterized by reverence for daily labors, it follows that activities that appear to us as either mundane or unpleasant work could be ritualized as symbolic labor within the Kaweah Colony's socialist vision. Mercyhurst University archaeology professor Mary Owoc describes how she views certain contexts of practice in the construction of British Bronze Age landscape features—digging, cutting sod, moving earth—as ritualized activities communally performed, and as products of shared memory and local contingency. She writes:

> The rules of ritual practice, which acquire their form and authority by reference to tradition, are moreover recognized, authorized, and transmitted by a community of participants. In this sense, ritualization, although performed by individuals, has an existence that goes beyond the individual performer. (Owoc 2005:262)

As long as the road was under construction, internal relations within the colony were relatively stable. The residential center at Advance, agricultural producers at East Branch, and workers at the road camp operated to support this collective effort that would support their planned future timber operation. After the road was completed and lumber operations at the Colony Mill were expected to support the development of a more permanent settlement downhill, changing the direction of focus and aspiration, relations were disrupted and inequalities became more problematic. Collective action, which had been focused on completion of the road, dispersed into many separate efforts that, although they may have been for the greater colony good, did not contribute to group cohesiveness. Rather than reinforcing colony unity, the move to the Kaweah town site may only have reinforced existing social distinctions between established families, among them the writers who envisioned a picturesque future highway, and more temporary residents, many of whom had spent long days sweating to realize others' poetic vision. At Kaweah, ideological factions who had previously been distant from one another at the smaller camps of Arcady, East Branch, and the road camps came into closer proximity with those from Advance, forcing them to confront their differences in opinion about the group's future direction.

Then, while experiencing the stress of internal dissent, loss of land access, and legal prosecution, the Kaweah Colony's leaders undertook significant physical relocations of industrial efforts from the Colony Mill, now unusable due to the federal government's forest reserve, to the leased Atwell's Mill many miles distant across the mountainous terrain. The economic and legal necessity to relocate logging efforts to Atwell's Mill removed members from the road that their physical, emotional, and financial sacrifices—their symbolic, ritualized labor—had contributed to building.

Civilizing Nature

Although the Kaweah Colony's ultimate goal was to build an industrial metropolis, members extolled the immediate superiority of their rustic environment over the urban centers many had left. After Kaweah's 1888 Christmas celebrations, a visitor wrote these glowing words of praise for the isolated settlement:

> What a jolly time we have had in spite of the wet weather, and how little we have missed the conveniences, comforts, and advantages of the city. Indeed, I have never enjoyed a Christmas more than this one I have just spent away up in the Sierras, in the tent-homes of the

Kaweah Colony. . . . Let our city friends only taste the pleasures of this peaceful life as an antidote to their eager thirst for wealth and power, which is so enslaving and delusive. (KC 18 January 1890)

The natural surroundings reportedly cured young Abbie Purdy's nervous exhaustion and delicate constitution in July 1890 (KC 5 July 1890) and inspired colonists and visitors alike to paint, sketch, photograph, and write poetry and prose expounding its virtues.

No matter how artistically and philosophically inspiring it was, the landscape was also something to be conquered and improved upon in the interest of colony goals. The natural world at Kaweah was, and remains, an unruly force (fig. 6.5). Level ground in the North Fork valley is rare, and is often so close to the river as to be too flood-prone for permanent building. Where unmanaged by fire or human activity, vegetation can be impassably thick, and poison oak covers many shady slopes. There are bears, rattle-snakes, tarantulas, and black-widow spiders. It was a challenging environment for the Kaweah colonists, and they approached that challenge with the colonial fervor of their late-Victorian milieu, ready to civilize the valley before them and create a safe, beautiful, parklike setting from this unpredictable and sometimes dangerous place.

Reporting on their Superintendent of Growing J. O. Knuckey's labors in the agricultural fields at the East Branch camp, a writer for the *Kaweah Commonwealth* reminded readers of the specific challenges of their situation:

People who live in the midst of untamed nature have to fight the elements under greater disadvantages than those who are located in places where nature has been subdued into working systematically for the use of man and became his obedient servant. (KC 5 July 1890)

Colonists had not yet tamed the landscape around them and were fighting an ongoing battle with nature to establish their settlement. Growing vegetable and fruit crops—melons, tomatoes, root vegetables, cabbage, peas, and lettuce—provided the satisfaction of a sense of self-sufficiency and productive labor. Planting exotic crops—fig trees, olive cuttings, English walnut, and Persian jujube "from trees that came originally from the garden of the Shah of Persia" (KC 4 March 1891)—brought the collecting ethic

Figure 6.5. Looking southwest down the North Fork of the Kaweah River, from North Fork Drive near the former location of the colony's "Progress" camp. Photo by author, 2007.

back into nature by establishing the collected specimens as living representatives of some colonists' hope to convey worldliness and taste.

Preferring an easily approachable, comfortably domesticated setting in the foreground with the more dangerous, rugged aspects of nature some distance in the background, colonists worked to establish a balance of wilderness and culture in their visual landscape. Anna Haskell, wife of colony cofounder Burnette Haskell, describes this layered view when she admires the tent village of Advance upon her first visit: the "long line of tents along

'Broadway', with its trim garden fronting the other side of the street and the everlasting mountains piercing to the clouds on every side" (KC 4 October 1890). The colonists' aesthetic approach to landscape around their residential camps was to improve upon the already scenic space by limiting and cutting back the existing vegetation while adding their own improvements. The "suburb" of Glen Park was settled in a thickly vegetated spot, where the "heavy growth of shrubbery, when properly trimmed up, will render the grounds very beautiful" (KC 19 April 1890). This refers not to simply making the area habitable but to grooming it into a popular standard of beauty. Dr. Hunter, whose Glen Park tent was already amply appointed with purchased furniture, carpeting, and other goods, carved the trunk of a living buckeye tree behind his tent into "rustic seats" (KC 10 May 1890). Based on other reports of Dr. Hunter's almost excessive quantity of furniture and household goods, we can assume that he did not need to augment his seating space. Rather, he exerted his power to make the natural world immediately outside his home into a more easily manageable place to live by transforming a natural into a domesticated object.

Colony members' individual and collective efforts to civilize nature were informed more by Victorian attitudes toward the landscape than by the socialist discourse that brought them into the valley. Children made collections of rocks, artifacts, and other curious specimens, and residents' enthusiasm for displaying nature under their command led to unrealized plans for a zoological garden and museum. The closest they came to such an institution were two unlucky specimens: a captured bear cub named McGinty, who was bottle-fed by member Mrs. Young and chained at the camp until he became too large to manage; and Polly Green, Miss Hildebrand's pet parrot, who survived less than a year in camp.

The Victorian impulse to control nature intersected with members' socialist philosophies as they attached symbolic names to some of the Giant Forest's most majestic sequoia trees during their hikes and camping excursions. Colonists gave the name of "Karl Marx" to the largest sequoia they encountered (O'Connell 1999:vii), and named other trees with equally philosophical and literary zeal. Lawyer and later congressman William Carey Jones recalls this practice in an article for the *Quarterly Journal of Economics*:

The Kaweah colonists have affixed the names of some of the apostles of socialism, such as Karl Marx and John Swinton, to the larger trees. Karl Marx, the largest one measured by the colonists, shows in a photograph twenty persons standing shoulder to shoulder with their backs against a face of the tree. Emerson and others, too, have been remembered by them in the names given to some of the larger and more beautiful trees. (Jones 1891:52)

The tree named "Karl Marx" would later be renamed "General Sherman" by what would become the National Parks Service and is now widely believed to be the world's largest living tree. A photo well known among scholars of the Kaweah Colony shows many members and visitors gathered together around the base of the Karl Marx tree (fig. 6.6). To capture this image, the group must have traveled together over a considerable distance of rocky, steep terrain in order to pose together in a picture of solidarity. They claimed an ancient representative of their muse and opponent, Nature, by naming it in honor of one of their ideological influences. The features of

Figure 6.6. Members and supporters of the Kaweah Colony gather at the base of the giant sequoia they named the Karl Marx tree. From the Kaweah Cooperative Colony Papers, 1886–1890, WA MSS S-1304, Yale Collection of Western Americana, Beinecke Rare Book and Manuscript Library, Yale University.

their environment that they could not domesticate with roads, gardens, or collections, they plied into cooperation with names and images.

Finding Advance

The longest occupied of the Kaweah Colony's tent villages, Advance was established in the spring of 1887 amid dense grasses, shrubs, and oaks on a broad, sloping plain to the east of the North Fork of the Kaweah River. Advance was intended to be a temporary camp, supporting the road crews and providing basic services while the colony's lumber operation was put into place. After achieving more economic stability, colony leaders planned to move the population downstream to Kaweah, where permanent buildings arranged on a street grid would be the start of their model city.

Within two years Advance had 32 full-time residents, a communal dining hall, and a school (fig. 6.7). It was here that members published the *Kaweah Commonwealth* and other promotional materials by steam press. Water piped from a nearby spring served the town's needs, which included ornamental flower gardens and a fountain. A few families also set up camp on the north side of the gulch adjacent to Advance, in a "suburb" that members called Glen Park. A writer for the *Kaweah Commonwealth* gave readers this verbal tour through Advance in the 5 April 1890 issue:

> Let us go up on the hill, where we can see the whole of Camp Advance to the best advantage. Looking down the gentle slope, we see a row of fifteen tents set close together, the lowermost and the largest being the printing house. Another row of five branches off to the south at right angles. All these are permanent. That other cluster, grouped near the store tent, belongs to the men who move to whatever point they are needed most. Just now the repairs to the road near by has brought them here, and our camp is larger than ever before. That wooden structure, covered with shakes, close by the printing house, is the stable, with accommodations for ten horses. It must be doubled in size before long. (KC 5 April 1890)

As dozens of Kaweah Colony members lived at the site of Advance for more than three years—with a communal kitchen, water pipes, blacksmith shop, printing press, and numerous fires and stoves—I expected the

Figure 6.7. Photo of Advance, ca. 1888. Kaweah Colony Views, BANC PIC 1905.13978. Courtesy of the Bancroft Library, University of California, Berkeley.

activities of their daily lives to have left significant archaeological traces in the form of trenches, trash dumps, privies, and general debris scatter.

Armed with historical photographs of the colony's tent village taken from a few perspectives, I visited the Bureau of Land Management property called Advance Site on the North Fork of the Kaweah River. Despite the sign's claims, it was difficult to visualize how the current landscape could be reconciled with the views in the archival photos. Given California trinomial CA-TUL-1791H in 1981, the only previously recorded archaeological features visible at the site are remnants of the buildings and roads built for a Civilian Conservation Corps (CCC) camp called Shreiber's Flat. To better locate the remains of the Kaweah Colonists' settlement of Advance, I employed a technique of superimposing a transparency of a historical photograph over a live view of the modern landscape called the Prince Principle, developed in the 1980s by Eugene Prince (Prince 1988). With

Figure 6.8. The ca. 1888 view of the tent village of Advance from figure 6.7 superimposed on the modern landscape. The hills and outcrops in the background were used to align and scale the two images.

a 35mm transparent slide of an archival photograph of Advance placed on the focusing plate of a 35mm single-lens reflex camera, I compared the view from several different points around the site. Landforms on the west side of the North Fork are clearly visible in both the old image and the modern landscape, but the angle and proportion of landmarks could not be aligned from any point on the site. This was not the location of Advance as photographed during the colony's days there.

Following written descriptions of the camp, I continued surveying the following spring south of a steep gulch and across the road from the marked "Advance Site." Again using the Prince Principle, in addition to digital photograph overlays capturing different angled views from four locations at the site, I concluded with little doubt that this was the site of Advance shown in the old photos (fig. 6.8).

With a volunteer crew, we began archaeological testing in the spring of 2005, with clearing and sampling in a dump on the steep slopes of the gulch north of Advance. On the slope where the heart of the tent colony grew, we conducted gradiometer survey, metal-detector survey with random sampling, systematic shovel testing, and hand excavation. The combined results of this site-level investigation showed low artifact density and a lack of any structural remains or features. All testing methods combined collected a total of 258 artifacts, 134 of which were nails. Dating evidence for the handful of diagnostic objects indicated that, however sparse, much of the assemblage represents colony-period occupation. There was an 1884 nickel. Sixty-three percent of the nails from the site were machine-cut, a manufacturing type that waned drastically in the last decade of the nineteenth century. This was definitely Advance, but where were the traces of the bustling camp? Some disturbance could certainly be attributed to the feet of grazing cattle and erosion from seasonal rains. These processes could definitely be expected to contribute to some mixing and stratigraphic disturbance at this site but not the wholesale disappearance of artifacts. Survey crews examined areas downslope from the camp's location, both in a seasonal drainage to the northeast and into the river valley to the west and north, but found no evidence of colony-related deposits apart from the intentional, and highly disturbed, trash dump at the bottom of the gulch across the road to the north.

The lack of structural remains and the small number of material finds at Advance prevented many of the kinds of spatial or statistical analyses, cross-mending studies, and economic and stylistic discussions typical of research efforts at richer historical archaeological sites. While frustrating to the archaeological mind, it is a problem that requires a creative approach to the sources—integrating those remains that are present with documentary sources to build a fuller picture of life at Advance, and to address the possible inconsistency in colonists' own claims suggested by the very scarcity of physical remains. I needed to reduce interpretation of many of the artifacts to a smaller scale—the level of individual artifacts, or small finds—that can support reasonable inferences about life at Advance. Monica Smith, studying the CCC camp at Bandelier National Monument (2001), and Diana DiPaolo Loren, considering dress practices in French colonial Louisiana (2003), have both demonstrated the utility of fully utilizing small finds from sparse deposits. At Advance, the most productive scale at which to interpret the smallest of personal and household objects was at the level of the personal body and the home tent.

By viewing the documentary record archaeologically, with a focus on the material construction of daily life at Advance, we can see how colonists

Figure 6.9. A September 1889 view of Advance residents and tents. The young people in the foreground are playing croquet, and the woman at the upper right is wearing dress-reform pantaloons. A 1961 handwritten description provided by former colonist A. E. Redstone on the copy in the Bancroft Library's collection reads "Mrs. Martin's tent is on the right. Al Redstone's is on the far left. In front of Martin tent with eyes shaded is Daisy Martin. To Daisy's right, holding croquett [sic] stick, her mother, Mrs. M. L. Martin." Kaweah Colony Views, BANC PIC 1905.2563. Courtesy of the Bancroft Library, University of California, Berkeley.

began to build their utopia. Even in this temporary location, high priority was placed on maintaining a sense of progress toward the goal. They imported wagonloads of goods to their temporary homes at Advance, installed a water distribution system of iron pipes to each tent, and planted ornamental gardens around their neighborhood. Institutions such as the school and band, and regular informal musical and artistic gatherings, began to organize social life along lines that were to be developed to fulfill the stated goals of Kaweah's organizational structure (fig. 6.9). Regular recitals, picnics, parties, and classes were part of a metropolitan world that otherwise existed in a largely imaginary realm. These frequent, rustic instantiations of the envisioned refined and civilized society reminded participants that one day they would have a proper meeting hall, a full orchestra, and a permanent school building. Their attempts to bring some standards of domesticity and comfort to Kaweah—rather than eschewing the comforts of home life—seem to be both a maintenance of habit and expectation for some members, as well as a deliberate effort to make the camps seem attractive and "civilized" to their supporters and prospective members. In the way Brook Farm's eclectic, homely buildings domesticated the Transcendentalists' radical ideas (Preucel 2006), the Kaweah colonists' familiar trappings of a cultured lifestyle could make their progressive economic and political ideas seem more feasible.

At Home in a Tent

Household members at Advance lived in canvas tents that belonged to each single individual, couple, or family and which served as the only private space for members living in the community. According to the colony by-laws, all "land, tools, material, crops, stores, and workshops" at the colony were to be collectively owned, while each resident member was entitled to a building site for "his own private use" as a tenant (Haskell 1889). Married couples shared a single membership fee, and therefore a single home lot. Tents were brought by members as private property but were not necessarily permanently held by specific individuals or families. Several tents changed ownership during their time at the colony as new members arrived and took the place of those who changed their minds about committing to the cause. Mr. and Mrs. Purdy and their two teenage children, Emma and Willie, moved to the colony from Colorado in June 1890 and bought the Theophilus's tent (KC 5 July 1890). Mrs. Purdy's daughter, Mrs. Boggs, and her family bought the Ashes' tent after that family returned to their home in Colorado (KC 14 June 1890). In the spring of 1891, George H. Stebbins sold his tent to Comrade Howard (George Stebbins to J. J. Martin, 27 March 1891, KCR) who was instructed to pay the seller $80 for the tent, stove, floor matting, and "wood on the premises" (J. J. Martin to William Howard, 27 March 1891, KCR). Stebbins was later paid $40 in cash and $40 in time-checks by the colony for its appraised value (Minutes of the Board of Trustees, 25 April 1891, KCR).

The Redstone family's tent at Advance is one of the few tents that were individually photographed at close range (fig. 6.10). It was also described in writing as a hub of social activity at Advance. An April 1890 *Kaweah Commonwealth* article about an evening's musical entertainment at the camp

Figure 6.10. The Redstone family tent at Advance, named "Alameda" after the family's previous city of residence in the San Francisco Bay area. Kaweah Colony Views, BANC PIC 1905.2561. Courtesy of the Bancroft Library, University of California, Berkeley.

reported that "entering into the canvas mansion of the Redstone family, you will doubtless find it crowded with thirty or forty people" (KC 26 April 1890), while Annie Haskell described the Redstone tent as "a stately edifice with two rooms and a half—very comfortable and cosy" (KC 4 October 1890). These reports give an impression of a relatively large canvas dwelling. However, photographs of the Redstone tent from the Bancroft Library collection show a more modest looking structure: a simple ridged canvas tent filled with furniture, in which it is a stretch of the imagination to picture 30 or 40 people standing, let alone singing and playing musical instruments. Did the *Kaweah Commonwealth*'s report exaggerate the number of attendees? Is this a different Redstone tent from the one described? Or did many spectators and participants actually join the festivities from outside the tent? If so, this blurs the boundary between inside and outside in defining the physical limits of a family's home, and is a departure from general interpretations of the Victorian distinctions between public and private space.

Archaeologists have emphasized the domestic unit—the house, its yard, and outside features—as a basic unit of study in our investigations of late nineteenth-century residential areas (e.g., Nassaney et al. 2001). The way Kaweah's colonists used space raises the possibility that this focus may be more an artifact of available maps, census, and property records, as well as our contemporary view of mainstream home life, than an accurate portrayal of how some communities occupied household places. Extended families at Kaweah, like those at the later Llano del Rio, interacted across multiple tents, shared laundry facilities, and dined with others in a communal kitchen. The community consisted, in a way, of several independently maintained but not mutually exclusive households within a larger, corporate household. Further interrogating the concept of private space inside nineteenth-century middle-class homes, we must assume that children and parents occupied closer quarters in their colony tents than even in small homes in their previous urban residences. In most Victorian homes, bedrooms were small chambers located in upstairs or back areas to preserve the privacy of the residents (Wright 1980:39). There are no descriptions of "bedrooms" or sleeping arrangements among the colonists' written reports of their homes at Advance, as propriety kept writers from exposing their most private activities in print. How family members of different ages and sexes arranged themselves for sleeping and dressing, within the boundaries of acceptable decorum, remains a question.

At Advance, many residents who had left middle-class city lifestyles idealized the labor of the working class, though certainly not their impoverished living conditions. These members could be heartened by the colony's desire to allow, even promote, individuality at the level of the home, maintaining secular American values of personal expression in distinct contrast with the fundamentally limiting domestic expectations for earlier nineteenth-century religious communalists such as the Shakers and Amana Inspirationists. In promotional literature Burnette Haskell asserts:

> Do not confuse this colony with any utopian communistic scheme; it is nothing of that kind; it is a co-operative colony. You will have fuller liberty there than you have now. The colony contemplates individual and not community homes,—the development of originality and differences of character rather than reducing all to a common level and self-same type. (C 24 November 1888:20)

Within their canvas walls, Kaweah Colony members were free to decorate according to their own tastes and abilities. For some, this meant bringing the material abundance they were used to in city life into their small, canvas colony homes. Popularly depicted Victorian domestic interior display before the 1890s involved eclectic collections of mass-produced, hand-crafted, and exotic objects in profusion around the public areas of the home—the decorative clutter we call bric-a-brac. As venues for social ceremony, parlors were decorated with special care according to complex aesthetic and symbolic standards. Erudition and worldliness were shown in reproductions of classical sculpture, natural history, and archaeological specimens (Mullins 2004:18). Exotic crafts from distant places lived alongside domesticity and morality, with handmade embroideries of religious passages and sentimental figurines. Natural objects dried, stuffed, and encased showed an appreciation for naturalistic forms and the desire to control and contain nature within a human dominion (Wright 1980:29).

An anonymous 1890 writer for the *Kaweah Commonwealth* shared that a home's decor did need to be pared down significantly at the colony, as

> here at Kaweah many of us have left the luxury of a comfortable and elegantly furnished house, replete with all the adornments appertaining to the fashionable society at any rate what the world calls the middle class, to come here and live in a tent. Before doing so most of these have disposed of personal properties of great commercial value and at financial sacrifices reserving only those small articles of little *avoirdupois* around which family ties are so entwined as to make it beyond their sympathetic powers to sever the connection. (KC 28 June 1890)

These "small articles" still consist of somewhat more than what modern campers might envision as necessities, as even though their current homes were made of canvas, the intentional community members of the Kaweah Colony planned for a permanent settlement in their valley. Shortly after arriving at the colony grounds, Anna Haskell wrote of Mr. and Mrs. Elford's tent that

> I felt as if I had been ushered into some snug New England home; two rooms, a kitchen and dining room in one, the other being the

sitting and bed room. The floors are carpeted and decorated with home-made rugs which look so cosy and the walls are lined with pretty carpet which seems like tapestry; there are pictures, baskets and all those little things which make up a house. The white spread bed, rocking chairs, sewing machine, all the household *Penates* that make home are here. (KC 4 October 1890)

Later that year, the report of a fire in "Mrs. Martin's tent" enumerated as its casualties an engraved silver urn "of very elegant and costly design," marble-topped bedroom furniture, a small personal library, and a working miniature stove that belonged to Martin's daughter, Daisy (KC 28 June 1890).

Unlike Martin and the Elfords, not all families at the colony had left behind an enviably comfortable Victorian home to join the colony and not all had one to return to later if the experiment failed. Annie Haskell's 10 January 1891 "Reflections" point to nuances in the material lives of "middle-class" women living in San Francisco through the late 1880s. She writes that

we lived in the city, some of us, before we came here;—the beautiful city with its theatres (which we couldn't afford,) with its gorgeous shop windows bedecked with wonderful silks and laces and plumes (we looked and sighed,) with its magnificent saloons to entice and destroy; with its thousand and one attractions and beauties, but they were for the rich. (KC 10 January 1891)

Annie Haskell wasn't writing from a working-class perspective but as the wife of a lawyer and activist newspaper editor whose experience of middle-class life in San Francisco was one of unfulfilled social and material aspirations. Striving to acquire indicators of success and belonging was part of the daily experience of women in Annie's circle, and yet the economic uncertainty of her life made this striving an exhausting routine rife with opportunities for failure. Her words remind readers that we can't interpret the material worlds of the Kaweah colonists, even those with marble-topped bedroom furniture, as unambiguous representations of either aspiration or resistance to Victorian domesticity (Wood 2004; Wilkie and Howlett 2006; Beaudry 2004).

Further, only a small number of members' tent homes are explicitly described as examples of comfort and refinement in the *Kaweah Common-wealth*'s pages. The publication's silence about other residents' domestic material comfort is just as informative. While certain homes were offered up as examples of successfully overcoming the general sacrifice of moving to Kaweah, those with less were thus constantly reminded of their own sacrifices, choices, and comparative disadvantage. While distant readers would have been impressed by the colonists' reports of comfort, the same reports may have been a source of discontent for local readers with fewer resources. The commitment to individual family autonomy at the colony exposed a potential weakness in the colonists' cooperative plan. Families who built and furnished their private tent homes more comfortably than their neighbors did drew praise and envy in equal measure, and highlighted the stubborn economic distinctions that seemingly couldn't be erased even in an ostensibly egalitarian experiment. Objects that families brought to furnish their colony homes were emblematic of the ideals and standards they were not willing to part with after joining the cooperative. Many of these objects' primary importance was not practical but aspirational. Musical instruments, books, and art supplies that are frequently mentioned as part of weekly routines at the colony likely signified education, the ability to use time for leisure activities, and the desire to use that leisure time in intellectual and artistic pursuits. As in urban domestic parlors (Mullins 2004), objects of symbolic significance communicated these values and aspirations to visitors and residents of Advance's tents. The potential meanings of such objects to different observers are complex, however. Some of Kaweah's residents most likely experienced ambivalence toward the silver urns and tapestry-like rugs in their midst, as those objects must have simultaneously communicated basic domestic comfort and inescapable inequality.

Archaeological testing and excavation at Advance found little evidence of the types of decorative household items reported in the colony newspapers' accounts of comfortable tent homes. In truth, furniture and knickknacks were unlikely to have been discarded, even if damaged, after accompanying their owners on the days-long journey to Kaweah. What we are left with, then, are accidentally lost traces of household display. Metal-detector survey at Advance in June 2005 did recover a small iron key, suited to a lock from a household chest or document box (fig. 6.11). Within the context

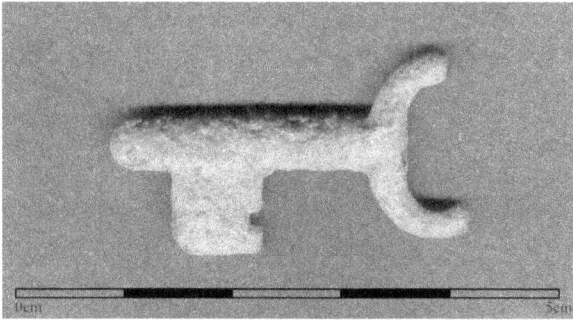

Figure 6.11. A key found by archaeologists near 180N 170E at Advance. Photo by author, 2007.

of a community for whom group cooperation and equal distribution of resources were paramount, the act of locking away one's private property suggests an individual's mistrust of his or her comrades, or the desire to keep something of personal value hidden from them lest it damage one's reputation as a member of the group. In any case, locks and keys where the only neighbors for several miles were supposed to be brothers and sisters in a common cause imply rips in the fabric of a community. Documentary evidence supports the interpretation that there may have been disunity and inequality in material property ownership at Kaweah. Colony policy ensured that all members shared equally in community property, with each single member or family paying the same membership fee, possessing a share, and, ideally, enjoying equal access to opportunity. Preexisting inequalities in wealth, though, were carried into the colony, as its policy did not extend to reach privately owned property or wealth except for that which was given to the colony in exchange for membership.

It was only after the colony's demise that Burnette Haskell printed a criticism of inequalities among personal property in the colony. In his description of the petty bickering and disorganization in many of their attempts to organize social institutions and activities, he writes, "People who had extra supplies bought with their private means brought them in closed boxes marked 'furniture,' and consumed them in secret for fear of adverse comment" (Haskell 1891:13). The 19 November 1891 installment of a multi-issue expose on the Kaweah Colony in the *Visalia Weekly Delta* accused the Martin family of hoarding canned meat, fruit, and milk under the floor of their tent, provisions that were only revealed in the smoking wreckage after the tent burned in June 1890.

Dining in Camp

According to the rules of genteel Victorian dining practices, individuality, restraint, and refinement were molded into matched sets of luncheon plates and celery salts, as personal place settings guided the manners of those who sat to dine. Archaeologist Robert Fitts remarks, "Following the proper manners while using these forms displayed one's knowledge of genteel etiquette and one's place in society. For the middle class, the general principles of segmented dining and the proper use of specialized vessels would have been a prerequisite for social success" (2002:8). Of course, neither the dishes (Scott 1997; Wilkie 1996, 2003; Fitts 2002) nor the practices (Praetzellis and Praetzellis 2001) necessarily indicated unnuanced participation in genteel dinners or teas. Food choices and dining practices are archaeologically visible as subject to socially constructed taste and meaning beyond basic nutrition (Praetzellis 2004). Food preparation and consumption at the Kaweah Colony were just as socially constructed and symbolic as in private, middle-class homes of the late nineteenth century, but they took a different form and referred to some distinctly different values. The colony dining room and its workers sought to move meals from the private table into the public sphere. At shared meals, members could gather to reinforce community bonds and recognize the labor of those who grew, canned, transported, and cooked the camp's food supplies. The simple recipes of regular daily fare, usually necessitated by the limited foodstuffs available to the cooking staff, celebrated and reinforced members' sense of pioneering spirit. At the same time, rules of etiquette were not suspended in the relatively rough surroundings, and, especially in the case of the children's dining room, group meals offered the opportunity for diners to learn and display high standards of deportment fitting the egalitarian, yet civilized, society they worked to build.

The tiny archaeological ceramic collection from Advance contains the remains of, at most, seven vessels from which to infer the dining practices of the site's residents. Even within these few vessels, however, the presence of three porcelain tableware fragments—one with a mold-relief floral pattern, one plain, and one banded—suggests that a variety of different decorative patterns were used at Advance. Porcelain, also, is a delicate material to incorporate into daily life in a tent camp, and its presence may suggest the desire to maintain a certain level of refinement and elegance at mealtimes. It is unclear if the ceramics recovered from Advance were used in the communal dining room or in the private homes of those residents who chose to cook their own meals.

Preparing meals for one's own family or for the community kitchen communicated and reinforced priorities of privacy and self-interest or of cooperation at the local scale. Cooking one's own meals required that a household own a stove and cookware, and could afford basic foodstuffs. Meals in the dining room were less costly—but were still not free to members. The published cost of meals for resident adult members at the colony restaurants varied between 10 cents and 20 cents per meal in 1889 and 1890 (C 1 August 1889; KC 15 February 1890). Meals for children were 5 cents as of October 1890 (KC 11 October 1890). An 1884 nickel recovered from Level 2 of Unit 8 represents the value of one child's meal, and reminds us in concrete terms that the colony's effort to replace the mainstream cash economy with the direct exchange of labor for goods and services was a work in progress. A system of time-checks had been devised by which members could pay their membership dues or trade the value of their labor for goods and services at the camps in denominations of 200, 1,000, and 5,000 minutes. However, cash was still the standard for expressing value, and was accepted at the colony alongside time-checks.

Despite the combined efforts of growing vegetable gardens, herding cattle and sometimes goats, hunting quail and deer, and preserving wild and local orchard fruit, maintaining a consistent food supply at all the colony camps was an ongoing challenge. Variable reporting of food quality and availability across different archival sources shows how colonists attempted to manage external perception of their well-being through their own publications. A March 1889 letter from young Daisy Martin to her father, the colony secretary in Visalia, reports that on a visit to the East Branch camp she had a glass of "real milk" (Advance, 24 March 1889, J. J. Martin Papers). Daisy's mention of this as a special event suggests that the youngster did not usually have access to fresh milk, and that her family, one of the most affluent of the community, had regular supplies of only canned milk. A 15

July 1891 letter from a resident colonist (possibly Haskell) to J. J. Martin in Visalia complains that

> we are entirely out of supplies of every kind here. They must also be entirely out at Atwell's of flour, sugar, and bacon. We had sent an order to Pogue on Saturday last for flour by Sam Bellah; had instructed Tousley when he brought up the team from Exeter with the Cable to fill out his load at Pogues with flour; Pogue refused to deliver the flour without a written order claiming that Bellah had not left him any on Saturday; so the team came up half loaded and they are without grub at the Mill; we have to keep the teams moving all the time and it is this idiotic disobedience and forgetfullness [sic] that causes all of our trouble. The stage absolutely must load itself down with flour, bacon, and whatever else Pogue has this trip; keep the picknicers [sic] off of the stage this trip and make Bellah load on all he can. (Minutes of the Board of Trustees, KCR)

In this case, at least, it appears that scarcity of some food resources on the colony grounds was a result of poor management and miscommunication more than it was of financial need, though Pogue's (a neighboring rancher and business owner) reticence to send flour to the camp may reflect the colony's failure to pay past bills. Complaints of scarcity were echoed in William Christie's 9 October 1891 letter, signed by 23 other resident colonists, to Secretary J. J. Martin, which reports that

> there are no supplies of any kind in the store. We are all out of tea, coffee, sugar, salt, baking powder, yeast, bacon, etc, and most of us are out of flower [sic] and meal as well. A few vegetables from the garden is the sole food of some of us, and all of us will soon be in the same state. (Kaweah Colony 1891)

When lacking other food sources, beans filled in the gaps in colonists' daily diets. Philip Winser (1931:90) recalls asking stage driver Frank Bishop about the local menu upon his arrival in February 1891, to which the driver replied, "Strawberries, generally." Winser later learned, to his disappointment, that this vernacular term actually referred to a pink-and-white bean. After a few months at the colony, Winser wrote to an acquaintance, John Orme, in England that "We are vegetarians as a rule, but I have not found the altered diet has had anything but a good effect on me" (13 May 1891, printed in Martin n.d., Section 8:3). This vegetarianism was likely not by conscious decision but by a lack of availability of regular meat.

Not surprisingly, the *Kaweah Commonwealth*'s food-related reporting tended to focus on small successes and colonists' resourcefulness, sometimes specifically denying actual shortages. Creative use of local produce was rewarded with mention in the "Colony Notes," as when Mrs. Taylor's summer squash fritters "created a sensation" at the Kaweah restaurant (KC 18 July 1891). At an ad hoc potluck-style Thanksgiving dinner in 1891, "there was no turkey, etc., but the plain provisions were worked up into such attractive forms that no one wished for anything better" (KC 5 December 1891). Even if food supplies were scarce at Advance, it is still noteworthy that archaeological testing at the site recovered little evidence of food containers and no food remains. Colonists are documented to have brought canned milk, corned beef, baking powder, oysters, and sardines to the site, in addition to the cans and jars of fruit produced by their own labors. Occasional beef, chicken, and fish dinners undoubtedly produced some bones. However, only one fragment of a milk-glass canning jar lid, one rim fragment likely from a commercial "jelly glass" (a container sold with a food product inside, designed for reuse as a drinking glass), and one rolled sheet-metal fragment that resembles a food can seam indicate possible food storage at Advance. There were no faunal remains. In contrast, archaeologists at site of the ca. 1914–1918 Llano del Rio Cooperative Colony in Los Angeles County found the remains of 257 food cans at 77 dwelling pads, and 57 other food storage containers such as canning jars and crocks at 39 dwelling pads (Van Bueren and Hupp 2000:75). Considered by Van Bueren and Hupp to be a relatively low incidence, these numbers place the paucity of such remains from the living areas at Advance in stark contrast.

So the question arises, where are the food remains from Advance? As the dining hall was located in the midst of several domestic tents (KC 5 April 1890), the remains of meals and tableware would not be physically far removed from individual families' domestic waste. Even if they were not cooking at home, members ate at Advance. The topography of the site provides one possible explanation. The steep gulch between Advance and Glen Park provided a convenient solution for colonists' trash disposal needs, and testing of the existing dump in the gulch did record ceramic, glass, and metal artifacts likely associated with the colony occupation intermixed with later twentieth-century refuse. Were the colonists at Advance very tidy and consistently cleaned the site of trash? We do not have documentary records about site cleaning at this location, though a later note from Redstone Park indicates that colonists there (many of whom previously lived at Advance) were not excessively fastidious about keeping trash out of sight: "there are not nearly so many tin cans around since the goat has been about" (KC February 1892). Of course, this latter quote comes from a period near the very end of the colony's lifespan, when fewer outside visitors may have come to evaluate the experiment than when Advance was the headquarters in more optimistic days. In the interest of image management, Advance's residents may well have kept a very clean "house" much of the time, so that outside reporters, prospective members, and concerned friends and visiting family would encounter pleasant surroundings.

Dismantling Advance

From food containers to tableware to building materials, why was there so little left behind by between 20 and 90 people living on a site for four years? Was the colony settlement at Advance neither as extensive nor as densely occupied as the reports in the *Commonwealth* and *Kaweah Commonwealth* led readers to believe? Did descriptions in the colony's newspapers exaggerate the level of activity, residence, development, and stability in the camp with the hope of inspiring greater nonresident membership and financial support?

As with the rest of the items in their newspapers, the "Colony Notes" were carefully constructed to reflect favorably on residents' daily lives at Kaweah. Both commonplace details, like frequent mentions of events such as "Social dances came off at the dining hall on Tuesday and Thursday evenings" (KC 29 March 1890), and more exciting news like "A fire occurred in the laundry department on Thursday the 20th. The prompt action of the fire department prevented much damage" (KC 22 March 1890), speak of success and progress. Social dances indicate a surplus of leisure time, and enough residents to participate in such entertainments. Simply having a laundry department and fire department is evidence of progress at the colony—demonstrating to readers that their experiment was not just a temporary camping trip but an earnest attempt to construct a fully functioning city. In their brevity, these short notices may not present all relevant information about colony life. For example, on 15 November 1890 the "Colony Notes" mentioned simply that "Advance has a very deserted appearance now" (KC 15 November 1890). Part of Annie Haskell's diary entry from the very same day reads: "This morning we went up to Advance—on business—hay + provisions—couldn't get the last—it looks pretty deserted up there, but still there are a number of tents remaining. I went in to see the Evans girls. Jennie was hungry as usual. said they had nothing but beans + flour." The "Colony Notes" would never have mentioned the Evans's girls' hunger; indeed, a later note in the 15 November paper reads: "A beef was killed at Kaweah on Monday, and we all said grace before meat" (KC 15 November 1890). Integrating these newspapers' reports with the information from other sources can give a more detailed picture of daily realities of colony life as experienced by those who did not write the news.

Documentary evidence suggests that the colonists experienced economic difficulty beginning in the fall of 1890 and lasting through to the demise of the colony in the spring of 1892. Limited access to food and household goods would encourage residents to conserve those resources at hand—potentially reusing household goods past a point when, if in the city, they might otherwise dispose of them. Beverage bottles could have been reused or even collected for recovering the deposit. Chipped ceramics may have remained on the meal table—or even put away in favor of cheaper, more durable enamelware. Dropped toys, buttons, and small personal objects would have been searched for, recovered, and reused. While their newspapers were promoting their successes to outside readers, colonists were developing different practical perspectives toward material value and waste during their time at Advance.

Three clothing buttons—one white ceramic "Prosser," one metal, and one hard rubber—were the only artifacts found at Advance that offered insight into colonists' dress and bodily adornment. If these modest buttons were lost from clothing still in use, they would have created a mild inconvenience for the wearer. The loss of a more ornate, decorative button was probably felt more sorely at Kaweah, as at least in one instance a member wanted to make sure one was reunited with the owner. "Found—A gold and pearl Collar Button. Owner may obtain same by applying at the print-ing office" (KC 4 October 1890). Dearer personal items lost at the camps were also sought by their owners. In August 1890, Mrs. Frost, who lived in a "canvas villa" at Glen Park (KC 3 May 1890), lost two diamond rings at the colony bathing place (KC 16 August 1890). Anna Haskell lost a silver pin at the colony later that year (KC 11 October 1890). These pieces of jewelry can be considered to have held more broadly recognizable mon-etary, decorative, and perhaps sentimental value within and outside of the colony than a few buttons, but near the last days of colonists' occupation even found buttons might have been valued articles.

In their deliberate progression toward the envisioned city at Kaweah, colonists at Advance packed away their tent homes and removed their im-provements to the site when they relocated to Kaweah in the autumn of 1890. The ornamental plants were dug out of the ground and taken to the Kaweah town site for replanting (KC 18 October 1890). The water pipes were removed from their trenches and taken to be used for linking a proposed reservoir to new residences at Kaweah (KC 27 January 1891). Colonists who had given much to risk their future with this communal experiment and condensed their worldly possessions into a wagonload of goods may understandably have scoured the site for all portable goods of any imaginable value as they dismantled their tents and packed their wag-ons once again.

Combined results of magnetometer survey, excavation, and metal-detec-tor survey support this interpretation. Linear magnetic anomalies recorded in March and October 2005 that correspond to visible trenches in photo-graphs of Advance may indicate the former location of the pipe, but exca-vation across the area of the anomaly showed that no actual pipe remains. The broken threaded end of an iron pipe found during metal-detector sur-vey in June 2006 also hints at the activity of stripping pipe, during which some workers may have cared more about removing the metal from the ground than preserving its integrity for future use. These archaeological traces show the shadow of improvements left after colony members erased their former home from view (fig. 6.12).

The scatter of machine-cut nails over the areas of Advance surveyed with metal-detector and shovel-testing programs could well represent the remains of this last activity of deconstruction and erasure at the site. A total

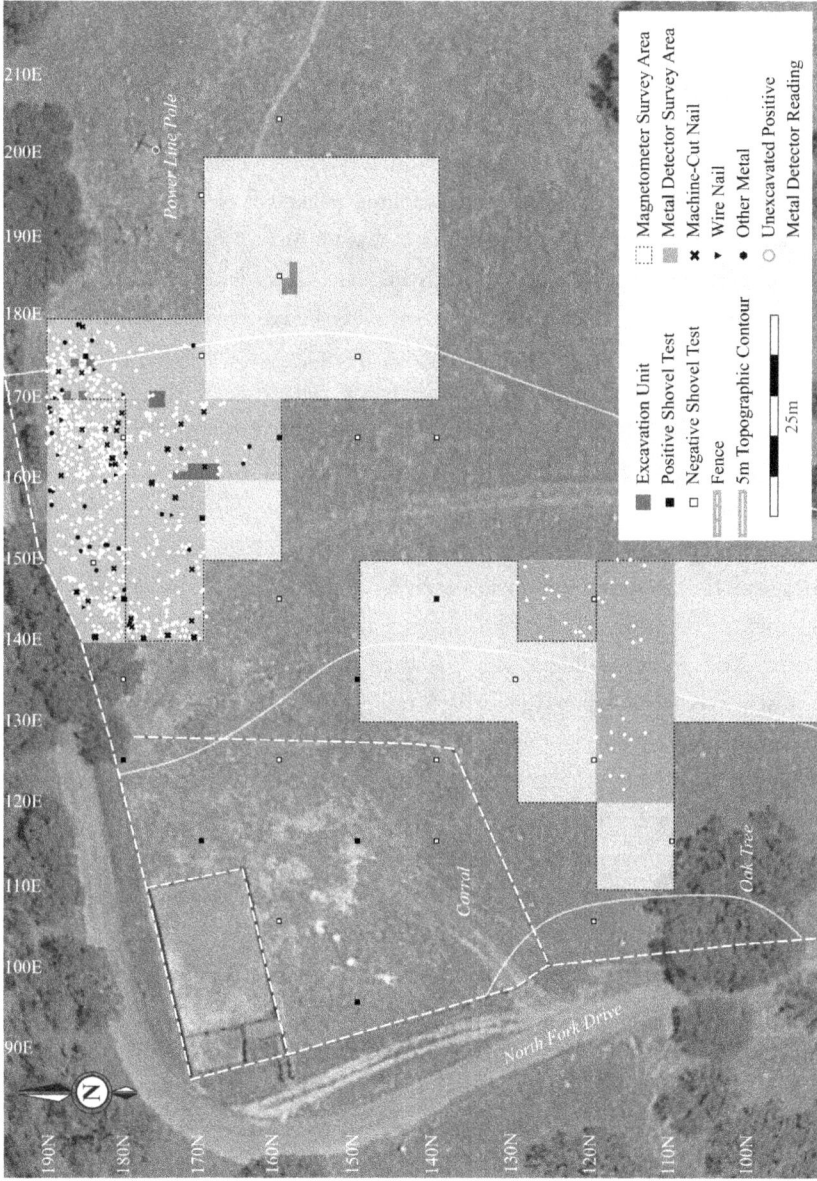

Figure 6.12. Overview map of archaeological survey and metal detector findings at Advance. Base aerial photo 2014, courtesy of Google Earth.

of 93 machine-cut nail fragments representing a minimum of 66 individual nails were recovered from the area formerly occupied by domestic tents. As 40 (41 percent) of the 98 artifacts recovered through metal-detector survey were machine-cut nails or fragments, and only a 10 percent sample of all positive metal-detector readings were randomly selected for excavation by shovel probe, there is a strong possibility that a similar proportion of the 604 unexcavated positive metal-detector readings are machine-cut nails or nail fragments. Among the 93 metal artifacts recovered from the nine excavated units at Advance, 45 (48 percent) are machine-cut nails or nail fragments, comprising one-third of the total assemblage from the excavated units. It is difficult to imagine the surface of Advance as littered with hundreds of nails and nail fragments while colonists lived there, with children running barefoot around the site (Daisy Martin to J. J. Martin, 17 June 1889, J. J. Martin Papers). Instead, the scatter of nails recorded at Advance more likely consists of nails removed from tent platforms, frames, and other temporary structures when they were dismantled through the autumn of 1890 to be removed to the new colony town of Kaweah. The majority of machine-cut nails from all survey and excavation activities are bent or broken, with only 11 specimens showing no evidence of use. The presence of a small number of unused nails in a scatter of bent and broken ones left largely by demolition activity is not incongruous. As they were tearing down their tents, colonists packed their belongings into trunks and shipping crates for the move. Some were traveling only as far as the Kaweah town site, while others packed to travel to Atwell's Mill or to leave the colony entirely. In the bustle of preparation as residents worked to pack and nail closed their crates for the journey, it is not a stretch to suggest that a few complete, unbent nails could have fallen and been left behind.

While abandoning Advance, families worked in their individual interest to collect and protect their own possessions. They also participated in the collective movement to push Kaweah's story forward—erasing the temporary story of a strong start and hard ending at Advance and pushing attention toward their new permanent home. This process of intentional site removal can be an informative case for the archaeological study of site abandonment in other contexts. As with Helaine Silverman's (1991) consideration of sparse domestic debris at the Nasca ceremonial pilgrimage center of Cahuachi, the site of Advance highlights the importance of deliberate dismantling as part of the social life of a residential location. Removing the tents, platforms, and pipes from Advance was definitely an economic necessity for those carrying on to the Kaweah town site, but it was also a way that members could assure their real settlement and its remains didn't contradict what they had reported in the *Kaweah Commonwealth*. Advance would not be left in ruins as a reminder of failed civilization for future observers, as Aldous Huxley later likened the scattered ruins of Llano del Rio to the plaintive vision of Shelley's *Ozymandias* (Klein 2001).

Focusing through the broadest scale of landscape, to household, to the level of the individual object we can see three different stories emerging about the Kaweah Co-operative Commonwealth. Burnette Haskell, John Redstone, J. J. Martin, and their comrades led dozens of hopeful socialists into a wild and challenging landscape to build their envisioned society. In the valley of the North Fork of the Kaweah River, visitors can still drive along road alignments first blasted by colony crews and hammered through rock by colony hands. At this scale, collective labor was celebrated in creating the road, the camps, and the mill that were planned to support a cooperative future, and in taming their corner of the vast Sierra wilderness into a picturesque park. Every action of colony labor can be considered part of a larger performance intended to display and reinforce unity in the group and to encourage outside members to maintain support. The results of this labor—whether a road, garden, or pamphlet—were held up as representations of the benefit of cooperation. Members reinforced their commitment to the group by their contribution of physical labor and activity, or resisted by withholding labor or acting in what they perceived to be their own interests. Difficulties in progress are visible in letters between trustees, and were built into the changing grade of sections along the road, but laborers overcame obstacles to achieve goals that were clear and shared. More philosophical and social tensions arose within the village of Advance at the level of the individual tent household and community dining services. Families who arrived at Advance with more wealth than others were not expected to relinquish that wealth to the collective, nor were they expected to live according to identical standards as their less affluent neighbors. Members' accounts of life in the camp share an enthusiasm for making do in their rustic surroundings but also maintaining a measure of comfort in their homes that required wagonloads of furniture and decor, musical instruments and small libraries, and all the small trappings of cultured domestic life. Reports from the dining hall show a collectivization of the same expectations. With glowing reports of cooks' resourcefulness under the pressure of limited supplies, the colonists laud each other's efforts to celebrate mainstream holidays like Thanksgiving and Christmas with as much bounty as they could muster. Rather than questioning the materialistic root of these holidays and of domestic interior display, the colonists whose voices are preserved in print strove to show how they could beat the competitive mainstream at its own game through cooperation. This optimistic but deeply contradictory view, constructed from personal accounts and colony newspaper reports, turns bleak at an archaeological level. There are no lasting traces of domestic comfort or material abundance at Advance. Instead, the sparse scatter of artifacts evidences the difficulties that colonists encountered when facing economic hardship and internal disparity.

After Kaweah: Nests and Webs of Colony Community

After a visit to the growing Kaweah Colony in April 1889, Burnette Haskell observed that although "there is work to do in the way of harmony and fraternity" (C 24 April 1889), colonists were beginning to let go of the competitive sentiments of their previous lives. Haskell and his contemporaries observed clearly, as we do now, that community building is a process that consists as much of building new habits and ways of relating as it does of releasing (or repressing) old ones. Members did not escape the uncertainties and unrest of urban life to an egalitarian utopia but to a new set of uncertainties, inequalities, and struggles intrinsic to the process of community building. Communities formed within the community at the Kaweah Colony as social dynamics developed, as homes were built, and as varied members joined the resident population. Separate camps, separate residential areas within the camps, occupational groups such as road workers, leisure activity groups such as the band, and age-related categories such as school children were all subcommunities with changing membership and different characteristics. As such, a full expression of cooperation was never realized at Kaweah, as members struggled daily to contribute meaningfully to the collective while providing for their own and their family's

needs. Further, they did not remove themselves from the political and economic discourse of late nineteenth-century America by moving to Kaweah;
rather, they continued to participate in a broader milieu of radicalism and
reform. Members contributed to a broader movement in which communal efforts and social reformers across the nation advocated change, and
extended their communal landscape far outside of the North Fork valley.

The most broadly overlapping social movement with the Kaweah Cooperative Commonwealth was the network of Nationalist clubs that grew
throughout the United States following the publication of Edward Bellamy's *Looking Backward* in 1888. Within a few years after its publication, more than 150 Nationalist Clubs had formed in 27 states (Passet
2005:309). Colony members established Nationalist clubs at Advance
and Avalon in late 1889 (C 1 November 1889), and their *Commonwealth*
advertised clubs in New York, Maryland, Ohio, Massachusetts, Kansas, Illinois, Connecticut, Minnesota, Michigan, Pennsylvania, New Hampshire,
Washington, and California (C 1 September 1889).

In the last year of the colony, the residents at Atwell's Mill resolved to
form a branch of the Farmers' Alliance at Kaweah (KC 15 August 1891),
joining the tradition of the Grange movement and allying with rural, agrarian populists. Comrades Weybright, Howard, and Smith planned to represent the growing group at a county convention in early 1892 (KC January
1892).

Members of socialist, utopian, and intentional communities were sometimes "serial" participants, moving from one colony to another as their relationships and interests changed, or as colonies rose and fell. Members of
the Kaweah Colony participated in this larger movement of intentional
communities and socialist discourse, and, for many, their time on the
North Fork was only one episode in a career of communalism. Louis Tox-
ward, who was elected to membership in the Kaweah Colony in 1889 (C 1
December 1889), traveled from the Puget Sound Co-operative Colony, an
experiment born out of Seattle's labor unrest (LeWarne 1995), to Kaweah
in April 1890 (KC 26 April 1890). While a member of Kaweah, George
Speed visited the Nehalem Valley Cooperative Colony (also known as the
Columbia Cooperative Colony) at Mist, Oregon, in the autumn of 1889
(KC 8 March 1890). One of the Nehalem Colony's founders, H. E. Girard,
wrote in both promotion and solidarity to the *Kaweah Commonwealth*:

"Extend the congratulations of the Nehalem cranks and dynamiters to the cranks and dynamiters of Kaweah, and, as you say, let us come a little closer together. We are doing the same work and should be in a manner related to each other" (KC 30 August 1890). Similar in structure and goals to the Kaweah Colony, the Nehalem Valley Cooperative Colony was formed in 1886 at a camp overlooking the Nehalem River in Mist, Oregon. The group aimed to provide employment and homes supported by a timber-based economy for up to 50 members able to pay the $500 fee (Miller 1990:421; C 1 December 1889). After leaving Kaweah, some colony members joined other existing colonies or attempted to start their own. Dr. H. S. Hubbard founded a cooperative colony near Santa Monica, California (KC 25 October 1890), that attracted fellow Kaweah members, the Miles family, to follow (KC 27 September 1890). In July 1891, sometimes-resident member Harry Hambly was reported by nonresident member Frank Jackson to have joined the Koreshan home in San Francisco (KC 25 July 1891), a short-lived ca. 1890–1891 branch of Dr. Cyrus Teed's spiritualist group whose largest community was in Estero, Florida (Landing 1997:262). M. A. Hunter, who had been the local editor of the *Kaweah Commonwealth* until a disagreement with Burnette Haskell in April 1890, left the colony in January 1891 to "join his fortunes with the Mrs. Washburn colony at San Jose" (KC 3 January 1891). After leaving Kaweah, W. B. Hunter wrote back to his comrades from Riverside, California, expressing his longing to return to the colony but also planning to join the Topolobampo Colony (KC February 1892). The brainchild of civil engineer and reform enthusiast Albert Kimsey Owen, the Credit Foncier of Sinaloa in Topolobampo, Mexico, was designed by its founder to provide a cosmopolitan city and major shipping port with railroad access reaching across the United States. Welcoming the first settlers in 1886, Owen and his followers continued their efforts to attract members and build a planned city displaying Moorish architecture until 1894 (Robertson 1947).

Former nonresident Kaweah member J. G. Wright was also a friend of Colorado Cooperative Company founder B. L. Smith. The Colorado experiment included an article on the third page of its February 1896 issue of the *Altrurian* (a name repeated in cooperative publications across the nation) titled "Lessons on Keweah [*sic*]," in which the reasons for the Kaweah Colony's failure are presented not as failures of the socialist ideal but of a particular group of people who were themselves unsuited to real-ize it. Even in seeming failure, the Kaweah Colony continued to inspire subsequent communities. The Colorado Cooperative experiment appears from its own publication to have been similar in many ways to Kaweah's, with a shared goal requiring long hours of heavy labor (in Colorado, a water supply ditch rather than a logging road) and commitment to pursuing arts and literacy in the members' leisure time (Clark 2001:67). Differences in their organization show a desire to avoid some of the pitfalls of Kaweah's experience. The Colorado group maintained a corporate structure overseen by an elected board of directors, and kept their belief in private ownership of land. Their motto, "Equity, Truth, and Fraternity," appears to be their own revision of the French revolutionary "Liberty, Equality, Fraternity," in which truth outweighed the importance of liberty. Perhaps their appraisal of Kaweah's experience led to the conclusion that too much liberty could be disruptive to fraternity, and truth was essential to maintaining equality when difficulties arose.

Although no living memories can attest to the achievements and lessons from the Kaweah Colony's short years in California, members' voices live on in their written words. Some left bitter and regretful memoirs, but some maintained a fervor against the competitive capitalist system that contin-ued to fuel forceful writing. For decades after leaving the colony, cofounder J. J. Martin and many of his former comrades believed that the U.S. gov-ernment owed them compensation for their labor and expense in building their road, which after most colonists left their camps became the public access route to Sequoia National Park. The single enduring representation of their collective effort, the Colony Mill Road, had been appropriated by the very mainstream government whose policies the colonists had hoped to reform. Martin continued to write of what he perceived as the government's conspiracy to destroy the Kaweah Colony, and on the topic of labor and co-operation in general. In 1936, he submitted a copy of his manuscript "The Curse of Capitalism" to prolific author and activist Upton Sinclair for his consideration. The work remains unpublished, but interested future read-ers can find a copy among Martin's papers in the collections of the Bancroft Library at the University of California, Berkeley.

As a modern researcher it is not easy to want to champion the cause of an organization whose official policies excluded Chinese workers and whose newspaper nameplate motto, "Men Made Here," so blatantly ignored the contributions of female workers. Indeed, the story told here of the Kaweah Colony can easily read as a sad tale of woe, of hopeless delusion and inevitable failure. But in telling this seeming cautionary tale, we must reveal one of our own. Historical archaeological perspectives can describe the different ways that intentional communities simultaneously drew strength, succeeded, and fell down at different scales of action during their attempts to reform society. By the very nature of our discipline, these communities exist in the past tense. With the exception of members of the modern Mormon church and a few living Shakers at Sabbathday Lake, Maine, the groups discussed in this volume have all been transformed into memories and museums. But the ideological thread of intentional community, which has been continuously woven through the history of American settlement and expansion, extends unbroken into our present. Intentional communities exist today, are formed according to principles relevant to modern society, and offer alternatives to institutionalized systems whose inequities and injustices many of us are so inured to as to be blind to the possibility of change. When we contribute to the voices telling past groups' stories for modern listeners, when we emphasize the past-tense nature of intentional communities, how do we contribute to their ongoing failure as attempts to change a society that has still not achieved many of the goals envisioned by hopeful community visionaries over two centuries? Can we, instead, join a different conversation? The following chapter investigates the various ways archaeological and historical representations portray past communities, and how the work of current and future researchers might transform the conversation from a bemused appreciation of history's quirks into a nuanced acknowledgment of a living lineage of radicalism and activism.

7

———★———

REMAKING COMMUNITIES

Concluding Thoughts

> The power to control the production of history is not necessarily a visible form of power, yet it is no less powerful than a political crusade, a riot, a strike.
>
> Stahlgren and Stottman 2007:131

Visiting Communities

In 1770, Moravians at Bethabara, North Carolina, erected a marker commemorating the location of a cabin used by their 1753 settlement. Replaced in 1806, this marker was the first in an array of standing testaments to the group's growth in the region and significance in building its social and economic base (South 1965:46). A little more than two centuries later, the Bethabara Historic District was nominated for National Historic Landmark status, and archaeological studies inform the public interpretation of the village's past industries (Clauser 1995). Today, visitors can see costumed interpreters in a reconstructed village, and the faithful can worship in the restored 1788 Moravian church. North Carolina's Moravians may have been early to recognize the historical import of their community, but they weren't alone in drawing public attention to their society. Shaker villages welcomed visitors with food and lodging, carefully maintaining their own separation from worldly guests while demonstrating the virtues of their lifestyle to potential converts. In the latter half of the nineteenth century, visiting Shaker villages became more popular with tourists than with the future faithful. Foodways historian Ruth Ann Murray writes of the New York Shakers' increased favor that "once persecuted, their farming, industry, and food were held up as models of perfection. Once dogged and driven out of towns by vengeful, angry, and sometimes dangerous mobs, their villages were now mobbed by tourists and writers who, along with their readers, could not get enough of them" (Murray 2012:91). Through this time Shaker village resident and recruitment numbers were also in irreversible decline. What was once a radical sect that divided families and overtook local economies was no longer perceived as a social and economic competitor. So began the long process of co-opting Shaker images into a narrative that emphasized their overlap with mainstream American history and values, rather than foregrounding the multiple ways intentional communities act to critique the cultural undergirdings of family structures, gender roles, and capitalist values.

Today there are dozens of American historical intentional community sites that welcome visitors, ranging in scale from isolated historical plaques like that marking Icaria-Speranza near Cloverdale, California, to fully staffed village museums like Canterbury Shaker Village in New Hampshire and Old Salem in North Carolina. Posters created by artist Katherine Milhous for the Work Projects Administration's Federal Art Project, a New Deal–era program that was itself somewhat utopian in its noble impulse and vision, encouraged tourists to visit Ephrata, Pennsylvania, in the late 1930s (fig. 7.1). But what do we learn from watching a candle-making demonstration at Ephrata Cloister, Pennsylvania, or in the Shaker Village of Pleasant Hill, Kentucky? That people in the eighteenth and nineteenth centuries made candles, and that despite their philosophical differences maybe Shakers and Ephratans weren't too different from our ancestors after all? Describing the ca. 1800 Winkler bakery at Old Salem, Gerald and Patricia Gutek write, "Bread is still being baked in the wood-fired domed brick bake oven attached to the south side of the building. Eighteenth-century baking processes are used to produce European-style breads, cakes, and cookies. The aroma of fresh-baked bread permeates the restored area" (1998:28). As well there is a shoemaker's shop displaying the tools of eighteenth-century shoemaking. Nearby these old-timey services lies Salem's God's Acre, a testament to the egalitarian and choir-based system of organization that structured the lives of Salem's Moravian residents. Are visitors invited to make the distinction between the communal, egalitarian features of Moravianism that were radical in their practice and those now-quaint characteristics that were commonplace in the eighteenth and nineteenth

Figure 7.1. A promotional poster for Historic Ephrata, one of a series created by Katherine Milhous between 1936 and 1941 for the WPA Federal Art Project in Pennsylvania. POS-WPA-PA .M54, no. 2a, Work Projects Administration Poster Collection, Library of Congress.

centuries? Do couples who now celebrate their weddings at the scenic locations of Pleasant Hill, South Union Shaker Village, or the Oneida Mansion House take a moment to toast the people who built their venue while specifically renouncing the mainstream institution of marriage? Clearly there are contradictions in how scholars and professionals affiliated with historical intentional community sites combine their interpretive themes with operational goals. When making decisions about how to present a site's radical or subversive past, curators and executives are faced not only with historical influences but with modern political and economic ones as well. Choosing not to represent specific aspects of a community's history, or to highlight those aspects that engender familiarity among mainstream visitors, is a political act that reengages the community's original dialogue of cultural critique.

Mark Leone's 1981 musings on the public historical site of Shakertown at Pleasant Hill, Kentucky, and Alison Wylie's 1985 response to his ideas both address these questions of public interpretation and are canonical literature in many historical archaeologists' postprocessual education. Leone takes the open air museum's designers, and in fact all of us as consumers of mass-produced assumptions about Shaker life, to task for assuming we could safely adopt Shaker efficiency and rationality as picturesque versions of qualities already valued in our modern capitalist society. Instead, Leone reminds us, the Shakers created productive communities supported by "agrarian industrialism" (1981:306), operating outside of and in some opposition to the worldly industrial capitalism against which they insulated all but their senior members. Leone's suggestion is to present a fuller vision of Shaker life—one that captures the industrial level of technology that brothers and sisters accomplished and puts it into context as an effort to remake society in an image much different from that we now enjoy (or alternately suffer), as heirs to mainstream capitalism. Not only should we reinterpret the Shakers, Leone suggests, but also we must expose the masking ideological processes by which we co-opt Shaker qualities as somehow ancestral to our own present (1981:309). Wylie extends and discusses Leone's views regarding the interpretation of historical sites. Her call is to critical theory, to archaeologists' awareness of "the constituted nature of knowledge claims" (Wylie 1985:144).

As Shaker sites continue to be the most visible public celebration of an intentional community available to most visitors, the dialogue continues about how best to preserve and present these places. Public history professor William D. Moore explores how Shaker village museums and historic sites developed through the 1950s and 1960s, demonstrating that the interpretations we have inherited from that earlier generation of museum professionals is perhaps more illuminating about midcentury

American culture than it is about the Shakers. At Pleasant Hill, Kentucky, the restoration's proponents stripped the site of evidence of the Shakers' nineteenth-century industries, creating an agrarian illusion to attract tourists. At nearby South Union, Kentucky, dramatic annual historical pageants brought together local theater and local history, while at Canterbury, New Hampshire, no actors were needed as the last remaining Shaker sisters were the main attraction until the early 1990s. Of the four villages Moore discusses in the article, he writes that "though they had all started with roughly the same raw material (that is to say, declining or abandoned Shaker villages), they achieved markedly different outcomes. . . . Whereas the Shakers had shaped the villages in accordance with their religious beliefs, the various Shaker village administrators had tailored them to fit decidedly different, secular visions" (2006:51). Most significant, Hancock Shaker Village in the Berkshires of western Massachusetts attracted the attention of vacationing affluent art aficionados whose modernist aesthetic and appreciation of American folk arts informed interpretation at the site. The publicity afforded by photographer William Winter's iconic images and Edward Deming Andrews and Faith Andrews's 1937 book, *Shaker Furniture: The Craftsmanship of an American Communal Sect*, set the popular tone for envisioning Shaker spaces. Perhaps more than any other site, this appropriated view of Hancock has influenced modern concepts of what Shakerism looked like. Recent developments in Hancock's interpretive plan show awareness of the site's role in skewing perspectives about Shaker history, and portray changes in Shaker belief and lifestyles over time while embracing several aspects of Shaker principles, such as "commitment to excellence, gender and racial equality, entrepreneurship, environmental management and spiritual and work ethics," considered relevant to contemporary American visitors (Cooper 2001:37). These are noble principles, indeed, though they are also modern societal ideals that many well-meaning Americans would like to associate with charismatic past societies.

Archaeologist Don Janzen, who conducted research at Pleasant Hill, Kentucky, in the 1970s, apparently preferred visitors to experience the passage of time at the site by viewing the "crumbled walls and fragments of pillars and posts" exposed in situ than more cleanly restored elements of the tourist areas (Parrish 2005:149). This is indeed one way to view the

Shakers in a less comfortable way—to distance ourselves by remembering that enough time has elapsed for even mainstream culture to have changed drastically across the past two centuries from what would likely be an unfamiliar America. Like Janzen, Kim McBride weighs in on the reconstruction at Pleasant Hill with mixed feelings. She acknowledges that the oversimplified current built environment gives an artificial impression of the village as it looked when occupied. Lacking are the small outbuildings and outdoor work areas that would have filled the now parklike spaces between larger reconstructed buildings. This simplicity, though, also heightens the sense of order at the site, a principle she sees as fundamental to the organization of Shaker life. In presenting an ordered landscape, she maintains, we are engaging with Shaker belief and social structure, not just admiring furniture design, and following from this,

> the better is the visitor's appreciation of the complexity of the American past(s), their awareness that myriad alternatives to mainstream capitalist society existed, and their understanding that the present is not so much a natural or inevitable outcome of a vague, distant and impersonalized past, but rather a more interesting outcome of struggles, successes, failures, and accommodations by individuals and groups some of whom you get to learn about at historic sites. (McBride 2010:268)

While McBride's experience of Pleasant Hill is of a peaceful space, David Starbuck and Paula Dennis complain that modern alterations have negatively impacted the experience of the landscape at Canterbury Shaker Village. Noise pollution and traffic from a nearby auto racetrack have made it less peaceful, while new roads and dams built according to modern safety regulations rather than traditional Shaker practices have made it less accurate (Starbuck and Dennis 2010:245–246). When approaching these reconstructed sites, it is important to remind ourselves of the fragmentary and impressionistic nature of historical preservation. No Shaker site can provide a true experience through sound, sight, and smell of the rattling mills and looms, animal pens and barns, steam from the sisters' syrup shop or laundry, or any of the other works to which residents put their hands in practice of their faith.

Also significant to modern visitor experience at sites such as Canterbury is that only the Church Family buildings and grounds generally remain for public view. The very intentional composition of Shaker villages, with a central Church Family insulated from outside contact by agricultural fields and outlying family compounds, is invisible to modern visitors (Starbuck 1988:7). This seems to be the norm for Shaker village museums. South Union, Kentucky, once had more than 220 buildings, of which 10 still stand (Gutek and Gutek 1998:74). The nonprofit corporation operating Mount Lebanon Shaker Village in eastern New York owns a total of 20 buildings from three Shaker families who occupied the village between 1787 and 1947—the North, Church, and Center Families—and welcomes visitors for tours of a small number of the standing buildings, while most are occupied by a currently operating private high school. Gutek and Gutek describe this as the "least restored of the Shaker museum villages" while paradoxically being a place where "visitors can truly experience a sense of a Shaker village" in large part because of its more distributed and less developed setting (1998:43).

As Shaker geographical spread was broad, and their infrastructure investments extensive, cultural resource management projects that encounter Shaker structures and infrastructure remains in the vicinity of village locations, like the Enfield Shaker Bridge in Lake Mascoma, New Hampshire (Switzer and Foley 2001; Starbuck 2006:187–188), can act to bring the extent of the Shakers' now invisible cultural landscape back into public view. As well, this issue of changing Shaker landscapes brings the opportunity for archaeologists to engage with time's passage in a way not usually well represented at public historic sites. Canterbury, New Hampshire, was one of the last occupied Shaker villages, with a handful of sisters remaining in residence until 1992. The encroachment of modern services and the shrinking of the village from its original four families and hundred buildings to the remaining 24 Church Family buildings enact an accurate representation of real Shaker experience, albeit a twentieth-century one. An even more current Shaker experience greets visitors at the Shaker Museum in the last remaining Shaker-occupied village, Sabbathday Lake, Maine. At the time of writing, the community had four residents, two brothers and two sisters, who participate in welcoming visitors to the museum while pursuing their faith in their daily vocations. Shakerism today, what members eat, wear, and build, is as different from Shakerism a century ago as the lives brothers and sisters led in 1900 was from their forebears' daily lives in 1800.

While the once oft-repeated pattern of multifamily Shaker villages is now obscured by fragmented land distribution, the Amana Inspirationists' unique seven-village landscape in Iowa has retained much of its form since the residents chose to change their structure from that of communal villages to a profit-sharing corporation in 1932. The built environment shows many transformations, including buildings and styles from the communal years, those built or renovated as families began to operate as independent units, and changes made in the interest of attracting tourist revenue. In the years after 1965, when Amana was declared a National Historic site, the number of businesses and buildings specifically catering to tourists increased. Working to attract more visitors to their establishments, local property owners beautified their businesses in ways they interpreted to represent Amana's, or at least Germanic, styles. In many cases, however, the new old look of these businesses was based more on an imagined history of Amana's appearance than reality. Amana historian Jonathan Andelson observes that modern shop owners attempted to copy what they perceived to be old Amana style but included elements never seen on the Inspirationists' buildings: "front porches, shutters, single-pane glass, painted wood facing, decorative wagon wheels, barrels serving as flower planters, and even *Fachwerk* (half-timbering) depart from traditional styles and precedents" (1986:53). Through the 1980s, work by the Amana Preservation Foundation actively encouraged a historic preservation ethos in the community, with education programs for preservation professionals and property owners. Older building exteriors have been restored to a more "original" (though never fully so) appearance, and functional elements such as grape trellises are preferred over decorative flourishes. However, Andelson stresses that "preservation never applies to all components of a built environment. Everyone engaged in the process exercises selectivity in what they preserve and what they allow to deteriorate or to remain modernized" (1986:55–56). Guidance in deciding what to preserve, restore, or reconstruct can come from archaeological views at the varying scales of landscape, built environment, and artifacts. For each community studied archaeologically, each of these scales addresses different questions and priorities related to a community's belief structure and development. At Amana, the existing broader landscape of villages interspersed with modernized versions of the colony's industrial plants is probably the strongest communicator of the Inspirationists as an intentionally unified social and economic body. Modern residential and tourist development has obscured most of the remains of the built environment, which most strongly structured the egalitarian relationships of multiple-family dwelling houses to each kitchen house. Only one remaining example of a communal-era kitchen house is maintained for visitors by the Amana Heritage Society, and though evocative of past times, this single building can't adequately illustrate how the communal kitchen system required a repeating pattern of many houses and kitchens throughout Inspirationists' villages.

The sites of intentional communities will necessarily continue to provide incomplete versions of history for the places and their people. True depictions aren't possible, and as Kim McBride suggests, might not even be desirable. Of Pleasant Hill, Kentucky, she muses, "If the experience was made more accurate, some of the audience might not want to come to the site, or at least might not want to come back" (McBride 1995:406). In an era when museums and historic sites need to sell themselves as destinations not only for community history enthusiasts but also group conferences, weddings, and other special events, organizations financially need people to want to visit, and to enjoy their experience enough to want to come back. So what is the best choice: to maintain an inaccurate portrayal and a viable operation, or to approach a fuller representation of the past at the risk of alienating some of the supporting public?

Historical Memory and Political Present

Just as there is no one unifying vision of the perfect society, there is no formulaic approach for studying and presenting the material histories of intentional communities. Each group left traces of the lives they lived while working for a better world, and in seeking those traces we need to decide how best to bring their vision through into our own interpretations. The documentary and material records we examine in our quest to learn about community lives aren't clear reflections of the past people and their actions but are representations constructed through the varying forces of instrumental action based on shared belief, routine activities, and the vagaries of preservation and publication. In his 2007 archaeological perspective on the English landscape tradition, Matthew Johnson reminds us that "both the archaeological and historical 'records' emerge as products and mediators of social action, rather than 'evidence' about a past to be 'reconstructed'" (2007:152). Writing about historic house museums in Louisville, Kentucky, where the city's racial history can be publicly engaged through archaeological practice, archaeologists Lori C. Stahlgren and M. Jay Stottman similarly assert that these institutions are products and perpetuators of the political climate when they're made, not objective presentations of neutral knowledge about the past. The points they make about museums, multivocality, and "giving voice to the silenced past in order to help change the present" (Stahlgren and Stottman 2007:148) are important considerations for sites of social critique and radicalism, such as intentional communities.

If what we choose to say about past communities is never a disinterested presentation of the evidence of past reality, and our own interpretations are as much produced and mediated by the material and documentary evidence of our research subjects and our modern milieu as the views of the people we are studying, then how do we choose which story to tell? The single example of carrots at Llano del Rio offers insight into how modern scholars can vary widely in their presentation of information from a past community. Journalist Lionel Rolfe, coauthor of *Bread and Hyacinths: The Rise & Fall of Utopian Los Angeles*, says in an AOL online documentary series episode of "What Remains" released on 17 August 2013 that the Llano colonists produced "tons of carrots—people got tired of carrots" as part of his story of rare economic successes at the colony. In an archaeological report, John M. Foster and Alex Kirkish offer the same carrot surplus as an example of extreme economic hardship, rather than agricultural success, at the colony: "Although enthusiasm was high, the food at the colony was neither palatable nor plentiful. Carrots were the only vegetable available for several weeks during one notable period" (Foster 2008:21; Foster and Kirkish 2009:3). Taking a longer view, documentary filmmakers Beverly

Lewis and Rick Blackwood credit early twentieth-century socialist activists, including the members of Louisiana's New Llano community and its previous incarnation, Llano del Rio in Southern California, with the lasting impact of broader Depression-era policy changes such as the 1935 Social Security Act and the 1938 Fair Labor Standards Act, which legislated a minimum wage. Lewis and Blackwood write:

> While Democrats and Republicans take credit for enacting these reforms, what is lost to history is the fact that these ideas did not originate with these mainstream groups. Such causes were initially proposed and championed long before they became politically popular by those who took great risks of being blackballed, beaten, deported, jailed, and ostracized. Socialists, communists, labor unions, and cooperative communities like Llano del Rio all played their roles in bringing the need for reform into the American consciousness. (1995:43)

So should we choose to see in Llano's carrot surplus a small victory or even a lucky break for Llano's colonists that helped them last another few weeks in their effort to improve society? Or was it a symptom of the broad infeasibility of their socialist goals? And how, as archaeologists, do we marshal these small details to point us toward some manifestly truer interpretation? How do we acknowledge our own biases, with appropriate humility, while also trying to question the assumptions of either the colonists themselves or mainstream culture today? When we study the activists of an earlier era, can archaeologists work among the ranks of modern social activists?

Working in the 1980s, both Wylie's and Leone's perspectives on Shaker site interpretation seem only to imagine a future practice in which archaeologists are honest about their own subjectivity and the ways in which those modern subjectivities shape our understanding and use of the past. While recognizing the Shakers' radicalism, they didn't yet recommend a radicalization of Shaker archaeology. Several established archaeological thinkers have, in recent years, called for an increase in social relevance and engagement by academics, professionals, and students in the field. Barbara J. Little sees archaeologists as potentially antimainstream radicals simply in our choice to practice and defend a discipline whose economic contribution to the gross domestic product is disproportionately low compared to the human hours spent and human connections made in creating our product and service. She writes that our

> willingness to stand against the powerful cultural tide of commercialism alone makes archaeology somewhat culturally subversive in the 21st century. I believe it can be culturally subversive in a most beneficial way. And as we insist that there is an alternative, better way to think about value, we are somewhat in line with others who want to work toward a society and a culture that benefit more people and support a more just and fair way of being in the world. (Little 2009:116)

In her call for true civic engagement in archaeology, Little recommends that we consider the potential impact of involving archaeological sites and projects in organizations like the International Coalition of Historic Site Museums of Conscience, whose goal is to help public audiences learn about and better understand historic places within the context of current social issues (Little 2007:6). Dozens of institutions in the United States across a broad spectrum of social issues belong to this coalition, including the *Brown v. Board of Education* National Historic Site in Topeka, Kansas; the Angel Island Immigration Station Foundation in San Francisco; and the Lower East Side Tenement Museum in New York City. Each of these sites, and the many others in the coalition, illuminate past generations' struggles to bring memory into present action for social justice.

Kentucky archaeologist M. Jay Stottman expresses a more tempered optimism for our potential to harness our knowledge about the past into present activism in the introduction to his appropriately titled 2010 edited volume *Archaeologists as Activists: Can Archaeologists Change the World?* When used as an agent for change in modern society, activist archaeology, Stottman writes, is "about understanding a community and integrating its needs and wants into our work and using the process of archaeology and the knowledge it produces to help satisfy community needs" (2010:8). The strongest skill archaeologists can contribute to such change, then, is advocacy, even though advocating on behalf of communities of which we aren't a part requires care and self-reflexivity (Stottman 2010:11).

Writing of historical archaeologies of nineteenth-century reform movements, SUNY Potsdam anthropology professor Hadley Kruczek-Aaron cautions that we should moderate our activist impulses with reflexivity, critique of the past and its scholarship, and consideration of whose interests our work will be serving. Her 2014 research illuminates distinctions between perfectionist Christian reform advocate Gerrit Smith's historical legacy and the archaeological evidence of reform settlements at Smithfield and North Elba, New York. Historical documentary sources seem to Kruczek-Aaron to overwhelmingly offer praise and recollections of success at Smithfield, a primarily white community in which Smith himself resided, while recalling what seemed the inevitable failure and decrepitude of North Elba, a primarily African American reformers' community also supported by Smith's ideas and donations. Digging deeper into primary documentary evidence, Kruczek-Aaron finds that conditions at Smithfield were not so ideal, after all, while the settlers at North Elba were inventive in their attempts to overcome structural difficulties. For example, she finds evidence of considerable disunity in attitudes to temperance in Smithfield, with tobacco pipes found in several contexts and different types of alcoholic beverage container fragments, especially wine, which was consumed by "partial" temperance advocates. These artifacts hint that Smith's fellow residents did not fully agree with his total abstinence rhetoric. Meanwhile, the predominantly African American settlers at the North Elba site of Timbuctoo, who were granted poor-quality farmland in the Adirondacks, marshaled the social connections from their previous homes for assistance and support. But it was not enough to overcome the inherent unproductivity of the soil, and the community faltered and dissolved after less than two decades. "By not acknowledging that struggles over reform were ongoing in Smithfield and by blaming Timbuctoo's failure on the settlers themselves, Smith's national reputation as an effective reform leader remained intact" (Kruczek-Aaron 2014:309). Subsequent historical writers upheld Gerrit Smith's efforts and ideals while suppressing the struggles inherent in his community residents' daily lives. Kruczek-Aaron's caution is to consider the actual outcomes and experiences of social movements before invoking them in modern social activism.

Colin Breen's archaeological landscape study of two Irish agricultural communities, Ralahine in County Clare and Carhoogariff in County Cork, similarly has a dual focus on both the past communities themselves and the cultural usage of the historical memory of those communities. Eight decades after its brief existence in the 1830s, Irish socialist-activist writers such as James Connolly invoked the community of Ralahine as an important experiment, and the town's story inspired the socialist ideals of some members of the Irish reunification activist party Sinn Féin (Breen 2006:37). Breen's research on the structure of Ralahine demonstrates that, though it was indeed intended to be an agricultural economic cooperative, in actuality resident members continued to pay rents to the landowner, Vandeleur. Living in an eighteenth-century house significantly larger than any of the renters' cottages, Vandeleur could observe the tenants from the upper levels of his private home. Dependent on one man's ownership of the land, the communal experiment collapsed after his personal fortunes were lost to gambling debts (Breen 2006:46). Like Ralahine, rather than having architecture reflective of a truly egalitarian cooperative, Carhoogariff featured a central tower in which the project's economic supporter could monitor residents' activities from an elevated perspective (Breen 2006:40). Both of these communities were established and supervised by middle-class, educated members of a social and economic elite who retained their class position while the resident members of the agricultural cooperatives toiled. Not strictly egalitarian, these were more like Owenite agricultural or company towns than true intentional communities or communal settlements. Breen cautions that the "extent to which radical concepts of socialist reform were central to the ideal communities of nineteenth-century Ireland has then to be questioned. Their pivotal place in later radical writing demonstrates the endurance of their myth but the reality of their structure and ideals were [sic] somewhat different to that ascribed to them by these commentators" (2006:36). Both Gerrit Smith's reform towns in New York and these Irish cooperative towns were held up by later writers as successful examples of certain kinds of reform—but examples that, in reality, seem not to fully support such claims. Hadley Kruczek-Aaron and Colin Breen expose others' myopic views of past communities, and in doing so remind us to adjust our own glasses when subtly extolling a social experiment's virtues or condemning its weaknesses with our interpretations of its material evidence.

Expressing hope that archaeologists will engage our writing in support of changing the narratives that inform most mainstream research processes and products, Paul Shackel cautions that "narratives that reinforce national stories or hegemonic power structures create an ideology whereby the narrative is seen as true and timeless" (2013:2). Socially disengaged archaeological practice can produce what Randall McGuire calls "secret writing," anonymously authored but seemingly authoritative texts purporting to present unbiased scientific perspectives, which more often than not are formative, or at least complicit, in perpetuating dominant ideological narratives. In North America, this often involves rationalizing the values and goals of individual capitalism (McGuire 2008:16; Duke and Saitta 2009:355). Authors in historic preservation and scholarship usually don't consciously try to perpetuate oppressive dominant messages but simply work to promote the relevance of their particular place or people of interest. Writing of the Oneida Mansion House as a visitor destination and educational opportunity, Bruce M. Moseley and Helen S. Schwartz write that "the extraordinary evolution of the Oneida Community from a religious experiment to a prospering industrial corporation both highlights and mirrors trends in American society as a whole" (2001:31). Moseley and Schwartz are absolutely aware of and express the Oneida Community's more radical history, but it seems that collaborative efforts with descendants and museum professionals to craft an interpretive plan for Oneida that would appeal to the widest audiences avoids the reality that the visiting public are heirs to a lifestyle that Oneida's members sacrificed much to reform.

Much more frequently than we appropriate a community's history to represent modern mainstream values, we conflate modern cultural attitudes with human nature to inadvertently naturalize the status quo. Stephen Warfel devoted years of research to the Ephrata Cloister in Pennsylvania, considering the lives of members who were, in his view, "quite ordinary" and thus subject to the same human weaknesses all of us encounter when attempting, and often failing, to live according to the high standards of behavior set by our religious and social institutions. He writes, "The Ephrata experiment was motivated by radical religious ideology, fueled by idealism, and tempered by reality" (Warfel 2009:150). To Warfel, Ephrata's members and contemporary supporters created a documentary record that emphasized successes and enforced desired behavior, a record that was embraced by later historians in what amounted to the perpetuation of a "romanticized" view of Ephrata's history (2009:149). In correcting this skewed historical portrayal with archaeological evidence that Ephrata's members were indeed more human than heavenly, Warfel may run the opposite risk of emphasizing their sameness at the cost of losing sight of the radicalism and idealism that inspired followers to live as a community for more than eight decades.

If we choose to engage in activist and critical archaeologies, by contrast, we can illuminate the potential of different possible paths throughout time, question the inevitability of our current reality, and "strengthen our license to participate in history" (Saitta 2007:5). Disrupting our existing national stories, some archaeologists are bringing into public view past bloody conflicts of class warfare where laborers clashed violently with mercenary or state armies bought to protect the interests of capital. Examples include the 1897 Lattimer Massacre in Pennsylvania (Roller 2013); the Ludlow, Colorado, Coal Field War of 1913–1914 (Ludlow Collective 2001); and the 1921 Battle of Blair Mountain in West Virginia (Nida 2013). Reintegrating knowledge of these events, and others like them, into our national memory changes the narratives about the legitimacy of industrial capital's power and the transforming face of labor in America and the world. In Randall McGuire, Dean Saitta, and their colleagues' work at Ludlow, the archaeologists' engagement with unionized workers in southern Colorado brought archaeological knowledge of local labor history into the modern discourse about labor and labor rights in the United States. McGuire's goal for praxis through such community collaboration in emancipatory archaeology is to free people from alienation. From his Marxist-inspired perspective, this necessarily involves a class-based orientation in which workers are alienated from the products of their labor, but alienation can occur in other social dimensions such as age, religion, and sexual orientation. Praxis, according to McGuire,

> refers to the distinctively human capacity to consciously and creatively construct and change both the world and ourselves. . . . To engage in praxis, people must entertain concepts of possibility and change. Praxis becomes emancipatory when it advances the interests

of the marginalized and the oppressed against the interests of the dominant. Praxis implies a process of gaining knowledge of the world, critiquing the world, and taking action to change the world. (2008:2–3)

This reads startlingly like a description of what many intentional communities' members aimed to achieve, reframed as a mission statement for best archaeological practices going forward into the future. If we take to heart these calls to reconstruct the narratives that structure our collective memory and that support our current national social and political context, we must also reconsider the base assumptions we have been working with when interpreting and presenting the pasts of intentional communities. There is a comforting benefit to interpreting community pasts as a series of fascinating, though historically irrelevant, destined failures: we can rest assured that our current status quo is the natural state of our society. Such interpretations gloss over not only the potential to shape other, alternative futures but also the influence that widely connected radical and experimental movements have had on forming the America we live in today. Our practice as archaeologists can recast historical memory and renew dialogues about the world we're working to build.

Seeing Community

With their fraught relationship to American history as sometimes-pioneers, sometimes-pariahs, Mormon settlers left an evocative landscape for their modern descendants, rich with possibilities for archaeological interpretation. Archaeologist Mark Leone has tied the reconstruction of the early Mormon temple and town at Nauvoo, Illinois, together with Colonial Williamsburg and Canada's Fortress of Louisbourg as examples of how "what the public gets out of archaeology is . . . the empirical substantiation of national mythology" (1973:129). In retellings of Mormon history, we see frontiers expanding westward, self-determination in the face of persecution and hardship, and an ultimately successful economic struggle won by virtue of hard work. We imagine the humble roots of persecuted migrants growing into the magnificence of the massive Nauvoo temple, rebuilt more than 150 years after it was burned by arsonists and its believers driven into the desert. Mormon scholars have since weighed in on the importance of Mormon archaeological sites, with one of the most outspoken of these, Benjamin C. Pykles, advocating the cultural value of these sites as reminders of the lives of Mormon forbears who "were impelled by a desire to practice their religion in peace and in isolation from those who had denied them this right" (2005:2). Migrating to the western frontiers in their search for freedom from oppression, Mormon pioneers can be seen as enacting what would become a typically American mythology.

While non-Mormon scholars like Leone bring Mormon archaeology to the attention of non-Mormon readers, Mormon institutions and scholars have devoted more effort in the past decades to discovering and interpreting their own history for modern congregations. Within the earliest years of historical archaeology's growth as a discipline, Virginia and J. C. Harrington participated in a Mormon-led effort to excavate the remains of the ca. 1846–1848 temple at Nauvoo. The 1971 report combines historical documentation with archaeological findings in an attempt to discern the construction methods and layout of the original temple basement, which contained the baptismal font, its water supply well, and smaller ancillary rooms. Their report on this site simultaneously contains one of the only archaeological considerations of the French-speaking intentional community of the Icarians. These followers of Etienne Cabet, French social reformer and author of the utopian novel *Voyage en Icarie*, occupied Nauvoo in 1850 after its previous Mormon residents fled in the wake of their prophet Joseph Smith and his brother Hyrum Smith's murders by an angry horde of denouncers. Among the Icarians' activities were attempts to construct communal service buildings within the ruins of the burned temple's basement, and to use some of the abundance of temple stone for constructing new buildings (Harrington and Harrington 1971:6, 10–11). It is particularly interesting to read a Mormon-sponsored report's portrayal of these post-Mormon activities. Of an iron stone chisel found beneath an Icarian-made stone pier, Harrington and Harrington write, "there is an excellent chance that it is Mormon, dating from the completion of the baptismal font. The work that the Icarians were doing in constructing the pier foundations was of a cruder sort than is suggested by this chisel, which would have been an appropriate tool for the work on the font" (1971:11). The authors also use the word "robbed" to describe stone salvaging in the temple ruins between

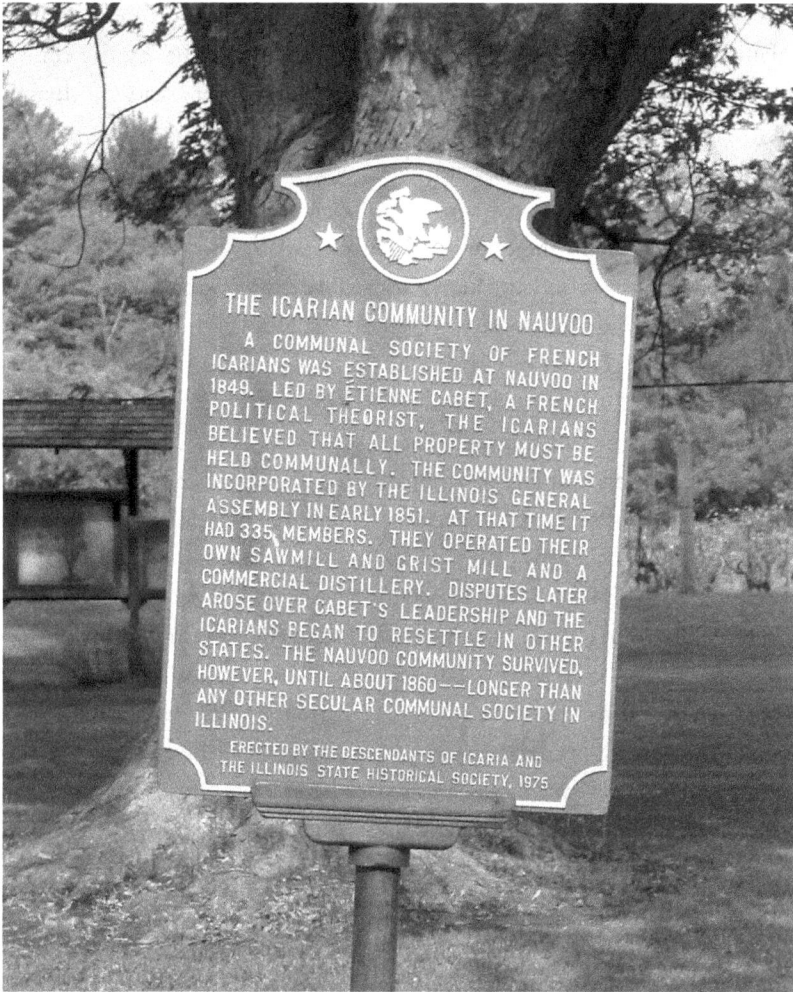

Figure 7.2. A sign commemorating the Icarian presence at Nauvoo, Illinois, stands amid the Mormon church historical site's features, which include a complete replica of the original temple destroyed by fire in 1848. Photo by author, 2005.

1850 and 1865, after the Mormons abandoned Nauvoo (1971:11). The perspective and language employed in the report serve to extend Mormons' metaphorical dominance over the site into interpretations of the later residents time there (fig. 7.2).

Benjamin Pykles explores the complex relationship between Mormon church leaders and historical archaeologists in his 2010 *Excavating Nauvoo,* a history of the competing interests in restoring the Mormon center of Nauvoo. Pykles chronicles two interpretive thrusts—one, by the church in recruiting converts and reinforcing members' beliefs, and another by non-Mormons promoting what they saw as the glorification of western expansionist history. Pykles writes that both religious and secular promoters "used the city and its history as a tool for proselytizing" (2010:136). Ultimately, it seems, the church's goals prevailed, and excavation of the Nauvoo temple was only the beginning. More than 30 sites were excavated across three decades in the city between 1961 and 1984, sponsored by the Church of Jesus Christ of Latter Day Saints and Reorganized Church of Jesus Christ of Latter Day Saints (2010:288).

As part of their 1980s investigations at Lower Goshen, Utah, discussed in chapter 3 as an example of an incompletely realized town based on Joseph Smith's Plat of the City of Zion, Dale Berge of Brigham Young University and his colleagues fully excavated three home sites and partially excavated five others to reveal foundation stone alignments and record the contents of artifact scatters within and around the structural remains. Excavators found that residents hauled logs and stones for several miles to construct wood homes with stone foundations rather than using adobe bricks from local clay. Berge asserts that the array of household artifacts recovered, from ceramic tablewares to bottles and buttons, "do[es] not suggest a poor community but rather a community of middle-class Americans using objects fashionable to the entire country" (1990:88). These interpretations, presented in a 1990 article within a volume of *BYU Studies*, serve the interests of a Mormon scholar working for a Mormon institution by presenting a comfortable image of Mormon settlers with whom their modern descendants can relate. Though their time at Lower Goshen was relatively short and the site conditions were poor for village settlement, residents of Goshen are presented as a hard-working group who could marshal the labor and tools to harvest lumber and load river rocks from distant locations in order to build their houses. They're remembered as middle-class consumers who, though separated from the reader by 130 years, are easier to imagine as the forebears of today's Mormon descendants than a bedraggled group of pioneers who uprooted their families multiple times, moving from one unsuitable home site to the next. This contrasts somewhat with an illustration facing the first page of Berge's 1983 article on the same site, which was published as part of a volume assembled for a primarily non-Mormon audience of scholars and archaeological professionals. The simple line drawing, presented without a caption or explanation, is of a presumably Mormon family consisting of one adult man and five adult women posing in front of a log cabin. If the group portrayed represents a Mormon settler with his wives, the image serves to separate the reader as an individual from Mormon history by illustrating polygamy, one of the oft-mentioned social practices that may serve to alienate modern North Americans from nineteenth-century Mormon families. No mention is made of polygamy, or family structure at all, in either of Berge's articles. The image's portrayal of an imagined family structure is, at best, irrelevant to the article's content and arguments. At worst, it confronts the reader with an assumption about Mormon settlers that plays on mainstream American aversions to Mormon polygyny, before she or he can read Berge's own words.

For the most part, the decades of excavations at Nauvoo and continuing studies at many other Mormon sites proceed more with the goals of historical restoration and reconstruction than with anthropological interpretation of past lifeways. These reconstructions, today, largely serve to authenticate Mormon history. As Pykles writes, "The Church's historical sites become three-dimensional witnesses to the supernatural events that underlie Mormon theology and identity" (2010:302). In the absence of physical evidence of the supernatural, the original and reconstructed buildings that stood during the lifetime of the Prophet Joseph Smith serve to legitimize a shared belief in Mormon history as it is currently understood. For those among us who are not Mormon and have not studied Mormon sites, it may be easy to see these church-based interpretations of history as some kind of misappropriation of reality. Archaeologists at American Mormon sites, however, use widely accepted methods to gather and analyze data and participate in the wider professional and academic communities of the discipline in a now decades-long dialogue regarding the uses of the past and the meaning of evidence.

Guided by physical and documentary evidence from African American burials at a Moravian Mission in Salem, North Carolina, Leland Ferguson (2011) provides an example of the kind of tempered advocacy that balances awareness of a past community's goals with nuanced understandings of the political realities facing nineteenth-century Moravians and twenty-first-century archaeologists. Though originating with a shared belief in the equality of all people, Moravians in North Carolina eventually came to buy enslaved persons and thereby participate in the broader American economy of inequality. In doing so, "the Brethren were caught between the egalitarian expressions of their religious faith and their slowly developing employment of slave labor" (Ferguson 2011:7). Ferguson and his colleagues' archaeological project aimed to record and identify African American people, both free and enslaved, Moravian and non-Moravian, who were buried in the graveyards of the St. Philips Church complex (fig. 7.3). This Moravian mission's church congregation was excluded from the larger Salem Congregation until 2010, and their graves and gravestones were neglected, and in some cases hidden under building remains, in the intervening years. Using historical and archaeological techniques, Ferguson and his colleagues literally brought to light an aspect of Moravian history that has been kept out of view. In exposing this aspect of Moravian history, and African American community participation, the project archaeologists aimed to contribute to the ongoing efforts toward reconciliation in this southern community. Ferguson is forthright about the origin of his interest in the Moravians, having grown up around Salem and thus personally experiencing the legacy of racial discrimination whose roots go back to the days before Salem was founded. He is not optimistic about the potential for religious idealists to achieve egalitarian goals in the face of evidence that communities such as the Moravians, whom he believes were not social or political activists, learned to accommodate local customs such as slavery when it eased their transition into a region (Ferguson 2011:195). He writes:

> The creation of an ideal Christian community was fundamental to early Moravians. I also appreciate the value of the early Moravians' commitment to a perfection of religious toleration and fellowship. My Christian experience has allowed me to understand and identify with this impossible goal and the temptation to claim success in achieving it, in spite of inevitable failure. (Ferguson 2011:16)

In exposing and sharing this part of Moravian history through archaeology, Ferguson champions values that seem to have been intended, if not fully lived, by Salem's early Moravian congregation. Even in his disillusionment,

Figure 7.3. Reconstruction of the 1823 African Moravian Log Church, Old Salem, North Carolina. Photo by Peter Merholz, 2005. Used with permission.

he connects the history and landscape of Moravian Salem with the lives of individual African Americans buried in their midst but outside of the village's own sacred space. In doing so, Ferguson brings the story forward to the 2010 reinclusion of the predominantly African American St. Philips Moravian Church in the Salem Congregation and contributes to dialogues of restorative justice.

Sometimes, bringing an archaeological project into modern social relevance can include bringing living descendants directly into the research process. As a graduate student at the University of Saskatchewan, Megan Brooks explored the Doukhobor pit house and village site of Ospennia, Saskatchewan, in partnership with a local community group of Doukhobor descendants (Brooks 2005) (see #26 in the Appendix). Occupied by Russian sectarian families between 1899 and 1904, the pit house was constructed as a temporary shelter for the new immigrant families while they built a more permanent village nearby. Modern Doukhobors, descendants of the village's original families, could discuss their own memories and oral traditions about their ancestors' early life in Saskatchewan while unearthing the material remains of those people's daily travails. Benefits and challenges accrue in equal measure when including descendant community members in our projects. Living members of the Doukhobor congregation are incontrovertible evidence that group beliefs and identity can persist long after an intentional community's coresidential structure falls apart. Their participation brings insights into the history and material remains that are inaccessible to researchers outside the Doukhobor faith and culture. At the same time, their interpretations can force us to consider our own biases, and to acknowledge the potential for ambiguity and subjectivity in our presentation of the past. Faced with a deepened contextual understanding of Doukhobor settlers' experience and beliefs, our academic and professional interpretation of what a liquor bottle or cow bone means in archaeological context can seem too simplistic. Our work with individuals who are also members of a broader community with its own history and relationships can act as a lens to bring into focus the complexity of that community. Modern Doukhobor descendants hold differing views on the issues of abstinence from tobacco and alcohol, vegetarianism, and communalism as they were practiced by their ancestors. Just as Doukhobor descendants are not a single united group in the present, surely Doukhobor belief and identity weren't monolithic in the past.

In cases where descendant communities aren't identifiable or are very dispersed, we also face the question of whose voices and perspectives to engage with in our archaeological process. Brooks was fortunate to work at a community site whose Doukhobor descendants are the grandchildren of original members, and many of whom still live within a short drive of their ancestors' home. The experience that the archaeologists studying the Ludlow Coal Field War encountered in trying to identify descendant communities could parallel a more likely experience in the search for intentional community descendants. Biological descendants of Ludlow's coal miners were geographically dispersed and socially disconnected from one another, as well as from their own families' mining past. The archaeologists identified instead the unionized workers of southern Colorado as their community collaborator, as these workers share geography, occupational class, and many of the same work-related struggles as their coalfield "ancestors" (Saitta 2007:93; Duke and Saitta 2009:356).

Our decisions are relatively clear when we're working toward representing organized labor's contributions, exposing past racial inequalities, and undoing the historical silencing of visible minorities. But not all social history as social action is as unambiguous. Barbara Little, providing the example of community-spurred housing legislation in a Virginia town that was essentially anti-immigrant, asks,

> When heritage places get identified, their stories told, the future of their past ensured, who is at the table? Who gets invited back? listened to? derided? dismissed? We can think of our own self-defined activism as intentional action to bring about social or political change, but we must be vigilant and continually self critical and questioning about the types of changes we advocate. If we aim our activism at progressive social change and social justice, we should understand that we may be aiming at a moving target. (2007:11)

Adding to the challenges of frequently divisive and changing modern goals for public engagement with our research, past communities were never one-dimensional representations of a single social or political goal. On weighing the successes and failures of the Koreshan Unity settlement at Estero, Florida, Sarah Tarlow writes, "If nothing else, they made many more people aware that there are alternatives to individualistic industrial capitalism" (2006:94). While convenient, stopping at this point would negate much that was significant in the lives of the Koreshans themselves. Tarlow continues in this vein with her suggestions that we rethink popular presentations of utopian societies to be fair and respectful to those past radicals whom we are representing, and to offer alternative histories to the mainstream view of nineteenth-century society and economy. This includes representing their religious beliefs; their family structures; their attitudes toward ethnic, racial, and gendered identities; and not only, for example, their anticapitalist and antimaterialist ideals that might appeal to activist scholars with Marxist perspectives. She writes, "Archaeologists have a duty to the people of the past to represent their views, values, and experiences as completely and subtly as we can" (Tarlow 2006:95–96).

Enough scholars are unforgiving, and even hostile, toward past visionaries' experiments that we have some work to do in achieving this balanced perspective. While formulating his ideas on space, representation, and ideology in Shaker and Mormon sites, Leone undermined the radicalism of all utopian ventures by arguing that they are essentially conservative outlets for reformation that can be easily reabsorbed into the mainstream once it begins fulfilling whatever need the utopian society identified (1977b:100). Much more recently, in the concluding paragraphs of their discussion of materials from a Theosophical Society dump near San Diego, California, Stephen Van Wormer and G. Timothy Gross use the word "cult" no less than six times to categorize this and other intentional communities (2006:117–118). This can be forgiven in Alice Felt Tyler's 1944 publication about social movements in American history, but the legacy of Jonestown and the Branch Davidians has since then loaded this term with negative meanings. The mildest dictionary definitions of the word "cult" emphasize a small group's religious devotion to or veneration of a person or idea. But our modern popular understanding of the term generally includes charismatic and deceptive leaders; persuasive indoctrination, or brainwashing, of members; and, ultimately, the perpetration of harmful acts within and outside the group. The term simply carries too much social and historical baggage not to be perceived as derogatory.

Historian Robert V. Hine stands as an example of a rare optimist, whose writing sometimes leans toward the poetic in its reluctance to place California's community visions solely into the past. Part of our work as historical researchers is to keep alive the hope for change, as he writes:

> The historical contribution lies in the continuous recall of utopian possibilities so that they may someday become realizable. And Godspeed their journey! If they walk through California's past, they will find there utopian experiments on every side, as variegated and extravagant as the natural environment that has bred them. (Hine 1983:xviii)

When advocating public engagement with the past of a nonmainstream sect whose members were very religious or overtly socialist, there will always be publics whose beliefs are at odds with those of the people whose voices we're bringing into the present. We need to be ready to accept that our role as publicly active scholars isn't going to be just that of the beneficent who undoes the wrongs perpetrated by oppressors of the past and their historian apologists. Starting a dialogue based on historical and archaeological knowledge is just as likely to create discord among interested publics as it is to spark unified action toward social justice. But just as the Mormons' westward movement and the Shakers' rational cottage industries feed our national mythology, the assumption that intentional communities, as individual examples or a broader set of movements, all ultimately end unfulfilled assures us that their alternative visions can't possibly compete with what feels like our inevitable current reality. Current intentional communities may very well have the potential to positively contribute to our own future, and past communities can teach lessons that are more than cautionary tales against unbridled optimism. If we as archaeologists perpetuate the idea that Utopia is ultimately unreachable, then we're complicit in discouraging today's visionaries from trying to create change.

The alternative visions espoused by community builders can shine a light (or throw shade) on many aspects of American mainstream society that continue to be part of our daily experience: persecution of minorities, institutional corruption, capitalism, competition, and individualism to name a few. Taking an archaeological approach toward the material remains and documentary records of past intentional communities illuminates the different ways individuals and groups negotiated the challenges of living together while trying to confront or reject these aspects of the broader world. Utilizing narrowing scales from the landscape, through architecture and the built environment, to the level of artifacts, we better understand how communities operated in dynamic ways. Shaker spaces were designed to reflect and reinforce an ordered vision, but maintaining order was an active process within which brothers and sisters continuously reworked their village landscapes by moving buildings, constructing paths, and building fences. Idealized urban plans met with the realities of local geography and resource availability as they were made real on the ground in Mormon towns and at the Llano del Rio Cooperative Colony. Repairs to the Ephrata Colony's Kedar show the building as part of a developing theology, which was physically changed as its builders' needs, abilities, and expectations changed. Differences between North Carolina Moravian ceramics produced for outside markets and those made for community use raise questions about the ongoing balance of identities engaged in by craftsmen and consumers in this sometimes proselytizing, sometimes insular group. In all these cases, the very materiality of our evidence, spanning the scales from citywide plans to single dishes, compels us to recognize the tangible legacy of intentional communities in the American experience. As the accumulated works of four decades of archaeological inquiry into the lives of intentional communities have demonstrated, we have much to learn from groups whose members worked together in pursuit of a shared ideal future.

APPENDIX

Archaeologically Studied Intentional Community Sites

1. Ephrata Community
Location: Lancaster County, Pennsylvania
Dates of Community: 1732–1813
Belief System: German Pietist ascetic
Archaeological Citations: Biever 1968; Warfel 1999, 2000, 2001, 2009

2. Bethlehem
Location: Lehigh and Northampton Counties, Pennsylvania
Dates of Community: 1742–1844
Belief System and Site: *Unitas Fratrum*, Moravian Protestant evangelical
Archaeological Citation: Foley 1965

3. Bethabara
Location: Forsyth County, North Carolina
Dates of Community: 1753–1766
Belief System: *Unitas Fratrum*, Moravian Protestant evangelical
Archaeological Citations: Clauser 1995; South 1965, 1999

4. Salem
Location: Forsyth County, North Carolina
Dates of Community: 1766–1857
Belief System: *Unitas Fratrum*, Moravian Protestant evangelical
Archaeological Citations: Ferguson 2011; South 1999; Thomas 1994

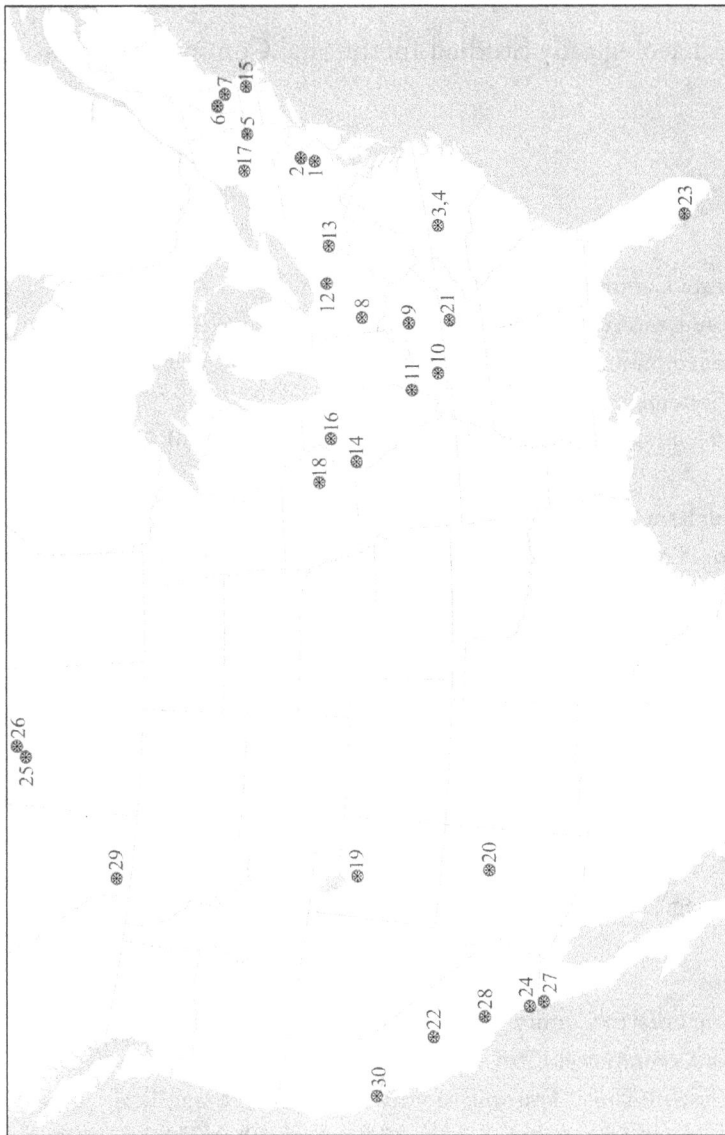

1. Ephrata, PA
2. Bethlehem, PA
3. Bethabara, NC
4. Salem, NC
5. Watervliet, NY
6. Enfield, NH
7. Canterbury, NH
8. Union Village, OH
9. Pleasant Hill, KY
10. South Union, KY
11. New Harmony, IN
12. Zoar, OH
13. Economy, PA
14. Nauvoo, IL
15. Brook Farm, MA
16. Bishop Hill, IL
17. Oneida, NY
18. Amana, IA
19. Lower Goshen, UT
20. Brigham City, AZ
21. Rugby, TN
22. Kaweah, CA
23. Estero, FL
24. Point Loma, CA
25. Kirilovka, SK
26. Ospennia, SK
27. Guadalupe, MX
28. Llano del Rio, CA
29. Bozhiya Milost, AB
30. Olompali, CA

Figure A.1. Locations of archaeologically studied intentional communities discussed in this book. North America base map created by Jared Benedict, 2004. Used under Creative Commons Attribution-ShareAlike License.

5. Watervliet Shaker Village
Location: Albany County, New York
Dates of Community: 1776–1926
Belief System: United Society of Believers in Christ's Second Appearing, millennialist Protestant
Archaeological Citation: Grygas 2011

6. Enfield Shaker Village
Location: Grafton County, New Hampshire
Dates of Community: 1792–1923
Belief System: United Society of Believers in Christ's Second Appearing, millennialist Protestant
Archaeological Citation: O'Connor 2015

7. Canterbury Shaker Village
Location: Merrimack County, New Hampshire
Dates of Community: 1792–1992
Belief System: United Society of Believers in Christ's Second Appearing, millennialist Protestant
Archaeological Citations: Starbuck 1986, 1988, 1998, 2004, 2006; Starbuck and Dennis 2010

8. Union Village Shakers
Location: Warren County, Ohio
Dates of Community: 1805–ca. 1920
Belief System: United Society of Believers in Christ's Second Appearing, millennialist Protestant
Archaeological Citations: Aument and Sewell 2009; Bennett et al. 2009; Sewell et al. 2009a, 2009b

9. Pleasant Hill Shaker Village
Location: Mercer County, Kentucky
Dates of Community: 1806–1910
Belief System: United Society of Believers in Christ's Second Appearing, millennialist Protestant
Archaeological Citations: Janzen 1981; McBride 1995, 2005, 2010; McBride and McBride 2008

10. South Union Shaker Village
Location: Logan County, Kentucky
Dates of Community: 1807–1922
Belief System: United Society of Believers in Christ's Second Appearing, millennialist Protestant
Archaeological Citations: Deiss 1987; Fiegel 1995; Tallent 2009

11. New Harmony
Location: Posey County, Indiana
Dates of Community: 1814–1827
Belief System: Harmonist (1814–ca. 1824), German Pietist, perfectionist; Owenite (1825–1827), socialist labor cooperative
Archaeological Citations: Strezewski 2011, 2013, 2014, 2015a, 2015b

12. Zoar
Location: Tuscarawas County, Ohio
Dates of Community: 1817–1898
Belief System: Separatist Society of Zoar, German Christian
Archaeological Citations: Herson et al. 2013; Sewell 2013; U.S. Army Corps of Engineers 2014

13. Economy
Location: Beaver County, Pennsylvania
Dates of Community: 1825–1905
Belief System: German Pietist
Archaeological Citations: De Cunzo et al. 1996 (Rapp's garden design); Heberling Associates 2008 (Rapp's garden design); Sewell et al. 2004 (Harmony Brickworks)

14. Nauvoo
Location: Hancock County, Illinois
Dates of Community: 1839–1860
Belief System: Church of Jesus Christ of Latter-day Saints, Mormon (1839–1846), Icarian Christian socialist (1846–1860)
Archaeological Citations: Harrington and Harrington 1971; Pykles 2006, 2010

15. Brook Farm
Location: Suffolk County, Massachusetts
Dates of Community: 1841–1847
Belief System: Transcendentalist (1841–1844), Fourierist socialist (1844–1847)
Archaeological Citations: Preucel 2006; Preucel and Pendery 2006; Savory 2013

16. Bishop Hill
Location: Henry County, Illinois
Dates of Community: 1846–1861
Belief System: Pietist-inspired Swedish Christian
Archaeological Citations: Mansberger 2002; McKay 1979; Safiran 1996, 2000; Van Ness 1973; Wagner 1974, 1975; Wilson and Wilson 1973

17. Oneida Perfectionists
Location: Madison County, New York
Dates of Community: 1848–1880
Belief System: Perfectionist Christian
Archaeological Citations: Van Wormer 2004, 2006

18. Amana Colonies
Location: Iowa County, Iowa
Dates of Community: 1855–1932
Belief System: Community of True Inspiration, German Pietist
Archaeological Citation: Andelson 1986 (architectural history and anthropology)

19. Lower Goshen
Location: Utah County, Utah
Dates of Community: 1860–1868
Belief System: Church of Jesus Christ of Latter-day Saints, Mormon
Archaeological Citations: Berge 1983, 1990

20. Brigham City
Location: Navajo County, Arizona

Dates of Community: 1876–1881
Belief System: United Order, Church of Jesus Christ of Latter-day Saints, Mormon
Archaeological Citations: Ferg 2005a, 2005b; Scarlett 2006

21. Rugby
Location: Morgan and Scott County, Tennessee
Dates of Community: 1880–1887
Belief System: Cooperative agriculture
Archaeological Citation: Avery 2001

22. Kaweah Colony
Location: Tulare County, California
Dates of Community: 1888–1892
Belief System: Socialist
Archaeological Citation: Kozakavich 2007

23. Estero
Location: Lee County, Florida
Dates of Community: 1894–1961
Belief System: Koreshan Unity
Archaeological Citations: Austin 1991; Baker and Wheeler 2000; Janus Research 1993; Tarlow 2002, 2006

24. Point Loma Theosophical Society
Location: San Diego County, California
Dates of Community: 1897–1942
Belief System: Blavatskyan Theosophy
Archaeological Citation: Van Wormer and Gross 2006

25. Kirilovka
Location: Saskatchewan, Canada
Dates of Community: 1899–ca. 1920
Belief System: Doukhobor, Russian Christian sectarian
Archaeological Citations: Kozakavich 1998, 2006

26. Ospennia
Location: Saskatchewan, Canada
Dates of Community: ca. 1902–1917
Belief System: Doukhobor, Russian Christian sectarian
Archaeological Citation: Brooks 2005

27. Guadalupe
Location: Baja California, Mexico
Dates of Community: 1905–
Belief System: Molokan, Russian Christian sectarian
Archaeological Citations: Muranaka 1992, 1995

28. Llano del Rio
Location: Los Angeles County, California
Dates of Community: 1914–1917
Belief System: Socialist
Archaeological Citations: Foster 2008; Foster and Kirkish 2009; Van Bueren 2006; Van Bueren and Hupp 2000

29. Bozhiya Milost
Location: Alberta, Canada
Dates of Community: ca. 1915–1937
Belief System: Doukhobor, Russian Christian sectarian
Archaeological Citations: Balcom 1991; Kennedy and Reeves 1986

30. Olompali
Location: Marin County, California
Dates of Community: 1967–1969
Belief System: Chosen Family Commune
Archaeological Citations: Fernandez and Parkman 2011; Parkman 2014, 2015

REFERENCES

Andelson, Jonathan. 1986. Three Faces of Amana: Architectural Change from Utopian Community to Tourist Attraction. In *Architecture in Cultural Change: Essays in Built Form & Culture Research*, ed. David G. Saile, 45–59. School of Architecture and Urban Design, University of Kansas, Lawrence.

———. 2002. Coming Together and Breaking Apart: Sociogenesis and Schismogenesis in Intentional Communities. In *Intentional Community: An Anthropological Perspective*, ed. S. L. Brown, 131–151. State University of New York Press, Albany.

Anderson, Varene. 1995. Land of Promise: The Icarian Experience in California. In *Icaria-Speranza: Final Utopian Experiment of Icarians in America, Proceedings of the 1989 Cours Icarien Symposium*. National Icarian Heritage Society, Corning, Iowa.

Andrews, Edward Deming. 1963. *The People Called Shakers: A Search for the Perfect Society*. 2nd ed. Dover, New York.

Arrington, Leonard J. 2005. *Great Basin Kingdom: An Economic History of the Latter-day Saints, 1830–1900, New Edition*. University of Illinois Press, Urbana.

Aument, Bruce, and Andrew R. Sewell. 2009. *Encountering the Shakers of the North Family Lot, Union Village, Ohio*. Vol. 1, *A Corner of Wisdom's Paradise—The North Family Lot Archaeological Project*. Prepared for the Ohio Department of Transportation Office of Environmental Services. Hardlines Design, Columbus, Ohio.

Austin, Robert J. 1991. *Archaeological Excavation at the Founder's House, Koreshan State Historic Site, Lee County, Florida*. Prepared for the Koreshan Unity Alliance by Piper Archaeological Research, St. Petersburg, Fla.

Avery, Paul Gordon. 2001. This Strangely Beautiful Solitude: An Archaeological and Historical Study of Uffington House, 40MO145, Rugby, Tennessee. Master's thesis, University of Tennessee, Knoxville.

Baker, Henry A., and Ryan Wheeler. 2000. *Archaeological and Historical Investigations at the Koreshan Community Laundry Site, Lee County, Florida*. Florida Bureau of Archaeological Research, Tallahassee.

Balcom, Rebecca J. 1991. Oldman River Dam Historical Sites Mitigation, 1989. In *Archaeology in Alberta 1988 and 1989, Provincial Museum of Alberta Occasional Paper No. 33*, ed. Martin Magne, 15–24. Archaeological Survey of Alberta, Alberta Culture and Multiculturalism, Historical Resources Division, Edmonton, Alb.

Baugher, Sherene. 2009. Historical Overview of the Archaeology of Institutional Life. In *The Archaeology of Institutional Life*, ed. April M. Beisaw and James G. Gibb, 5–16. University of Alabama Press, Tuscaloosa.

Baxter, Jane Eva. 2012. The Paradox of a Capitalist Utopia: Visionary Ideals and Lived Experience in the Pullman Community 1880–1900. *International Journal of Historical Archaeology* 16(4): 651–665.

Beaudry, M. C. 2004. Doing the Housework: New Approaches to the Archaeology of Households. In *Household Chores and Household Choices: Theorizing the Domestic Sphere in Historical Archaeology*, ed. Kerri Barile and Jamie C. Brandon, 254–262. University of Alabama Press, Tuscaloosa.

Beisaw, April M., and James G. Gibb, eds. 2009. *The Archaeology of Institutional Life*. University of Alabama Press, Tuscaloosa.

Bennett, Patrick M., Thomas Grooms, Andrew R. Sewell, and Bruce Aument. 2009. *Encountering the Shakers of the North Family Lot, Union Village, Ohio. Vol. 4, Simplicity Comes in All Forms—The Shaker Ceramic Industries of Union Village*. Prepared for the Ohio Department of Transportation Office of Environmental Services. Hardlines Design, Columbus, Ohio.

Berge, Dale L. 1983. Lower Goshen: A Historic Mormon Community in Central Utah. In *Forgotten Places and Things: Archaeological Perspectives on American History*, ed. Albert E. Ward, 173–184. Center for Anthropological Studies, Albuquerque, N.Mex.

———. 1990. Lower Goshen: Archaeology of a Mormon Pioneer Town. *BYU Studies* 30(2): 67–89.

Bellamy, Edward. 1967 [1888]. *Looking Backward: 2000–1887*, ed. J. L. Thomas. Harvard University Press, Cambridge, Mass.

Berry, Brian J. L. 1992. *America's Utopian Experiments: Communal Havens from Long-Wave Crises*. University Press of New England, Hanover, N.H.

Biever, Dale E. 1968. *The Historical Significance of Archaeology at the Ephrata Cloister, Ephrata, Pennsylvania*. Master's thesis, Kutztown State College. University Microfilms, Ann Arbor, Mich.

Bowen, Marshall E. 2006. Two Russian Molokan Agricultural Villages in the Intermountain West. In *Yearbook of the Association of Pacific Coast Geographers* 68:53–78.

Boyer, Paul S. 1997. Foreword. In *America's Communal Utopias*, ed. Donald E. Pitzer, ix–xiii. University of North Carolina Press, Chapel Hill.

Breen, Colin. 2006. Social Archaeologies of "Utopian" Settlements in Ireland. *International Journal of Historical Archaeology* 10(1): 35–48.

Brooks, Meagan. 2005. Public Archaeology with a Doukhobor Descendant Community. Master's thesis, University of Saskatchewan, Saskatoon.

Broome, Isaac. 1902. *The Last Days of the Ruskin Co-operative Association*. C. H. Kerr, Chicago.

Brown, Susan Love. 2002a. Introduction. In *Intentional Community: An Anthropological Perspective*, ed. S. L. Brown, 1–15. State University of New York Press, Albany.

———. 2002b. Community as Cultural Critique. In *Intentional Community: An Anthropological Perspective*, ed. S. L. Brown, 153–180. State University of New York Press, Albany.

Brunwasser, Matthew. 2009. Digging the Age of Aquarius. *Archaeology* 62(4): 30–33.

Buchli, Victor. 1999. *An Archaeology of Socialism*. Berg, Oxford.

Burning Man Project. 2016. Event FAQ. Electronic document, http://burningman.org/event/preparation/faq/.

Burton, Kelli Whitlock. 2012. Striving for Perfection. *American Archaeology* 16(3): 37–43.

Casella, Eleanor Conlin. 2007. *The Archaeology of Institutional Confinement*. University Press of Florida, Gainesville.

Claeys, Gregory, and Lyman Tower Sargent. 1999. *The Utopia Reader*. New York University Press, New York.

Clark, Pamela J. 2001. A Study of *The Altrurian* Newspaper and Its Attempts to Establish or Reinforce Community Core Values in the Cooperative Colony Established by the Colorado Cooperative Company in Nucla, Colorado, from 1895 to 1901. Ph.D. diss., University of Wyoming, Laramie.

Clauser, John W., Jr. 1995. Test Excavations at the Bethabara Brewery Site. *North Carolina Archaeological Society Newsletter* 5(1): 1–3.

Clifton, A. R. 1918. History of the Communistic Colony Llano del Rio. *Annual Publication of the Historical Society of Southern California* 11:80–90.

Cooper, Matthew. 2001. Representing Historic Groups Outside the Mainstream: Hancock Shaker Village. *CRM* 24(9): 36–37.

Cross, Ira B. 1935. *A History of the Labor Movement in California*. University of California Press, Berkeley.

De Cunzo, Lu Ann. 2009. The Future of the Archaeology of Institutions. In *The Archaeology of Institutional Life*, ed. April M. Beisaw and James G. Gibb, 206–214. University of Alabama Press, Tuscaloosa.

De Cunzo, Lu Ann, Therese O'Malley, Michael J. Lewis, George E. Thomas, and Christa Wilmanns-Wells. 1996. Father Rapp's Garden at Economy: Harmony Society Culture in Microcosm. In *Landscape Archaeology: Reading and Interpreting the American Historical Landscape*, ed. Rebecca Yamin and Karen B. Metheny, 91–117. University of Tennessee Press, Knoxville.

Deiss, R. W. 1987. Shaker Brick Types from South Union, Kentucky. *Proceedings of the Symposium on Ohio Valley Urban and Historic Archaeology*. Vol. 5. Ed. D. Ball and P. J. DiBlasi, 90–95. University of Louisville.

Doctor, Joseph E. 1968. Why Kaweah Failed. *Los Tulares* 78:1–4.

Duke, Philip, and Dean Saitta. 2009. Why We Dig: Archaeology, Ludlow, and the Public. In *The Archaeology of Class War: The Colorado Coalfield Strike of 1913–1914*, 351–361. University Press of Colorado, Boulder.

Egerton, John. 1977. *Visions of Utopia: Nashoba, Rugby, Ruskin, and the "New Communities" in Tennessee's Past*. University of Tennessee Press, Knoxville.

Ellsworth, Rodney Sydes. n.d. Rodney Sydes Ellsworth Papers: Papers relating to the Kaweah Cooperative Colony Co., 1926–1931. Manuscript collection BANC MSS 81/27 c, Bancroft Library, University of California, Berkeley.

Evans, Kenn. 2005. Sunset Fort and the Sunset Pioneer Cemetery. *Archaeology Southwest* 19(2): 9.

Fairchild, C. C. n.d. Surveyors File R-183: I.176. Saskatchewan Archives Board.

Ferg, Alan. 2005a. Brigham City, Winslow, and Prospects for Renewal. *Archaeology Southwest* 19(2): 6.

———. 2005b. Brother Behrman's Pottery. *Archaeology Southwest* 19(2): 7.

———. 2005c. Obed: Death of a Mormon Colony. *Archaeology Southwest* 19(2): 8.

Ferguson, Leland. 2011. *God's Fields: Landscape, Religion and Race in Moravian Wachovia*. University Press of Florida, Gainesville.

Fernandez, Elizabeth R., and E. Breck Parkman. 2011. The Commune Era of Olompali: Challenging Our Assumptions of the Hippie Lifestyle. *Proceedings of the Society for California Archaeology* 25.

Fiegel, K. H. 1995. A Summary of the 1991–1995 Archaeological and Archival Investigations at the South Union Shaker Village in Logan County, Kentucky. In *Historical Archaeology in Kentucky*, ed. K. A. McBride, W. S. McBride, and D. Pollack, 369–390. Kentucky Heritage Council, Frankfort.

Fitts, Robert K. 2002. Becoming American: The Archaeology of an Italian Immigrant. *Historical Archaeology* 36(2): 1–17.

Fogarty, R. S. 1990. *All Things New: American Communes and Utopian Movements, 1860–1914*. University of Chicago Press, Chicago.

Foley, Vincent P. 1965. Historic Sites Investigations in Bethlehem, Pennsylvania. *Florida Anthropologist* 18(3): 61–64.

Foster, John M. 2008. *Data Recovery Report: Llano del Rio, CA-LAN-2677H, State*

Route 138 Widening Project Task Order No. 8. Report prepared for Caltrans District 7, Division of Environmental Planning, Los Angeles by Greenwood and Associates, Pacific Palisades, Calif.

Foster, John M., and Alex Kirkish. 2009. Another Look at the Llano del Rio Colony. *Proceedings of the Society for California Archaeology* 23:1–8.

Francis, Richard. 1997. *Transcendental Utopias: Individual and Community at Brook Farm, Fruitlands, and Walden*. Cornell University Press, Ithaca, N.Y.

Fretageot, Nora C., and W. V. Mangrum. 1914. *Historic New Harmony Official Guide, Centennial Edition*. Published by the authors.

Gibbs, Martin. 2010. Landscapes of Redemption: Tracing the Path of a Convict Miner in Western Australia. *International Journal of Historical Archaeology* 14(4): 593–613.

Gorby, Christine. 2005. Pincushions, Dormitory Gardens, and Seed Gardens: Gender Identity and Spiritual Place at the West Union Shaker Village. In *Gender and Landscape: Renegotiating Morality and Space*, ed. L. Dowler, J. Carubia, and B. Szczygiel, 162–181. Routledge, Taylor and Francis Group, New York.

Gronlund, Laurence. 1965 [1884]. *The Cooperative Commonwealth in Its Outlines: An Exposition of Modern Socialism*. Harvard University Press, Cambridge, Mass.

Grygas, Joseph. 2011. *Life at the Watervliet Shaker Village: An Archaeological and Historical Approach*. Master's thesis, University at Albany, State University of New York. University Microfilms, Ann Arbor.

Guarneri, Carl. 1991. *The Utopian Alternative: Fourierism in Nineteenth-Century America*. Cornell University Press, Ithaca, N.Y.

Gutek, Gerald, and Patricia Gutek. 1998. *Visiting Utopian Communities: A Guide to the Shakers, Moravians, and Others*. University of South Carolina Press, Columbia.

Gyrisco, Geoffrey M. 1979. *Excavating Utopia: The Archaeology of American Communal Societies, An Annotated Bibliography*. Information Related to Responsibilities of the Secretary of the Interior Section 3, Executive Order 11593, Vol. 4, No. 4. Heritage Conservation and Recreation Service, Washington, D.C.

Harrington, Virginia S., and J. C. Harrington. 1971. *Rediscovery of the Nauvoo Temple: Report on Archaeological Excavations*. Nauvoo Restoration, Nauvoo, Ill.

Haskell, Burnette G. 1889. A Pen Picture of the Kaweah Co-Operative Colony Co. Limited, a Joint Stock Company, Located in Kaweah Canyon, and the Giant Forest of Tulare Co. Cal. Supplement to the *Commonwealth*, 24 April 1889. Advance, Calif.

———. 1891. How Kaweah Fell. *San Francisco Examiner*, 29 November.

Hayden, D. 1976. *Seven American Utopias: The Architecture of Communitarian Socialism, 1790–1975*. MIT Press, Cambridge, Mass.

Heberling Associates. 2008. *Archaeological and Historical Investigations in the Great House Garden, Old Economy Village, Final Report, Old Economy Village Historic Landscape Study, Ambridge, Pennsylvania.* Prepared for Pennsylvania Historical and Museum Commission, Division of Architecture and Preservation, Harrisburg by Heberling Associates, Pittsburgh.

Hendon, Julia A. 2000. Having and Holding: Storage, Memory, Knowledge, and Social Relations. *American Anthropologist* 102:42–53.

Herson, Chandler S., Linda Pansing, and Bill Pickard. 2013. Cobblestone Pavement Discovered during Archaeological Investigations at the Bimeler House in Zoar Village. *Current Research in Ohio Archaeology 2013.*

Hewitt, Geoff. 2007. "Archaeologies of Utopia?" *Journal of Historical and European Studies* 1:105–123.

Hinds, William Alfred. 1908. *American Communities and Co-operative Colonies.* Second Revision. Charles H. Kerr, Chicago.

Hine, Robert V. 1981. *California Utopianism: Contemplations of Eden.* Boyd & Fraser, San Francisco.

———. 1983. *California's Utopian Colonies.* University of California Press, Berkeley.

———. 1997. California's Socialist Utopias. In *America's Communal Utopias*, ed. Donald E. Pitzer, 419–431. University of North Carolina Press, Chapel Hill.

Hoehnle, Peter. 2000. Communal Bonds: Contact Between the Amana Society and Other Communal Groups, 1843–1931. *Communal Societies* 20:59–80.

Holloway, Mark. 1966. *Utopian Communities in America, 1680–1880.* Dover, Mineola, N.Y.

Janus Research. 1993. *Koreshan State Historic Site Mapping Project and Archaeological Management Plan.* Prepared for the Koreshan Unity Alliance, Estero, by Janus Research, Tampa Bay, Fla.

Janzen, Donald E. 1981. *The Shaker Mills on Shawnee Run: Historical Archaeology at Shakertown at Pleasant Hill, Report of Archaeological Investigations, 1975–1978.* Pleasant Hill Press, Harrodsburg, Ky.

Johnson, J. K. 1907. Letter to Frank Oliver, 11 March. Department of the Interior RG15, D-II-1, Vol. 755, File 494483, Pt. 6, National Archives of Canada, Ottawa.

Johnson, Matthew. 2007. *Ideas of Landscape.* Blackwell, Malden, Mass.

Jones, William Carey. 1891. The Kaweah Experiment in Co-operation. *Quarterly Journal of Economics* 6:47–73.

Kanter, Rosabeth M. 1972. *Commitment and Community: Communes and Utopias in Sociological Perspective.* Harvard University Press, Cambridge, Mass.

Kaweah Commonwealth [KC]. 1890–1892. Weekly newspaper of the Kaweah Cooperative Commonwealth at Advance and Kaweah, Calif.

Kaweah Co-operative Colony Company Records [KCR]. 1886–1892. Manuscript collection BANC MSS C-A 303, Bancroft Library, University of California, Berkeley.

Kennedy, Margaret, and Brian O. K. Reeves. 1986. *Phase II Archaeological and Historical Resources Study, Oldman River Dam*. Vol. 1, *Historic Period Resources Inventory and Impact Assessment*. Archaeological Survey of Alberta Permit 85-47C.

Klein, Kerwin L. 2001. Westward, Utopia: Robert V. Hine, Aldous Huxley, and the Future of California History. *Pacific Historical Review* 70(3): 465–476.

Kopp, James J. 2009. *Eden within Eden: Oregon's Utopian Heritage*. Oregon State University Press, Corvallis.

Kozakavich, Stacy C. 1998. A State of Change: An Historical Archaeology of Doukhobor Identity at Kirilovka Village Site (FcNs-1). Master's thesis, University of Saskatchewan, Saskatoon.

———. 2006. Doukhobor Identity and Communalism at Kirilovka Village Site. *Historical Archaeology* 40(1): 119–132.

———. 2007. *The Center of Civilization: Archaeology and History of the Kaweah Co-operative Commonwealth*. Ph.D. diss., University of California, Berkeley. University Microfilms, Ann Arbor.

Kruczek-Aaron, Hadley. 2014. Making Change Materialize: An Archaeology of Social Reform in the Age of Obama. *International Journal of Historical Archaeology* 18(2): 299–315.

Kryder-Reid, Elizabeth. 1996. The Construction of Sanctity: Landscape and Ritual in a Religious Community. In *Landscape Archaeology: Reading and Interpreting the American Historical Landscape*, ed. Rebecca Yamin and Karen B. Metheny, 228–248. University of Tennessee Press, Knoxville.

Landing, James E. 1997. Cyrus Reed Teed and the Koreshan Unity. In *America's Communal Utopias*, ed. Donald E. Pitzer, 251–264. University of North Carolina Press, Chapel Hill.

Leary, Timothy. 1966. *Turn On, Tune In, Drop Out*. Record album produced by ESP Disk, New York.

Leone, Mark P. 1973. Archeology as the Science of Technology: Mormon Town Plans and Fences. In *Research and Theory in Current Archeology*, ed. Charles L. Redman, 125–150. John Wiley & Sons, New York.

———. 1977a. The New Mormon Temple in Washington, D.C. In *Historical Archaeology and the Importance of Material Things*, ed. Leland Ferguson, 43–61. Society for Historical Archaeology Special Publication Series, No. 2.

———. 1977b. The Role of Primitive Technology in 19th Century American Utopias. In *Material Culture: Styles, Organization, and Dynamics of Technology*, ed. Heather Lechtman and Robert S. Merrill, 87–107. West, St. Paul, Minn.

———. 1981. The Relationship between Artifacts and the Public in Outdoor History Museums. In *The Research Potential of Anthropological Museum Collections*, ed. Anne-Marie E. Cantwell, James B. Griffin, and Nan A. Rothschild, 301–313. New York Academy of Sciences, New York.

———. 2005. Mormon Town Plans. *Archaeology Southwest* 19(2): 14.

LeWarne, Charles Pierce. 1995. *Utopias on Puget Sound 1885–1915*. University of Washington Press, Seattle.

Lewis, Beverly, and Rick Blackwood. 1995. American Utopia: Louisiana's New Llano Colony. *Louisiana Cultural Vistas* 5(4).

Lewis, Pierce. 1999. Axioms for Reading the Landscape: Some Guides to the American Scene [1979]. In *Material Culture Studies in America*, ed. Thomas J. Schlereth, 174–182. Altamira Press, Lanham, Md.

Lipow, Arthur. 1982. *Authoritarian Socialism in America: Edward Bellamy and the Nationalist Movement*. University of California Press, Berkeley.

Little, Barbara J. 2007. Archaeology and Civic Engagement. In *Archaeology as a Tool of Civic Engagement*, ed. Barbara J. Little and Paul A. Shackel 1–22. Altamira Press, Lanham, Md.

———. 2009. What Can Archaeology Do for Justice, Peace, Community, and the Earth? *Historical Archaeology* 43(4): 115–119.

Llano del Rio Company of Nevada. 1916. The Gateway to Freedom through Cooperative Action. *Western Comrade* 3(12): 2–3.

Loren, Diana DiPaolo. 2003. Refashioning a Body Politic in Colonial Louisiana. *Cambridge Archaeological Journal* 13(2): 231–237.

Ludlow Collective. 2001. Archaeology of the Colorado Coal Field War, 1913–1914. In *Archaeologies of the Contemporary Past*, ed. Victor Buchli and Gavin Lucas, 94–107. Routledge, London.

Mansberger, Floyd. 2002. *Phase III Data Recovery Plan (DRP) for Foundation Repair at the Bjorklund Hotel, Bishop Hill, Illinois (Archaeological Site 11HY113)*. Prepared for the Illinois Historic Preservation Agency, Historic Sites Division, Springfield, by Fever River Research, Springfield.

Martin, James John. n.d. J. J. Martin Papers, 1880–1972. Manuscript collection BANC MSS C-B 363, Bancroft Library, University of California, Berkeley.

Martineau, Harriet. 1837. *Society in America*. Vol. 1. Baudry's European Library, Paris.

McBride, Kim A. 1995. Archaeology at the Shaker Village at Pleasant Hill, Kentucky: Rediscovering the Importance of Order. In *Historical Archaeology in Kentucky*, ed. K. A. McBride, W. S. McBride, and D. Pollack, 391–408. Kentucky Heritage Council, Frankfort.

———. 2005. Sidebar 13: Lessons from Two Shaker Smoking Pipe Fragments. In *Unlocking the Past: Celebrating Historical Archaeology in North America*, ed. Lu

Ann De Cunzo and John H. Jameson Jr., 136–139. University Press of Florida, Gainesville.

———. 2010. The Importance of an Ordered Landscape at Pleasant Hill Shaker Village: Past and Present Issues. In *Archaeology and Preservation of Gendered Landscapes*, ed. Sherene Baugher and Suzanne M. Spencer-Wood, 251–271. Springer, New York.

McBride, Kim A., and W. Stephen McBride. 2008. Historic Period. In *Kentucky Heritage Council State Preservation Comprehensive Plan Report No. 3*. Vol. 2, *The Archaeology of Kentucky: An Update*, ed. David Pollack. Kentucky Heritage Council, Frankfort.

McGuire, Randall H. 2008. *Archaeology as Political Action*. University of California Press, Berkeley.

McKay, Joyce. 1979. An Analysis of Archaeological Excavations at Bishop Hill 1972–1975. Unpublished manuscript in the collection of the Illinois Historic Preservation Agency, Historic Sites Division, Springfield.

Miller, Timothy. 1990. *American Communes 1860–1960: A Bibliography*. Garland, New York.

———. 1998. *The Quest for Utopia in Twentieth Century America*. Vol. 1, *1900–1960*. Syracuse University Press, Syracuse, N.Y.

Minturn, Leigh. 1995. Communes as Moralnets. *Cross-cultural Research: The Journal of Comparative Social Science* 29(1): 5–13.

Mohn, Kelly. 2001. The Ephrata Cloister: Enigmatic Oasis. *CRM* 24(9): 24–26.

Moore, William D. 2006. Interpreting the Shakers: Opening the Villages to the Public, 1955–1965. *CRM: The Journal of Heritage Stewardship* 3(1): 49–69.

Moseley, Bruce M., and Helen S. Schwartz. 2001. Developing the Interpretive Plan for the Oneida Community Mansion House. *CRM* 24(9): 29–32.

Mowers, Charlene Donchez. 2012. National Historic Landmarks Program Nomination (NPS Form 10-900), Historic Moravian Bethlehem Historic District. National Historic Landmarks Program, National Park Service.

Mullins, P. 2004. Consuming Aspirations: Bric-a-Brac and the Politics of Victorian Materialism in West Oakland. In *Putting the "There" There: Historical Archaeologies of West Oakland, I-880 Cypress Freeway Replacement Project*, Vol. 2, ed. Mary Praetzellis and Adrian Praetzellis, 85–116. Prepared for the California Department of Transportation, Contract 04AO583, Task Order 15 by the Anthropological Studies Center, Sonoma State University, Rohnert Park, Calif.

Munson, Cheryl Ann. 2013. "Where's the Porch" and Other Intersections between Archaeology and Historic Preservation. In *Historic Preservation in Indiana: Essays from the Field*, ed. Nancy R. Hiller, 128–145. Indiana University Press, Bloomington.

Muranaka, Therese Adams. 1992. *The Russian Molokan Colony at Guadalupe, Baja California: Continuity and Change in a Sectarian Community.* Ph.D. diss., University of Arizona, Tucson. University Microfilms, Ann Arbor.

———. 1995. An Archaeological Study of the Russian Colony of the Guadalupe Valley. *Estudios Fronterizos* 35–36:93–125.

Murphy, James. 1978. Shaker Reed Stem Tobacco Pipes. *Pennsylvania Archaeologist* 48(1–2): 48–52.

Murray, Ruth Ann. 2012. *Through Their Stomachs: Shakers, Food, and Business Practices in the Nineteenth Century.* Ph.D. diss., Boston University. University Microfilms, Ann Arbor.

Nassaney, M. S., D. Rotman, D. Sayers, and C. Nikolai. 2001. The Southwest Michigan Historical Landscape Project: Exploring Class, Gender, and Ethnicity from the Ground Up. *International Journal of Historical Archaeology* 5(3): 219–261.

Nida, Brandon. 2013. Demystifying the Hidden Hand: Capital and the State at Blair Mountain. *Historical Archaeology* 47(3): 52–68.

Nordhoff, Charles. 1966 [1875]. *The Communistic Societies of the United States.* Dover, New York.

Noyes, John Humphrey. 1870. *History of American Socialisms.* J. B. Lippincott, Philadelphia.

O'Connell, Jay. 1999. *Co-operative Dreams: A History of the Kaweah Colony.* Raven River Press, Van Nuys, Calif.

O'Connor, Michael. 2015. ESM's First Archaeological Dig: Archaeological Dig and Field School Looks at the Church Family Trustees' Office. *The Friends' Quarterly: Newsletter of the Enfield Shaker Museum* (Summer): 1, 3.

O'Connor, Shaun. 2000. On the Road to Utopia: The Social History and Spirituality of Altruria, an Intentional Religious Community in Sonoma County, California, 1894–1896. Ph.D. diss., Graduate Theological Union, Berkeley, Calif.

Okugawa, Otohiko. 1983. Intercommunal Relationships among Nineteenth-Century Communal Societies in America. *Communal Societies* 3:68–82.

Orser, Charles E., Jr., ed. 2002. *Encyclopedia of Historical Archaeology.* Routledge, New York.

Oved, Yaacov. 1988. *Two Hundred Years of American Communes.* Transaction Books, New Brunswick, N.J.

Owoc, M. 2005. From the Ground Up: Agency, Practice, and Community in the Southwestern British Bronze Age. *Journal of Archaeological Method and Theory* 12(4): 257–281.

Parkman, E. Breck. 2014. A Hippie Discography: Vinyl Records from a Sixties Commune. *World Archaeology* 46(3): 431–447.

————. 2015. *The Last Song at Olompali*. Science Notes No. 208, California State Parks Bay Area District, Petaluma.

Parrish, Thomas. 2005. *Restoring Shakertown: The Struggle to Save the Historic Shaker Village of Pleasant Hill*. University of Kentucky Press, Lexington.

Passet, J. E. 2005. Reading Hilda's Home: Gender, Print Culture, and the Dissemination of Utopian Thought in Late-Nineteenth-Century America. *Libraries and Culture* 40(3): 307–323.

Pitzer, Donald E. 1997. Introduction. In *America's Communal Utopias*, ed. Donald E. Pitzer, 1–8. University of North Carolina Press, Chapel Hill.

————. 2012. Introduction to the 2012 Reprint Edition. In Arthur Bestor, *Backwoods Utopias: The Sectarian Origins and the Owenite Phase of Communitarian Socialism in America, 1663–1829*, xi–xl. 2nd ed. Wipf & Stock, Eugene, Ore.

Pitzer, Donald E., and Josephine M. Elliott. 1979. New Harmony's First Utopians, 1814–1824. *Indiana Magazine of History* 75(3): 225–300.

Pitzer, Donald E., and Connie A. Weinzapfel. 2001. Utopia on the Wabash: The History of Preservation in New Harmony. *CRM* 24(9): 18–20.

Praetzellis, Adrian. 2004. Consumerism, Living Conditions, and Material Well-Being. In *Putting the "There" There: Historical Archaeologies of West Oakland, I-880 Cypress Freeway Replacement Project*, Vol. 2, ed. Mary Praetzellis and Adrian Praetzellis, 47–83. Prepared for the California Department of Transportation, Contract 04AO583, Task Order 15 by the Anthropological Studies Center, Sonoma State University, Rohnert Park, Calif.

Praetzellis, Adrian, and Mary Praetzellis. 2001. Mangling Symbols of Gentility in the Wild West: Case Studies in Interpretive Archaeology. *American Anthropologist* 103(3): 645–654.

Preucel, Robert. 2006. *Archaeological Semiotics*. Blackwell, Malden, Mass.

Preucel, Robert W., and Steven R. Pendery. 2006. Envisioning Utopia: Transcendentalist and Fourierist Landscapes at Brook Farm, West Roxbury, Massachusetts. *Historical Archaeology* (40)1: 6–19.

Prince, Gene. 1988. Photography for Discovery and Scale by Superimposing Old Photographs on the Present-Day Scene. *Antiquity* 62(234): 112–116.

Promey, Sally M. 1993. *Spiritual Spectacles: Vision and Image in Mid-Nineteenth-Century Shakerism*. Indiana University Press, Bloomington.

Pykles, Benjamin C. 2005. Mormon Heritage and Archaeological Sites. *Archaeology Southwest* 19(2): 2.

————. 2006. "The Archaeology of the Mormons Themselves": The Restoration of Nauvoo and the Rise of Historical Archaeology in America. Ph.D. diss., University of Pennsylvania, Philadelphia.

————. 2010. *Excavating Nauvoo: The Mormons and the Rise of Historical Archaeology in America*. University of Nebraska Press, Lincoln.

Rathje, William L., and Cullen Murphy. 1992. *Rubbish!: The Archaeology of Garbage*. Harper Collins, New York.

Rathje, William L., W. W. Hughes, D. C. Wilson, M. K. Tani, G. H. Archer, R. G. Hunt, and T. W. Jones. 1992. Archaeology of Contemporary Landfills. *American Antiquity* 57(3): 437–447.

Rhoads, Jonathan. 1900. *A Day with the Doukhobors*. William H. Poles Sons, Philadelphia.

Rhodes, Harold V. 1967. *Utopia in American Political Thought*. University of Arizona Press, Tucson.

Robertson, Thomas A. 1947. *A Southwestern Utopia*. Ward Ritchie Press, Los Angeles.

Roller, Michael P. 2013. Rewriting the Narratives of Labor Violence: A Transnational Perspective of the Latimer Massacre. *Historical Archaeology* 47(3): 109–123.

Rothschild, Nan A., and Diana diZerega Wall. 2014. *The Archaeology of American Cities*. University Press of Florida, Gainesville.

Safiran, Edward T. 1996. Archaeological Excavations at the Boy's Dormitory Site, Bishop Hill, Illinois. Unpublished manuscript in the collection of the Illinois Historic Preservation Agency, Historic Sites Division, Springfield.

———. 2000. A Very Brief History of Archaeology at Bishop Hill SHS. Unpublished manuscript in the collection of Bishop Hill State Historic Site, Bishop Hill, Ill.

Saitta, Dean. 2007. *The Archaeology of Collective Action*. University Press of Florida, Gainesville.

Sargisson, Lucy, and Lyman Tower Sargent. 2004. *Living in Utopia: New Zealand's Intentional Communities*. Ashgate, Burlington, Vt.

Savory, Samantha. 2013. Brook Farm: A Ceramic Analysis of a Short Lived Utopia. Master's thesis, Indiana University of Pennsylvania.

Savulis, Ellen. 1992. Alternative Visions and Landscapes: Archaeology of the Shaker Social Order and Built Environment. In *Text-Aided Archaeology*, ed. B. Little, 195–204. CRC Press, Boca Raton, Fla.

———. 2003. Zion's Zeal: Negotiating Identity in Shaker Communities. In *Shared Spaces and Divided Places: Material Dimensions of Gender Relations and the American Historical Landscape*, ed. Deborah L. Rotman and Ellen Savulis, 160–189. University of Tennessee Press, Knoxville.

Saxton, Alexander. 1971. *The Indispensable Enemy: Labor and the Anti-Chinese Movement in California*. University of California Press, Berkeley.

Scarlett, Timothy James. 2006. Globalizing Flowscapes and the Historical Archaeology of the Mormon Domain. *International Journal of Historical Archaeology* 10(2): 109–134.

Scarlett, Timothy James, Robert J. Speakman, and Michael D. Glascock. 2007. Pottery in the Mormon Economy: An Historical, Archaeological, and Archaeometric Study. *Historical Archaeology* 41(4): 72–97.

Scott, Elizabeth M. 1997. "A Little Gravy in the Dish and Onions in a Tea Cup": What Cookbooks Reveal About Material Culture. *International Journal of Historical Archaeology* 1(2): 131–155.

Sewell, Andrew R. 2013. *Executive Summary: Baseline Planning Assessments for Zoar Levee & Diversion Dam, Dam Safety Modifications Study, Historic Property Baseline Study, Lawrence Township, Tuscarawas County, Ohio.* Prepared for the Huntington District, U.S. Army Corps of Engineers, Huntington, West Virginia. Hardlines Design, Columbus, Ohio.

Sewell, Andrew, Roy Hampton, R. Joe Brandon, and Amy Case. 2004. *Archaeology at the Harmony Brickworks, Leetsdale, Pennsylvania.* Prepared for the Pittsburgh District, U.S. Army Corps of Engineers, Pittsburgh. Hardlines Design, Columbus, Ohio.

Sewell, Andrew, Roy A. Hampton III, and Rory Krupp. 2009a. *Encountering the Shakers of the North Family Lot, Union Village, Ohio.* Vol. 2, *A Clean and Lively Appearance—Landscape and Architecture of the North Family Lot.* Prepared for the Ohio Department of Transportation Office of Environmental Services. Hardlines Design, Columbus, Ohio.

———. 2009b. *Encountering the Shakers of the North Family Lot, Union Village, Ohio.* Vol. 3, *Tracing Prosperity and Adversity—A Social History of the North Family Lot.* Prepared for the Ohio Department of Transportation Office of Environmental Services. Hardlines Design, Columbus, Ohio.

Shackel, Paul A. 2013. Changing the Past for the Present and the Future. *Historical Archaeology* 47(3): 1–11.

Shaw, Albert. 1884. *Icaria: A Chapter in the History of Communism.* George M. Putnam's Sons, New York.

Shor, Frances Robert. 1997. *Utopianism and Radicalism in a Reforming America, 1888–1918.* Greenwood Press, Westport, Conn.

Silverman, Helaine. 1991. Ethnography and Archaeology of Two Andean Pilgrimage Centers. In *Pilgrimage in Latin America*, ed. N. Ross Crumrine and Alan Morinis, 215–228. Greenwood Press, New York.

Smith, Monica L. 2001. The Archaeology of a "Destroyed" Site: Surface Survey and Historical Documents at the Civilian Conservation Corps Camp, Bandelier National Monument, New Mexico. *Historical Archaeology* 35(2): 31–40.

South, Stanley. 1965. Excavating the 18th Century Moravian Town of Bethabara, North Carolina. *Florida Anthropologist* 18(3): 45–48.

———. 1999. *Historical Archaeology in Wachovia: Excavating Eighteenth-Century Bethabara and Moravian Pottery.* Kluwer Academic Publishers, New York.

Spann, Edward K. 1994. Review of *America's Utopian Experiments: Communal Havens from Long-Wave Crises*, by Brian J. L. Berry. *Annals of Iowa* 53(4): 369–371.

Spencer-Wood, Suzanne M. 1999. The World Their Household: Changing Meanings of the Domestic Sphere in the Nineteenth Century. In *The Archaeology of Household Activities*, ed. Penelope M. Allison, 162–189. Routledge, New York.

Stahlgren, Lori C., and M. Jay Stottman. 2007. Voices from the Past: Changing the Culture of Historic House Museums with Archaeology. In *Archaeology as a Tool of Civic Engagement*, ed. Barbara J. Little and Paul A. Shackel, 131–150. Altamira Press, Lanham, Md.

Starbuck, David R. 1986. The Shaker Mills in Canterbury, New Hampshire. *Journal of the Society for Industrial Archaeology* 12(1): 11–38.

———. 1988. Documenting the Canterbury Shakers. *Historical New Hampshire* 43(1): 1–20.

———. 1998. New Perspectives on Shaker Life: An Archaeologist Discovers "Hog Heaven" at Canterbury Shaker Village. *Expedition* 40(3): 3–16.

———. 2000. Waiting for the Second Coming: The Canterbury Shakers, an Archaeological Perspective on Blacksmithing and Pipe Smoking. *Northeast Historical Archaeology* 29(2):83–106.

———. 2004. *Neither Plain nor Simple: New Perspectives on the Canterbury Shakers*. University Press of New England, Lebanon, N.H.

———. 2006. *The Archaeology of New Hampshire: Exploring 10,000 Years in the Granite State*. University of New Hampshire Press, University Press of New England, Lebanon.

Starbuck, David R., and Paula J. Dennis. 2010. The Dynamics of a Shaker Landscape in Canterbury, New Hampshire. In *Archaeology and Preservation of Gendered Landscapes*, ed. Sherene Baugher and Suzanne M. Spencer-Wood, 233–249. Springer, New York.

State of Florida Department of Environmental Protection. 2003. *Koreshan State Historic Site Unit Management Plan*. Division of Recreation and Parks, Department of Environmental Protection, State of Florida, Tallahassee.

Stein, Pat. 2005. The Mormon Lake Dairy, Sawmill, and Tannery. *Archaeology Southwest* 19(2): 10.

Stein, Stephen J. 1992. *The Shaker Experience in America: A History of the United Society of Believers*. Yale University Press, New Haven, Conn.

Stottman, M. Jay. 2010. Introduction: Archaeologists as Activists. *Archaeologists as Activists: Can Archaeologists Change the World?*, ed. M. Jay Stottman, 1–18. University of Alabama Press, Tuscaloosa.

Strezewski, Michael. 2011. Excavations at the Harmonist Redware Kiln. *Indiana Archaeology* 6(1): 164–166.

———. 2013. *"An Exceedingly Industrious Race of People": Investigations at the Harmonist Redware Kiln Site, Posey County, Indiana.* Archaeology Laboratory Reports of Investigations 13-01. University of Southern Indiana, Evansville.

———. 2014. *Excavations at the Wolf House and Harmonist Warehouse Sites, New Harmony, Indiana.* Archaeology Laboratory Reports of Investigations, 14-05. University of Southern Indiana, Evansville.

———. 2015a. Harmonist Demography and Town Planning in New Harmony, Indiana. *Communal Societies* 35(1): 1–28.

———. 2015b. *Excavations at the Harmonist Dormitory #1 Complex, New Harmony, Indiana.* Archaeology Laboratory Reports of Investigations 14-02. University of Southern Indiana, Evansville.

Sutton, Robert P. 1985. Translation of Etienne Cabet's *Travels in Icaria* [originally published 1840 as *Voyage en Icarie*]. Unpublished manuscript in collection of the Center for Icarian Studies, Western Illinois University.

———. 1995. Cabetian Orthodoxy Asserted: Past Practices and *Voyage en Icarie* in Icaria-Speranza, 1880–1886. In *Proceedings of the 1989 Cours Icarien Symposium.* National Icarian Heritage Society, Nauvoo, Ill.

———. 2003. *Communal Utopias and the American Experience: Religious Communities, 1732–2000.* Praeger, Westport, Conn.

———. 2004. *Communal Utopias and the American Experience: Secular Communities, 1824–2000.* Praeger, Westport, Conn.

Sweeny-Justice, Karen. 2001. Thomas Hughes'"Rugby": Utopia on the Cumberland Plateau. *CRM* 24(9): 13–15.

Switzer, David C., and Brendan P. Foley. 2001. Underwater Study of Enfield Shaker Bridge. Report prepared for New Hampshire Department of Transportation.

Tallent, Daniel. 2009. Communion in the South Union: An Archaeological Analysis of a Shaker Colony. Honors thesis, Western Kentucky University.

Tarasoff, Koozma J. 1972. Doukhobors—Their Migration Experience. *Canadian Ethnic Studies* 4(1): 1–12.

———. 1977. *Traditional Doukhobor Folkways: An Ethnographic and Biographic Record of Prescribed Behavior.* National Museum of Man Mercury Series, Canadian Centre for Folk Culture Studies Paper No. 20. Ottawa, Ont.

Tarlow, Sarah. 2002. Excavating Utopia: Why Archaeologists Should Study "Ideal" Communities of the Nineteenth Century. *International Journal of Historical Archaeology* 6(4): 299–323.

———. 2006. Representing Utopia: The Case of Cyrus Teed's Koreshan Unity Settlement. *Historical Archaeology* 40(1): 89–99.

Teed, Cyrus (Koresh). 1905. *Cellular Cosmogony, or, the Earth a Hollow Globe, Estero Enlarged Edition.* Guiding Star Publishing House, Estero, Fla.

Thomas, Brian W. 1994. Inclusion and Exclusion in the Moravian Settlement in North Carolina, 1770–1790. *Historical Archaeology* 28(3): 15–29.

Tomaso, Matthew S., Richard F. Veit, Carissa A. DeRooy, and Stanley L. Walling. 2006. Social Status and Landscape in a Nineteenth-Century Planned Industrial Alternative Community: Archaeology and the Geography of Feltville, New Jersey. *Historical Archaeology* 40(1): 20–36.

Tracie, Carl J. 1996. *Toil and Peaceful Life: Doukhobor Village Settlement in Saskatchewan, 1899–1918*. Canadian Plains Research Center, Regina, Sask.

Trahair, Richard C. S. 1999. *Utopias and Utopians: An Historical Dictionary*. Greenwood Press, Westport, Conn.

Turney-High, Harry Holbert. 1968. *Man and System: Foundations for the Study of Human Relations*. Appleton-Century-Crofts, New York.

Tyler, Alice Felt. 1944. *Freedom's Ferment: Phases of American Social History to 1860*. University of Minnesota Press, Minneapolis.

United Society of Believers. 1892. *The Manifesto*. United Society of Believers, Canterbury, N.H.

Upton, Dell. 2005. What the Mormon Cultural Landscape Can Teach Us. *Journal of Mormon History* 31(2): 1–29.

U.S. Army Corps of Engineers, Huntington District, Great Lakes & Ohio River Division. 2014. *Draft Dam Safety Modification Report and Draft Environmental Assessment, Zoar Levee and Diversion Dam, an Appurtenance to Dover Dam, Tuscarawas River, Muskingum River Basin, Tuscarawas County, Ohio*. NIDID: OH00003-ZL.

Van Bueren, Thad M. 2006. Between Vision and Practice: Archaeological Perspectives on the Llano del Rio Cooperative. *Historical Archaeology* 40(1): 133–151.

Van Bueren, Thad M., and Jill Hupp. 2000. *Searching for Utopia: Results of Archaeological and Historical Investigations at the Llano del Rio Colony (CA-LAN-2677H) near Pearblossom, Los Angeles County, California*. Report prepared for Caltrans District 7, Environmental Planning Branch, Los Angeles.

Van Bueren, Thad M., and Sarah Tarlow. 2006. The Interpretive Potential of Utopian Settlements. *Historical Archaeology* 40(1): 1–5.

Van Ness, John R. 1973. *The Bjorklund Stable Site, Bishop Hill, Illinois*. Knox College Historical Archaeology Project Site Report. Unpublished manuscript in the collection of the Illinois Historic Preservation Agency, Historic Sites Division, Springfield.

Van Wormer, Heather. 2004. Ideology in All Things: Material Culture and Intentional Communities. Ph.D. diss., Michigan State University.

———. 2006. The Ties That Bind: Ideology, Material Culture, and the Utopian Ideal. *Historical Archaeology* 40(1): 37–56.

Van Wormer, Stephen R., and G. Timothy Gross. 2006. Archaeological Identification of an Idiosyncratic Lifestyle: Excavation and Analysis of the Theosophical Society Dump, San Diego, California. *Historical Archaeology* 40(1): 100–118.

Vassault, F. I. 1890. Nationalism in California. *Overland Monthly and Out West Magazine* 15(90): 659–661.

Wagner, Jon. 1974. The Old Colony Church Site, Bishop Hill, Illinois. Knox College Historical Archaeology Project Site Report. Unpublished manuscript in the collection of the Illinois Historic Preservation Agency, Historic Sites Division, Springfield.

———. 1975. The Knox College Bishop Hill Historical Archaeology Project, 1975 Site Report. Unpublished manuscript in the collection of the Illinois Historic Preservation Agency, Historic Sites Division, Springfield.

———. 1997. Eric Jansson and the Bishop Hill Colony. In *America's Communal Utopias*, ed. Donald E. Pitzer, 297–318. University of North Carolina Press, Chapel Hill.

Walker, Mark. 2004. Aristocracies of Labor: Craft Unionism, Immigration, and Working-Class Households. In *Putting the "There" There: Historical Archaeologies of West Oakland, I-880 Cypress Freeway Replacement Project*, Vol. 2, ed. Mary Praetzellis and Adrian Praetzellis, 207–236. Prepared for the California Department of Transportation, Contract 04AO583, Task Order 15 by the Anthropological Studies Center, Sonoma State University, Rohnert Park, Calif.

Wall, Diana diZerega. 1991. Sacred Dinners and Secular Teas: Constructing Domesticity in Mid-19th-Century New York. *Historical Archaeology* 25(4): 69–81.

Walters, Ronald G. 1997. *American Reformers, 1815–1860*. Hill and Wang, New York.

Warfel, Steven G. 1999. *Historical Archaeology at Ephrata Cloister: A Report on 1998 Investigations*. Pennsylvania Historical and Museum Commission, Harrisburg.

———. 2000. *Historical Archaeology at Ephrata Cloister: A Report on 1999 Investigations*. Pennsylvania Historical and Museum Commission, Harrisburg.

———. 2001. *Historical Archaeology at Ephrata Cloister: A Report on 2000 Investigations*. Pennsylvania Historical and Museum Commission, Harrisburg.

———. 2009. Ideology, Idealism, and Reality: Investigating the Ephrata Commune. In *The Archaeology of Institutional Life*, ed. April M. Beisaw and James G. Gibb, 137–152. University of Alabama Press, Tuscaloosa.

Wiegenstein, Steve. 2006. The Icarians and Their Neighbors. *International Journal of Historical Archaeology* 10(3): 283–289.

Wilkie, Laurie A. 1996. Medicinal Teas and Patent Medicines: African-American Women's Consumer Choices and Ethnomedical Traditions at a Louisiana Plantation. *Southeastern Archaeology* 15(2): 119–131.

———. 2003. *The Archaeology of Mothering*. Routledge, New York

Wilkie, Laurie A., and Kat Howlett Hayes. 2006. Engendered and Feminist Archaeologies of the Recent and Documented Pasts. *Journal of Archaeological Research* 14:243–264.

Wilson, Carolyn Anderson, and Hiram Wilson. 1973. Bjorklund Hotel Privy Site, Bishop Hill, Illinois. Unpublished manuscript in the collection of the Illinois Historic Preservation Agency, Historic Sites Division, Springfield.

Winser, Philip. 1931. Memories. Unpublished manuscript in the collection of Huntington Library, San Marino, Calif.

W.J.A.B. 1852. The Icarian Community. *Christian Examiner and Religious Miscellany* 53(3): 378.

Wood, M. C. 2004. Working-class Households as Sites of Social Change. In *Household Chores and Household Choices: Theorizing the Domestic Sphere in Historical Archaeology*, ed. Kerri Barile and Jamie C. Brandon, 210–232. University of Alabama Press, Tuscaloosa.

Wooster, E. S. 1924. *Communities of the Past and Present*. Llano Colonist, Newllano, La.

Wright, Gwendolyn. 1980. *Moralism and the Model Home: Domestic Architecture and Cultural Conflict in Chicago, 1873–1913*. University of Chicago Press, Chicago.

Wurst, LouAnn. 2002. "For the Means of Your Subsistence . . . Look Under God to Your Own Industry and Frugality": Life and Labor in Gerrit Smith's Peterboro. *International Journal of Historical Archaeology* 6(3): 159–172.

Wylie, Alison. 1985. Putting Shakertown Back Together: Critical Theory in Archaeology. *Journal of Anthropological Archaeology* 4:133–147.

Yamin, Rebecca, and Karen Bescherer Metheny. 1996. Preface: Reading the Historical Landscape. *In Landscape Archaeology: Reading and Interpreting the American Historical Landscape*, ed. Rebecca Yamin and Karen B. Metheny, xiii–xx. University of Tennessee Press, Knoxville.

Youngs, Isaac N., and George Kendall. 1835. *Sketches of the various Societies of Believers in the states of Ohio & Kentucky*. Library of Congress Geography and Map Division. http://hdl.loc.gov/loc.gmd/g3706em.gct000206.

INDEX

STACY KOZAKAVICH is a project director with PaleoWest in Orinda, California. She lives with her family in Oakland, California.

THE AMERICAN EXPERIENCE IN ARCHAEOLOGICAL PERSPECTIVE
Edited by Michael S. Nassaney, Founding Editor
Krysta Ryzewski, Co-editor

The American Experience in Archaeological Perspective series was established by the University Press of Florida and founding editor Michael S. Nassaney in 2004. This prestigious historical archaeology series focuses attention on a range of significant themes in the development of the modern world from an Americanist perspective. Each volume explores an event, process, setting, institution, or geographic region that played a formative role in the making of the United States of America as a political, social, and cultural entity. These comprehensive overviews underscore the theoretical, methodological, and substantive contributions that archaeology has made to the study of American history and culture. Rather than subscribing to American exceptionalism, the authors aim to illuminate the distinctive character of the American experience in time and space. While these studies focus on historical archaeology in the United States, they are also broadly applicable to historical and anthropological inquiries in other parts of the world. To date the series has produced more than two dozen titles. Prospective authors are encouraged to contact the Series Editors to learn more.

The Archaeology of Collective Action, by Dean J. Saitta (2007)

The Archaeology of Institutional Confinement, by Eleanor Conlin Casella (2007)

The Archaeology of Race and Racialization in Historic America, by Charles E. Orser Jr. (2007)

The Archaeology of North American Farmsteads, by Mark D. Groover (2008)

The Archaeology of Alcohol and Drinking, by Frederick H. Smith (2008)

The Archaeology of American Labor and Working-Class Life, by Paul A. Shackel (2009; first paperback edition, 2011)

The Archaeology of Clothing and Bodily Adornment in Colonial America, by Diana DiPaolo Loren (2010; first paperback edition, 2011)

The Archaeology of American Capitalism, by Christopher N. Matthews (2010; first paperback edition, 2012)

The Archaeology of Forts and Battlefields, by David R. Starbuck (2011; first paperback edition, 2012)

The Archaeology of Consumer Culture, by Paul R. Mullins (2011; first paperback edition, 2012)

The Archaeology of Antislavery Resistance, by Terrance M. Weik (2012; first paperback edition, 2013)

The Archaeology of Citizenship, by Stacey Lynn Camp (2013; first paperback edition, 2019)

The Archaeology of American Cities, by Nan A. Rothschild and Diana diZerega Wall (2014; first paperback edition, 2015)

The Archaeology of American Cemeteries and Gravemarkers, by Sherene Baugher and Richard F. Veit (2014; first paperback edition, 2015)

The Archaeology of Smoking and Tobacco, by Georgia L. Fox (2015; first paperback edition, 2016)

The Archaeology of Gender in Historic America, by Deborah L. Rotman (2015; first paperback edition, 2018)

The Archaeology of the North American Fur Trade, by Michael S. Nassaney (2015; first paperback edition, 2017)

The Archaeology of the Cold War, by Todd A. Hanson (2016; first paperback edition, 2019)

The Archaeology of American Mining, by Paul J. White (2017; first paperback edition, 2020)

The Archaeology of Utopian and Intentional Communities, by Stacy C. Kozakavich (2017; first paperback edition, 2023)

The Archaeology of American Childhood and Adolescence, by Jane Eva Baxter (2019)

The Archaeology of Northern Slavery and Freedom, by James A. Delle (2019)

The Archaeology of Prostitution and Clandestine Pursuits, by Rebecca Yamin and Donna J. Seifert (2019; first paperback edition, 2023)

The Archaeology of Southeastern Native American Landscapes of the Colonial Era, by Charles R. Cobb (2019)

The Archaeology of the Logging Industry, by John G. Franzen (2020)

The Archaeology of Craft and Industry, by Christopher C. Fennell (2021)

The Archaeology of the Homed and the Unhomed, by Daniel O. Sayers (2023)

www.ingramcontent.com/pod-product-compliance
Lightning Source LLC
Chambersburg PA
CBHW071733270326
41928CB00013B/2656